"In a country where journalists critical of the government have a way of meeting untimely deaths, Ms. Gessen has shown remarkable courage in researching and writing this unflinching indictment of the most powerful man in Russia. . . . Although written before the recent protests erupted, the book helps to explain the anger and outrage driving that movement."
                                                    —*The Wall Street Journal*

"Powerful and gracefully written . . . Gessen's book flows on multiple tracks, tracing Putin's life back to boyhood, the story of his hometown of St. Petersburg, and finally the last quarter-century of Russian history. . . . For all of the ghoulish detail, Gessen's account of Putin's Russia is not overwrought. . . . [She] displays impressive control of her prose and her story, painting a portrait of a vile Putin without sounding polemical."
                                                    —*San Francisco Chronicle*

"Written in English but with Russian heart, Gessen focuses on the places and institutions that bred the nation's most resolute leader since Stalin . . . Some might say that Gessen's interpretation is political. Of course it is . . . But more importantly, it is thorough. She has seen fellow journalists killed, has been harassed herself, and yet continues to write from Russia . . . Her urgency is felt on nearly every page."
                                                    —*Bookforum*

"[Gessen] shines a piercing light into every dark corner of Putin's story . . . Fascinating, hard-hitting reading."
                                                    —*Foreign Affairs*

"Although Gessen is enough of an outsider to write beautifully clear and eloquent English, she is enough of an insider to convey, accurately, the wild swings of emotions, the atmosphere of mad speculation, the paranoia, and, yes, the hysteria that pervade all political discussion and debate in Moscow today."
                                                    —*The New York Review of Books*

"What Gessen sees in Putin is a troubled childhood brawler who became a paper-pushing KGB man and, by improbable twists and turns, rose to the top in Russia. . . . [She] does not attempt to weigh up Putin's record but rather examines his biography, mind-set, and methods . . . as a thug loyal to the KGB and the empire it served who never had a clue about the earth-shattering events that blew the Soviet Union apart."   —*The Washington Post*

"Masha Gessen steps into the fray with a perceptive account of the new czar."   —*The Daily Beast*

"Part psychological profile, part conspiracy study. As a Moscow native who has written perceptively for both Russian and Western publications, Gessen knows the cultures and pathologies of Russia . . . [and has] a delicious command of the English language . . . A fiercely independent journalist . . . Gessen's armchair psychoanalysis of Putin is speculative. But it is a clever and sometimes convincing speculation, based on a close reading of Putin's own inadvertently revealing accounts of his life, and on interviews with people who knew Putin before he mattered."   —*The New York Times Book Review*

"[An] incisive bildungsroman of Putin and his regime . . . Alongside an acute apprehension of the post-Soviet dynamics that facilitated Putin's rise, Gessen balances narratives of Putin-as-bureaucrat and Putin-as-kleptocrat with a wider indictment of the 'Mafia clan' that retains him solely as its Godfather."   —*The Daily*

"Illuminating . . . It is with [the] explosive revelations that Gessen truly excels. . . . An electrifying read from what can only be described as an incredibly brave writer."   —*Columbia Journalism Review*

"Engrossing and insightful."   —*Bloomberg*

"A chilling and brave work of nonfiction. . . . With *The Man Without a Face*, Gessen has succeeded in convincingly portraying the forces that made Putin who he is today . . . [a] crafty, canny, power-hungry man whose hold on Russia shows no sign of slacking."   —*BookPage*

THE MAN WITHOUT A FACE

The Unlikely Rise of
VLADIMIR PUTIN

Masha Gessen

RIVERHEAD BOOKS
New York

RIVERHEAD BOOKS
Published by the Penguin Group
Penguin Group (USA) Inc.
375 Hudson Street, New York, New York 10014, USA

USA / Canada / UK / Ireland / Australia / New Zealand / India / South Africa / China

Penguin Books Ltd., Registered Offices: 80 Strand, London WC2R 0RL, England
For more information about Penguin Group, visit penguin.com

The Library of Congress has catalogued the Riverhead hardcover edition as follows:

Gessen, Masha.
The man without a face : the unlikely rise of Vladimir Putin /
Masha Gessen.
p.   cm.
ISBN 978-1-59448-842-9
1. Putin, Vladimir Vladimirovich, 1952– .   2. Presidents—Russia (Federation).
3. Russia (Federation)—Politics and government—1991– .   I. Title.
DK510.766.P87G47   2012   2011047578
947.086'2092—dc23
[B]

First Riverhead hardcover edition: March 2012
First Riverhead trade paperback edition: March 2013
Riverhead trade paperback ISBN: 978-1-59448-651-7

PRINTED IN THE UNITED STATES OF AMERICA

20 19 18 17 16 15 14 13 12

Cover design by Alex Merto
Cover phogograph © Stephane Lavoue / Pasco
Book design by Amanda Dewey

CONTENTS

PROLOGUE

I woke up because someone was shaking me. Kate's face looked terrified. "They are saying something about Galina on the radio," she half whispered. "And a gun. I think . . . I don't understand."

I got out of bed and stumbled into the tiny kitchen, where Kate had been making breakfast and listening to Echo Moskvy, the country's best news and talk radio station. It was a Saturday morning, unusually light and crisp for November in Moscow. And I was not worried: somehow, Kate's fear did not impress me. Whatever she had heard—or, with her limited Russian, misheard—might be the beginning of yet another great story. As the chief correspondent for Russia's leading newsmagazine, *Itogi*, I felt all great stories were my fiefdom. And there were a lot of great stories. In a country that was inventing itself, every city, every family, and every institution was, in some sense, uncharted territory. The year was 1998. Since the early 1990s, virtually every piece I wrote was a tale no one had told before: I spent about half my time outside Moscow, traveling to conflict zones and gold mines, orphanages and universities, abandoned villages and burgeoning oil towns, writing their stories. The magazine, which was owned and financed by the same magnate as Echo Moskvy, rewarded me by never questioning my extravagant travel schedule and by frequently placing my stories on the cover.

In other words, I was one of those young people who had gained everything in the 1990s. Many people older and younger than I was had paid dearly for the transition. The older generation had lost its savings to hyperinflation and its identities to the apparent destruction of all Soviet institutions. The younger generation was growing up in the shadow of its parents' fear and, often, failure. But I had been twenty-four years old the year the Soviet Union collapsed, and my peers and I had spent the 1990s inventing our careers and what we thought were the ways and institutions of a new society. Even as violent crime seemed to become epidemic in Russia, we felt peculiarly secure: we observed and occasionally described the criminal underworld without ever feeling that it might affect our existence. Plus, I was certain that things would only get better: I had recently bought a dilapidated former communal apartment in the very heart of Moscow, and I was now renovating it before moving out of the flat I rented with Kate, a British editor working for an oil trade publication. I envisioned myself starting a family in that new apartment. And this particular Saturday, I had an appointment with the contractor to go shopping for bathroom fixtures.

KATE GESTURED AT THE BOOM BOX as though it were a source of toxins, and looked at me questioningly. Galina Starovoitova, whose name the newscaster was repeating over and over, was a member of the lower house of parliament, one of Russia's best-known politicians, and a friend. In the late 1980s, when the empire teetered on the brink of collapse, Starovoitova, an ethnographer, became a pro-democracy activist and the most prominent spokesperson for the people of Nagorno-Karabakh, an Armenian exclave in Azerbaijan that was then engulfed in the first of many armed ethnic conflicts that would mark the dissolution of the Eastern Bloc. Like several other academics turned politicians, she had seemed to emerge in the spotlight instantly. Though she had lived in Leningrad since she was an infant, the people of Armenia nominated her as their representative to the first quasi-democratically elected Supreme Soviet, and in 1989 she was voted into office by an overwhelming majority. In the Supreme Soviet, she became a leader of the Interregional Group, a minority pro-democracy faction whose leadership also included Andrei Sakharov and Boris Yeltsin. As soon as Yeltsin was elected president of Russia in 1990—at that point largely a ceremonial and even aspirational post—Galina became his closest adviser, counseling him officially on ethnic issues and unofficially on everything else, including government appointments. In 1992, Yeltsin was considering Galina for the post of minister of defense; such an appointment, of a civilian and a woman whose views bordered on the pacifist, would have been a grand gesture in classic early-1990s Yeltsin style, a message that nothing would ever be the same in Russia and perhaps in the world.

That nothing should ever be the same was the crux of Galina's agenda, radical even by early-nineties pro-democracy activist standards. As part of a small group of lawyers and politicians, she tried unsuccessfully to put the Communist Party of the USSR on trial. She authored a draft law on *lustratsiya* (lustration), the word deriving from the ancient Greek for "purification," a concept that was now coming into use in former Eastern Bloc countries to denote the process of banning former Party and secret police operatives from holding public office. In 1992, she learned that the KGB had reconstituted an internal Party organization—a direct violation of Yeltsin's August 1991 post–failed-coup decree outlawing the Russian Communist Party. At a public meeting in July 1992, she tried to confront Yeltsin with this fact, and he had rudely dismissed her, signaling both the end of Galina's career in his administration and his own increasingly conciliatory stance toward the security services and the many die-hard Communists who remained in power or close to it. Dismissed from the administration, Galina made a push for the lustration law, which failed, and then left Russian politics altogether and decamped to the United States, first to the U.S. Institute for Peace in Washington, and then to teach at Brown University.

THE FIRST TIME I SAW GALINA. I could not see her: she was obscured by hundreds of thousands of people who came out into Moscow's Maya-kovsky Square on March 28, 1991, to take part in a rally in support of Yeltsin. Soviet president Mikhail Gorbachev had recently publicly dressed down Yeltsin; he had also issued a decree forbidding protests in the city. Tanks rolled into Moscow that morning and were positioned in such a way as to make it as difficult as possible for people to make their way to the banned pro-democracy rally. The organizers, in response, split their rally into two, to make it easier for people to find a way to at least one of the locations. It was my first visit to Moscow after ten years as an émigré; I happened to be staying at my grandmother's apartment near the Mayakovsky Square site. With the main street, Tverskaya, blocked off, I wound my way through a series of courtyards, diving out through an archway and immediately finding myself in the thick of a crowd. I could see nothing but the backs of people's heads and a series of almost identical gray and black woolen coats. But I could hear a woman's voice booming over the crowd, speaking about the inviolability of the constitutional right to assembly. I turned to a man standing next to me; he was holding a yellow plastic bag in one hand and a child by the hand with the other. "Who is speaking?" I asked. "Starovoitova," he responded. Just then the woman began leading the crowd in a five-syllable chant that reverberated, it seemed, through the entire city: "Ros-si-ya! Yel-tsin!"

In less than half a year, the Soviet Union would effectively collapse and Yeltsin would become the leader of a new, democratic Russia. That this was inevitable had become clear to many people, including me, that March day, when the people of Moscow had defied the Communist government and its tanks and insisted on having their say in the public square.

I do not actually remember when I met Galina in person, but we became friendly the year she was teaching at Brown: she was a frequent guest at my father's house in the Boston area; I was shuttling back and forth between the United States and Moscow, and Galina became something of a mentor to me in the world of Russian politics, though she occasionally protested that she had completely returned to academe. Those protestations must have ended in December 1994, when Yeltsin launched a military offensive in the breakaway republic of Chechnya: the people advising him now apparently assured him that the insurgency could be tamed quickly and painlessly for the federal center. Galina perceived the new war as the certain disaster it was, and as the biggest threat yet to Russian democracy. In the spring she went to the Urals to chair a congress aimed at resurrecting her political party, Democratic Russia, which had once been the country's most potent political force. I covered the congress for the leading Russian newspaper at the time, but on my way to the city of Chelyabinsk—a journey that involved a three-hour flight, followed by a three-hour bus ride—I managed to get myself robbed. I arrived in Chelyabinsk close to midnight, shaken and penniless, and ran into Galina in the hotel lobby: she had just emerged from a long day of tense meetings. Before I had a chance to say anything, she pulled me up to her room, where she placed a glass of vodka in my hands and sat down at a glass coffee table to make me a bunch of tiny salami sandwiches. She lent me money for the ticket back to Moscow.

Galina clearly felt motherly toward me—I was the same age as her son, who had moved to England with his father just as his mother was becoming a major politician—but the scene with the sandwiches was part of something else too: in a country where political role models ran from leather-jacketed commissar to decrepit apparatchik, Galina was trying to be an entirely new creature, a politician who was also a human. At a Russian feminist conference, she shocked the audience by lifting her skirt to display her legs: she was trying to prove that a male politician who had accused her of being bowlegged was wrong. She spoke to one of the first Russian glossy magazines about the difficulty someone who is seriously overweight, as she was, has choosing clothes. At the same time, she pursued her legislative agenda furiously, stubbornly. In late 1997, for example, she again tried to push through her lustration bill—and failed again. In 1998 she immersed herself in an investigation of campaign financing of some of her most powerful political enemies, including the Communist speaker of the Duma, the lower house of parliament. (The Communist Party was legal again, and popular.)

I had asked her why she had decided to return to politics, when she knew full well she would never again have the kind of influence that had once been hers. She had tried to answer me several times, always stumbling over her own motivation. Finally, she called me from a hospital where she was going to have surgery; about to go under anesthesia, she had been trying to fix her view of her life and had finally found an image she liked. "There is an ancient Greek legend about harpies," she told me. "They are shadows that can come to life only if they drink human blood. The life of a scholar is the life of a shadow. When one participates in making the future happen, even a small part of the future—and this is what politics is about—that is when one who was a shadow can come to life. But for that, one has to drink blood, including one's own."

I FOLLOWED KATE'S STARE to the boom box, which crackled slightly, as though the words emerging from its speakers were causing it strain. The newscaster was saying Galina had been shot dead several hours earlier, in the stairway of her apartment building in St. Petersburg. She had flown in from Moscow in the evening. She and her legislative aide, Ruslan Linkov, had stopped by Galina's parents' house for a short visit before continuing to her apartment building on the Griboyedov Embankment, one of the city's most beautiful streets. When they entered the building, the stairway was dark: the gunmen waiting on the stairs had removed the lightbulbs. They continued up the steps nonetheless, speaking about a court case recently filed against Galina by a nationalist political party. Then there was a clapping sound, and a flash of light; Galina's speech halted. Ruslan screamed, "What are you doing?" and ran at the source of light and sound. He took the next two bullets.

Ruslan had apparently lost consciousness briefly and then regained it long enough to call a journalist from his cell phone. It was the journalist who called the police. And now, the voice from the boom box was telling me, Galina was dead and Ruslan, whom I also knew and liked, was in the hospital, in critical condition.

IF THIS BOOK WERE A NOVEL, my character probably would have dropped everything upon hearing the news of her friend's death and, already knowing that life had changed forever, would have rushed off to do something—anything to give the moment its due. In real life, we rarely know when our lives are changed irrevocably or how to act when tragedy strikes. I went shopping for bathroom fixtures for my new apartment. It was when the construction crew leader who went with me said, "Have you heard about Starovoitova?" that I stopped in my tracks. I remember staring down at my boots and the snow, gray and packed hard under the feet of thousands of aspiring home-owners. "We were under contract to build a garage for her," he said. Somehow, it was then, when I thought how my friend would never need that garage, that I knew just how helpless, scared, and angry I felt. I hopped in my car, drove to the train station, and went to St. Petersburg to try to write the story of what happened to Galina Starovoitova.

Over the following couple of years, I would spend weeks on end in St. Petersburg. Here was another story no one had told before—but it was a much bigger story than any I had written, a much bigger story even than that of the murder, in cold blood, of one of the country's best-known politicians. What I found in St. Petersburg was a city—Russia's second-largest city—that was a state within a state. It was a place where the KGB—the organization against which Starovoitova had waged her most important and most hopeless battle—was all-powerful. Local politicians and journalists believed their phones and offices were tapped, and it seemed they were right. It was a place where the murder of major political and business players was a regular occurrence. And it was a place where business deals gone sour could easily land someone behind bars. In other words, it was very much like what Russia itself would become in a few years, once it came to be ruled by the people who ruled St. Petersburg in the 1990s.

I never found out who ordered the killing of Galina Starovoitova (the two men who were convicted of the murders years later were merely hired hands). Nor did I ever find out why. What I did find was that throughout the 1990s, while young people like me were constructing new lives in a new country, a parallel world had ex-isted alongside ours. St. Petersburg had preserved and perfected many of the key features of the Soviet state: it was a system of gov-ernment that worked to annihilate its enemies—a paranoid, closed system that strove to control everything and to wipe out anything that it could not control. It was impossible to determine what had gotten Starovoitova killed, precisely because her standing as an enemy of the system had made her a marked woman, a doomed one. I had been to many war zones, I had worked under shrapnel fire, but this was the most frightening story I ever had to write: never before had I been forced to describe a reality so emotionless and cruel, so clear and so merciless, so corrupt and so utterly void of remorse.

Within a few years, all of Russia would be living inside this reality. How that came to be is the story I will tell in this book.

One

THE ACCIDENTAL
PRESIDENT

I magine you have a country and no one to run it. This was the predicament that Boris Yeltsin and his inner circle thought they faced in 1999.

Yeltsin had been very ill for a long time. He had suffered several heart attacks and had undergone open-heart surgery soon after he was elected for a second term in 1996. Most people believed he drank heavily—a common and easily recognizable Russian affliction, though some of those close to him insisted that Yeltsin's occasional bouts of disorientation and withdrawal stemmed from his persistent physical ailments and not from drinking. Whatever the reason, Yeltsin had become incoherent or gone missing during several state visits, devastating his supporters and disappointing his voters.

By 1999, Yeltsin, his popularity rating dipping into the single digits, was not half the politician he had been. He still used many of the tools that had once made him great, making unexpected political appointments, alternating periods of hands-on and laissez-faire governance, strategically applying his larger-than-life persona—but by now he most resembled a boxer gone blind, flailing in the ring, striking imaginary targets and missing real ones.

In the second half of his second term, Yeltsin reshuffled his administration repeatedly and frantically. He fired a prime minister who had been in office for six years, replacing him with a thirty-six-year-old unknown, only to bring the old prime minister back six months later—to replace him again in three weeks. Yeltsin anointed one successor after another, only to grow disenchanted with each of them in a very public manner that had a way of embarrassing both the object of Yeltsin's displeasure and anyone who witnessed the display of disaffection.

The more erratic the president became, the more enemies he made—and the more his enemies banded together. A year before his second and final term was to expire, Yeltsin found himself at the top of a very fragile pyramid. His many reshufflings had forced out several political generations' worth of professionals; many ministry and federal agency heads were now young mediocrities who had been sucked into the vacuum at the top. Yeltsin's trusted allies were now so few and so cloistered that the press called them the "Family"; they included Yeltsin's daughter, Tatyana; his chief of staff, Alexander Voloshin; his former chief of staff, Valentin Yumashev, whom Tatyana would later marry; another former chief of staff, the economist and architect of Russian privatization Anatoly Chubais; and the entrepreneur Boris Berezovsky. Of the half-dozen so-called oligarchs—the businessmen who had grown superrich under Yeltsin and had repaid him by orchestrating his reelection campaign—Berezovsky was the only one to remain firmly by the president's side.

Yeltsin had no legal right to seek a third term, nor was he well enough to try, and he had every reason to fear an unfriendly successor. Yeltsin was not just an unpopular president: he was the first politician whom Russians had ever trusted—and the disappointment his people felt now was every bit as bitter as the support he had once enjoyed had been inspiring.

The country was battered, traumatized, and disappointed. It had experienced hope and unity in the late 1980s, culminating in August 1991, when the people beat back the junta that had threatened Gorbachev's rule. It had placed its faith in Boris Yeltsin, the only Russian leader in history to have been freely elected. In return, the people of Russia got hyperinflation that swallowed up their life savings in a matter of months; bureaucrats and entrepreneurs who stole from the state and from one another in plain sight; and economic and social inequality on a scale they had never known. Worst of all, many and possibly most Russians lost any sense of certainty in their future—and with it, the sense of unity that had carried them through the 1980s and early 1990s.

The Yeltsin government had made the grave mistake of not addressing the country's pain and fear. Throughout the decade Yeltsin, who had been a true populist, riding the buses and mounting the tanks—whichever the situation happened to require—increasingly withdrew into an impenetrable and heavily guarded world of black limousines and closed conferences. His first prime minister, the brilliant young economist Yegor Gaidar, who came to epitomize post-Soviet economic reform, made it plain and public that he considered the people too dumb to engage in any discussion about reform. The people of Russia, essentially abandoned by their leaders in their hour of pain, sought solace in nostalgia—not so much in Communist ideology, which had used up its inspirational potential decades earlier, but in a longing to regain Russia's superpower status. By 1999, there was palpable aggression in the air, and this was a large part of the reason Yeltsin and the Family were rightly terrified.

Hurt and aggression have a way of rendering people blind. So the people of Russia were largely oblivious to the actual accomplishments of the Yeltsin decade. Notwithstanding the many, many wrong turns made along the way, Russia had succeeded in privatizing much enterprise—and the biggest privatized companies had been turned around and made competitive. Despite an increase in inequality, a great majority of Russians had experienced overall improvement in their lives: the number of households with televisions, washing machines, and refrigerators grew; the number of privately owned cars doubled; the number of people traveling abroad as tourists nearly tripled between 1993 and 2000. In August 1998, Russia had defaulted on its debts, and this had caused a short but significant spike in inflation; but since then, the economy had been growing.

The media were flourishing: in an uncannily short period of time, Russians had taught themselves to make sophisticated, beautiful television, and had also created an inordinate number of print outlets and several budding electronic publications. Many though certainly not all of the country's infrastructure problems had been addressed: intercity trains were once again running on time, the postal service was working, the number of households with telephone landlines was growing. One Russian company, a cellular service provider founded in 1992, had placed its stock on the New York Stock Exchange and done very well.

Yet the government seemed entirely incapable of convincing the people that things were indeed better than they had been a couple of years earlier, and certainly better than a decade earlier. The sense of uncertainty Russians had felt ever since the Soviet Union crumbled under their feet was so great that any losses seemed to confirm their expectation of doom, while any gains were transformed into fears of further loss. Yeltsin had only his populist ways to fall back on: he could not challenge or reshape expectations; he could not lead the country in finding new ideals and a new rhetoric. He could only try to give the people what they wanted.

And what they wanted was decidedly not Yeltsin. Tens of millions of Russians held him personally responsible for every misfortune they had encountered over the previous ten years, for their lost hopes and their shattered dreams—even, it seemed, for their vanished youth—and they hated him passionately. Whoever came to lead the country after Yeltsin could win easy popularity by prosecuting him. What the ailing president feared most was that a political party called Otechestvo—Vsya Rossiya (Fatherland—All Russia; the name, a hybrid of two political titles, sounds as inelegant in Russian as it does in English), headed by a former prime minister and several mayors and governors, would come to power and exact revenge on Yeltsin and the Family—and that he would spend his final days in jail.

That is where Vladimir Putin came in.

As Berezovsky tells it, the Family was casting about for a successor. Incongruities of scale haunt this story. A tiny group of people, besieged and isolated, were looking for someone to take over the world's largest landmass, with all its nuclear warheads and all its tragic history—and the only thing smaller than the pool of candidates seems to have been the list of qualifications required of them. Anyone with any real political capital and ambition—anyone with a personality commensurate with the office—had already abandoned Yeltsin. The candidates were all plain men in gray suits.

Berezovsky claims that Putin was his protégé. As he told it to me at his villa outside London—I kept my promise to forget its specific location as soon as I returned to the city—Berezovsky had met Putin in 1990, when he was looking to expand his business to Leningrad. Berezovsky was an academic turned car dealer. His business was selling the Lada—the name Russians slapped on a car shoddily made on the basis of a long-outdated Fiat. He was also importing used European cars and building service stations to fix what he sold. Putin, then a deputy of City Council chairman Anatoly Sobchak, had helped Berezovsky arrange to open a service station in Leningrad, and had declined a bribe—and that was enough to make Berezovsky remember him. "He was the first bureaucrat who did not take bribes," Berezovsky assured me. "Seriously. It made a huge impression on me."

Berezovsky made it a habit to "run by" Putin's office whenever he was in St. Petersburg—given Berezovsky's frenetic nature, these were most likely truly run-by visits during which the oligarch would storm in, chatter excitedly, and storm out, possibly without registering much of his host's reaction. When I spoke with Berezovsky, he was hard-pressed to recall anything Putin had said to him. "But I perceived him as a sort of ally," he said. He was impressed, too, that Putin, promoted to deputy mayor of St. Petersburg when Sobchak became mayor, later refused a position with the new mayor when Sobchak failed to be reelected.

When Putin moved to Moscow in 1996 to take an administrative job at the Kremlin, the two began to see each other more frequently, at the exclusive club Berezovsky maintained in the center of the city. Berezovsky had used his connections to arrange for "No Entry" traffic signs to be placed on both ends of a city block, essentially marking a segment of a residential street as his own. (Residents of the several apartment buildings across the street could no longer legally drive up to their homes.)

But by early 1999, Berezovsky was a man under siege—like the rest of the Family but more so: he was the only one of them who valued his place in Moscow society. Locked in a desperate and apparently losing power struggle with former prime minister Yevgeny Primakov, who led the anti-Yeltsin political alliance, Berezovsky had become something of a pariah. "It was my wife's, Lena's, birthday," he told me. "And we decided not to invite a lot of people because we didn't want anyone to have to strain their relationship with Primakov. So it was just friends. And then my security tells me, 'Boris Abramovich, Vladimir Vladimirovich Putin will be arriving in ten minutes.' And I said, 'What happened?' And he said, 'He wants to wish Lena a happy birthday.' And he showed up ten minutes later, with a bouquet of flowers. And I said, 'Volodya,* what are you doing this for? You have enough problems as it is. Are you just making a show of it?' And he says, 'I am making a show of it, yes.' And this was how he cemented our relationship. Starting with the fact that he would not accept a bribe. Then refusing to abandon Sobchak. And then this incident, which made me sure that he was a good, direct man—a KGB man, yes, but still a man." It went straight to Berezovsky's head.

Berezovsky was made in the same mold as other early Russian entrepreneurs. Like all of them, he was very intelligent, well educated, and a risk lover. Like most of them, he was Jewish, which had marked him as an outsider from the time he was a small child. Like all of them, he had outsize ambition and boundless energy. He was a mathematics Ph.D. who had started in business with a car import-export and service company. By leveraging credit against hyperinflation, he had essentially swindled Russia's largest carmaker out of millions of dollars. In the early and middle 1990s he got into banking, continued to keep a hand in the car business, acquired part of a large oil company, and, most important, placed himself at the helm of Russian Public Television, or Channel One, the country's most-watched television channel—which gave him unfettered access to 98 percent of Russia's households.

Like other oligarchs, Berezovsky invested in Yeltsin's 1996 re-election campaign. Unlike the rest of them, he parlayed his access into a series of political appointments. He shuttled around the country, brokering political deals, negotiating for peace in Chechnya, and reveling in the spotlight. He cultivated the image of a kingmaker, certainly exaggerating his influence and just as certainly believing half of what he said or implied as he said or implied it. A couple of

---

*"Volodya," "Vova," "Volod'ka," and "Vovka" are all diminutive forms of "Vladimir," listed here in increasing order of familiarity.

consecutive generations of foreign correspondents in Russia believed that Berezovsky was the country's shadow ruler.

NO ONE IS EASIER to manipulate than a man who exaggerates his own influence. As the Family looked for Russia's future leader, a series of meetings between Berezovsky and Putin commenced. By this time, Putin was the head of Russia's secret police. Yeltsin had obliterated the top brass everywhere, repeatedly, and the FSB—the Federal Security Service, as the successor agency to the KGB was now called— was no exception. If Berezovsky is to be believed, he was the one who mentioned Putin to Valentin Yumashev, Yeltsin's chief of staff. "I said, 'We've got Putin, who used to be in the secret services, didn't he?' And Valya said, 'Yes, he did,' and I said, 'Listen, I think it's an option. Think about it: he is a friend, after all.' And Valya said, 'But he's got pretty low rank.' And I said, 'Look, there is a revolution going on, everything is all mixed up, so there . . .'"

As a description of the decision-making process for appointing the head of the main security agency of a nuclear power, this conversation sounds so absurd, I am actually inclined to believe it. Putin's rank was indeed low: he had left active duty as a lieutenant colonel and had received an automatic upgrade to colonel while in reserve. He would claim to have been offered a general's stars when he took over the FSB and to have turned the honor down. "It doesn't take a general to order colonels around," was how his wife explained his decision. "It takes someone who is capable of doing it."

Whether he was capable or not, Putin clearly felt insecure in his job at the FSB. He quickly began appointing people he knew from the Leningrad KGB to top positions in the federal structure. Meanwhile, he did not even feel safe in his own office: whenever he met with Berezovsky, the two would take their conversations to a disused elevator shaft behind Putin's office; this was the only place in the building Putin believed their discussions would not be recorded. In this desolate and dysfunctional setting, Berezovsky met with Putin almost every day to talk about his battle with former prime minister Primakov—and, eventually, about becoming president of Russia. The potential candidate was skeptical at first, Berezovsky recalled, but he was willing to listen. One time Putin carelessly shut the door that separated the shaft from the hallway in front of his office, and the pair got locked in the elevator shaft. Putin had to pound on the wall for someone to let them out.

In the end, Berezovsky, who fully felt he represented Russia, courted Putin. In July 1999, Berezovsky flew to Biarritz, in southwest France, where Putin was vacationing. "I called him ahead of time," Berezovsky remembered. "I told him I wanted to come and discuss something serious with him. I got there; he was vacationing with his wife and two daughters, who were still very young at the time, in these very modest condominium-type accommodations. It was like an apartment building slash apartment hotel. A small kitchen, a bedroom or a few bedrooms. Really very modest." By this time, Russian millionaires, of whom Putin no doubt was one, had become accustomed to taking their vacations in giant villas on the Côte d'Azur: this was why Berezovsky was so impressed with Putin's unassuming holiday arrangement.

"We spent an entire day in conversation. In the end, he said, 'All right, let's give it a shot. But you do understand that Boris Nikolayevich [Yeltsin] has to be the one to say it to me.'"

All of this resembled an old shtetl joke. A matchmaker calls on an aging tailor to discuss the possibility of arranging his middle daughter's marriage to the heir to the Rothschild empire. The tailor puts up several objections: he has no business marrying off his middle daughter before the older ones have found a match, he does not want his daughter to move far from home, he is not so sure the Rothschilds are as pious as his daughter's husband ought to be.

The matchmaker counters each argument with his own: this is, after all, the heir to the Rothschild fortune. Finally, the old tailor relents. "Excellent," says the matchmaker. "Now all I have to do is talk to the Rothschilds."

Berezovsky reassured Putin. "I said, 'Volodya, what are you talking about? I was sent here by him, just to make sure there was no misunderstanding, so it wouldn't happen that he would say it to you and you responded, like you have to me on many occasions, by saying you don't want this.' So he agreed. I returned to Moscow and told Yumashev about our conversation. And a short time later—I no longer remember exactly how many days later—Putin returned to Moscow and met with Boris Nikolayevich. And Boris Nikolayevich had a complicated reaction. At least, I remember his saying one thing to me: 'He seems all right, but he is kind of small.'"

Yeltsin's daughter, Tatyana Yumasheva, remembers the story differently. She recalls Yeltsin's then chief of staff, Voloshin, locked in an argument with a former chief of staff, Chubais: both agreed Putin was a good choice for successor, but Chubais did not believe the Russian parliament would confirm Putin as prime minister. While both were presenting their cases to Yeltsin, Berezovsky flew to Biarritz to pop the question—because he wanted Putin and the rest of the country to believe he was the kingmaker.

Like the other participants in the presidential selection process, however, Tatyana Yumasheva remembers the panic with which they viewed the political situation and the country's future. "Chubais believed that the Duma would not confirm Putin. There would be three votes and then the dissolution of parliament.* Communists, united with [former premier] Primakov and [Moscow mayor Yuri]

---

*The Russian constitution allowed Yeltsin to force three votes on the prime minister's candidacy and then dissolve parliament.

Luzhkov would garner a firm majority in the next election, possibly even a constitutional majority. After that, the country would be on a slippery slope to catastrophe, and it could go as far as civil war. The best possible scenario was a neo-Communist regime, slightly adapted to more modern conditions; but business would be nationalized again, borders would be closed, and many media outlets would be shut down."

"The situation was bordering on catastrophe," was how Berezovsky described it. "We had lost time, and we had lost our positional advantage. Primakov and Luzhkov were organizing countrywide. Around fifty governors [out of eighty-nine] had already signed on to their political movement. And Primakov was a monster who wanted to reverse everything that had been accomplished in those years."

Why, if the Family saw the situation as desperate, did they see Putin as their savior? Chubais said he was an ideal candidate. Berezovsky clearly thought he was a brilliant choice. Who did they think Putin was, and why did they think he was qualified to run the country?

POSSIBLY THE MOST BIZARRE FACT about Putin's ascent to power is that the people who lifted him to the throne knew little more about him than you do. Berezovsky told me he never considered Putin a friend and never found him interesting as a person—a strong statement from a man so ebullient that he tends to draw anyone with intellectual ambition firmly and enthusiastically into his orbit and hold him there by sheer magnetism. The fact that Berezovsky never found Putin attractive enough to try to pull him close suggests he never perceived a spark of curiosity in the other man. But when he considered Putin as a successor to Yeltsin, he seemed to assume that the very qualities that had kept them at arm's length would make

Putin an ideal candidate: Putin, being apparently devoid of personality and personal interest, would be both malleable and disciplined.
Berezovsky could not have been more wrong.

As for Chubais, he had known Putin briefly when he served as
an economic adviser to Mayor Sobchak in St. Petersburg and Putin
had just been appointed deputy. He remembered Putin as he had
been during his first year of working for the mayor: it had been
a uniquely charged year, and Putin had been uncharacteristically energetic and curious, always asking questions. Chubais had left St.
Petersburg in November 1991 to join the government in Moscow,
and his initial impressions had remained untempered.

And what did Boris Yeltsin himself know about his soon-to-be-
anointed successor? He knew this was one of the few men who had
remained loyal to him. He knew he was of a different generation: unlike Yeltsin, his enemy Primakov, and his army of governors, Putin had
not come up through the ranks of the Communist Party and had not,
therefore, had to publicly switch allegiances when the Soviet Union
collapsed. He looked different: all those men, without exception,
were heavyset and, it seemed, permanently wrinkled; Putin—slim,
small, and by now in the habit of wearing well-cut European suits—
looked much more like the new Russia Yeltsin had promised his
people ten years earlier. Yeltsin also knew, or thought he knew, that
Putin would not allow the prosecution or persecution of Yeltsin himself once he retired. And if Yeltsin still possessed even a fraction of his
once outstanding feel for politics, he knew that Russians would like
this man they would be inheriting, and who would be inheriting them.

Everyone could invest this gray, ordinary man with what they
wanted to see in him.

On August 9, 1999, Boris Yeltsin named Vladimir Putin prime
minister of Russia. A week later he was confirmed in that position
by a wide majority of the Duma: he proved just as likable, or at least
unobjectionable, as Yeltsin had intuited.

Two

THE ELECTION WAR

You know, some people are saying the FSB is behind the bombings," my editor, one of the smartest people I knew, said to me when I walked in one afternoon in September 1999. "Do you believe it?"

For three weeks, Moscow and other Russian cities had been terrorized by a series of explosions. The first occurred on August 31 in a crowded shopping mall in the center of Moscow. One person died, and more than thirty people were injured. But it was not immediately clear that this explosion was anything more frightening than a giant prank, or perhaps a shot fired in a business dispute.

Five days later, an explosion brought down a large part of an apartment block in the southern city of Buynaksk, not far from Chechnya. Sixty-four people were killed and one hundred and forty-six injured. But all of the building's residents were Russian military officers and their families—so, although the dead included twenty-three children, the blast did not have the effect of making civilians, especially civilians living in Moscow, feel vulnerable and scared.

Four days later, however, at two seconds before midnight on September 8, a giant blast sounded in a bedroom neighborhood outside Moscow's city center. A densely populated concrete city block was ripped in half, two of its stairwells—seventy-two apartments in total—completely obliterated. Exactly one hundred people died; nearly seven hundred more were injured. Five days later, another explosion brought down another building, on the outskirts of Moscow. The eight-story brick building folded in on itself like a house of cards; the journalists in the crowd that rushed to the building that morning talked about the fact that concrete buildings apparently explode outward, while brick ones collapse inward. The blast came at five in the morning, which meant that most residents were home at the time; almost all of them were killed: one hundred twenty-four people were dead and seven injured.

Three days after that, on September 16, a truck blew up in the street in Volgodonsk, a city in southern Russia. Nineteen people died, and over a thousand were injured.

Panic set in all over the country. Residents of Moscow and other Russian cities formed neighborhood patrols; many people went out into the streets simply because it felt safer than sleeping in their apartments. Volunteers stopped anyone they considered suspicious, which often meant everyone who was not a part of the patrol. At least one group of Moscow volunteers stopped everyone walking a dog—to check the dog. The police all over the country were inundated with calls from people who thought they had seen suspicious activity or suspicious objects. On September 22, police responding to a call in Ryazan, a city about a hundred miles from Moscow, found three bags of explosives planted under the stairway of an apartment building.

In a country stricken with fear and grief, no one doubted that the

Chechens had done it, and I was not an exception. I had spent the previous couple of days driving around Moscow visiting Chechen families: refugees, professionals who had settled there long ago, temporary workers living in dormitories. All of them were terrified. Police in Moscow were rounding up young Chechen men, detaining hundreds of them in connection with the bombings. Many of the men I interviewed not only stopped going outside but refused even to open their apartment or dormitory-room doors. One family's child had come home from school saying the teacher had written the Russian words for "explosion" and "Chechens" side by side on the chalkboard.

I knew the police were detaining hundreds of innocent men, but I could easily imagine that whoever was guilty was a Chechen or a group of people who came from Chechnya. I had covered the 1994–1996 war in Chechnya from beginning to end. The first time I ever heard a bomb explode within yards of where I was standing, I was in the stairway of an apartment building for the blind on the outskirts of Grozny, the Chechen capital. It was January 1995—the first month of the war—and I had gone to that particular quarter of the city because the Russian army claimed it was not bombing civilians; I could imagine no one who fit the very definition of *civilian* better than the residents of that building: blind, helpless, unable to leave the city. When I stepped outside the building, I saw bodies and body parts strewn around.

The many children I saw on the streets of Grozny on that day and on subsequent days had seen the same thing. They were the children who would be hanging around the open fires on Grozny's sidewalks in the coming weeks, watching their mothers prepare food. These were the same children who would then spend years cooped up in tiny apartments—packed half a dozen to a room, because so many of the buildings had been bombed out of existence—and forbidden to go outside for fear of hitting a land mine or a Russian soldier, who might rape a girl or detain a boy. And still they went outside and were raped, detained, tortured, disappeared—or saw it happen to their sisters, brothers, and friends. These children were young adults now, and I had no trouble believing some of them would be capable of horrific revenge.

Most Russians had not seen what I had seen, but they saw television footage of the explosion sites, each one more terrifying than the last. The war in Chechnya had never really ended: the arrangement brokered three years earlier by Berezovsky, among others, amounted to a cease-fire. Russians were very much a nation at war, and, like all nations at war, they believed the enemy to be both less than human and capable of inflicting unimaginable horror.

On September 23, a group of twenty-four governors—more than a quarter of all governors in the federation—wrote a letter to President Yeltsin asking him to yield power to Putin, who had been in office as prime minister for just over a month. The same day, Yeltsin issued a secret decree authorizing the army to resume combat in Chechnya; the decree was also illegal, because Russian law forbids the use of regular troops within the country's borders. That day, Russian military planes once again began bombing Grozny, starting with the airport, the oil refinery, and residential neighborhoods. The following day, Putin issued his own order authorizing Russian troops to engage in combat in Chechnya; this time the order was not classified, though Russian law in fact gives the prime minister no authority over the military.

The same day, Putin made one of his first television appearances. "We will hunt them down," he said of the terrorists. "Wherever we find them, we will destroy them. Even if we find them in the toilet. We will rub them out in the outhouse."

Putin was using rhetoric markedly different from Yeltsin's. He was not promising to bring the terrorists to justice. Nor was he expressing compassion for the hundreds of victims of the explosions.

This was the language of a leader who was planning to rule with his fist. These sorts of vulgar statements, often spiced with below-the-belt humor, would become Putin's signature oratorical device. His popularity began to soar.

BEREZOVSKY THE PH.D. and his small propaganda army formed of highly educated men seemed to see no contradiction between their stated goal of securing Russia's democratic future and the man in whom they had chosen to vest their hopes for this future. They worked tirelessly on their campaign, using the might of Berezovsky's Channel One to smear former prime minister Primakov and his governor allies. One memorable program explained Primakov's recent hip surgery in repulsive anatomical detail. Another focused on Moscow mayor Yuri Luzhkov's ostensible resemblance to Mussolini. But in addition to discrediting his opponents, Putin's allies—who thought of themselves more as his authors than his supporters—had to create and put forth an image of their own candidate.

Strictly speaking, Putin was not running a campaign—the presidential election was not expected for nearly a year, and Russia did not have a political culture of protracted campaigns—but the people who wanted to see him become president were very much campaigning. An influential political consulting firm called the Foundation for Effective Politics, located in one of the city's most beautiful historic buildings, just across the river from the Kremlin, was tasked with creating the image of Putin as a young, energetic politician who would advance much-needed reform. "Everyone was so tired of Yeltsin, it was an easy job to do," a woman who had been instrumental in the campaign told me.

Her name was Marina Litvinovich, and like many people who worked at the Foundation for Effective Politics, she was very young, very smart (she had just graduated from one of the best universities), and very inexperienced in politics, even naive. She had come to work at the foundation part-time when she was still a student, and three years later she was a key person on the presidential campaign team. She believed herself to be entirely devoted to democratic ideals, and yet she saw nothing wrong with the way the future president was being invented and sold to the public: she simply trusted the people who had thought the whole thing up. "There were some articles coming out saying he was from the KGB," she told me years later, "but the headquarters was staffed with liberals and we were convinced these were the people who would make up his inner circle."

Nor did one have to be young and naive to believe that. In the late summer of 1999, I had a memorable dinner with Alexander Goldfarb, an old acquaintance who had been a dissident in the 1970s; he had played the role of Andrei Sakharov's translator, become an émigré, spending the 1980s in New York, and turned into a highly effective social activist in the 1990s. He had served as billionaire philanthropist George Soros's adviser on Russia; he had then launched a campaign to publicize and fight Russia's epidemic of drug-resistant tuberculosis, bringing it to the world's attention almost single-handedly. Now Alex and I were having dinner and talking about Putin. "He is the KGB's flesh and blood," I said to him, then still testing a theory more than making an argument. "But I hear from Chubais that he is smart, effective, and worldly," Alex countered. Even a former dissident was nearly convinced that Putin was the modern young politician the Foundation for Effective Politics was inventing.

The more the military campaign in Chechnya escalated, the more the entire country seemed to be in thrall. Berezovsky, meanwhile, came up with the idea of a new political party, one that would be entirely devoid of ideology. "Nobody would hear the words if we said them," he told me nine years later, still apparently convinced this had been a stellar invention. "I decided we would replace ideology with faces." Berezovsky's people cast about for faces and came up with a couple of celebrities and one cabinet minister. But the face that mattered most belonged to the man who had been faceless just weeks earlier: as Putin's popularity soared, so did the new political party's. In the parliamentary election on December 19, 1999, nearly a quarter of the voters chose the two-month-old bloc called Yedin-stvo (Unity) or Medved (The Bear), making it the largest faction in the lower house of parliament.

To cement Putin's lead, someone in the Family—no one seems able to recall who it was any longer—proposed a brilliant move: Yeltsin should resign early. As prime minister, Putin would, by law, become acting president, turning into an instant incumbent in the upcoming race. His opponents would be caught by surprise, and the lead time to the election would be shortened. In fact, Yeltsin should do it on December 31. It would be a very Yeltsin move: he would up-stage the millennium, the Y2K bug, and any other news story that might occur almost anyplace in the world. It would also come on the eve of the traditional two-week New Year's and Christmas hiatus, making the time available for Putin's opponents to prepare for the vote that much shorter.

NEW YEAR'S. a secular holiday, had long since superseded all other occasions as Russia's biggest family holiday. On this night, Russians everywhere would gather with friends and family; just before the end of the year they would assemble in front of their television sets to watch the clock on one of the Kremlin towers strike midnight—to raise their glasses of champagne and only then to sit down to a tra-ditional meal. In the minutes leading up to midnight, the nation's leader would give a speech; this had been a tradition in the Soviet Union, and it had been picked up by Boris Yeltsin on December 31, 1992 (on December 31, 1991, as the Soviet Union officially ended its existence, the nation was addressed by a comedian).

Yeltsin appeared on television twelve hours ahead of schedule. "My friends," he said. "My dears. Today is the last time I am going to address you on New Year's Eve. But that is not all. Today is the last time I address you as the president of Russia. I have made a decision. I spent a long and difficult time thinking about it. Today, on the last day of this century, I am going to resign. . . . I am leaving. . . . Russia should enter the new millennium with new politicians, new faces, new, smart, strong, energetic people. . . . Why should I hold on to my seat for six more months when the country has a strong person who deserves to become president and to whom virtually every Russian has linked his hopes for the future?"

Then Yeltsin apologized. "I am sorry," he said, "that many of our dreams failed to come true. That things we thought would be easy turned out to be painfully hard. I am sorry that I did not live up to the hopes of people who believed that we could, with a single effort, a single strong push, jump out of our gray, stagnant, totalitarian past and into a bright, wealthy, civilized future. I used to believe that myself. . . . I have never said this before, but I want you to know. I felt the pain of each of you in my heart. I spent sleepless nights, painful periods thinking about what I could do to make life just a little bit better. . . . I am leaving. I have done all I could. . . . A new generation is coming; they can do more, and better."

Yeltsin spoke for ten minutes. He looked bloated, heavy, barely mobile. He also looked dejected, helpless, like a man who was burying himself alive in plain view of over a hundred million people. His facial expression barely changed throughout the speech, but his voice cracked with emotion as he signed off.

At midnight, it was Vladimir Putin who appeared on television. He looked noticeably nervous at first, and even stuttered at the beginning of his speech, but seemed more confident as he went on. He spoke for three and a half minutes. Remarkably, he did not seem to use the opportunity to give his first stump speech. He made no promises and said nothing that could be interpreted as being inspiring. He said instead that nothing would change in Russia and assured viewers that their rights were well protected. In closing, he proposed Russians raise a glass to "Russia's new century"—though he had no glass of his own to raise.

Putin was now acting president, and the election campaign was officially under way. Putin, recalled Berezovsky, was disciplined and even docile: he did as he was told—and he was told not to do much. He was already so popular that this was, in essence, a non-campaign campaign, leading up to a non-election election. All Putin had to do was never seem too different from whatever it was voters wished to see in him.

On January 26, 2000, exactly two months before the election, the moderator of a Russia panel at the annual World Economic Forum in Davos, Switzerland, asked, "Who is Mr. Putin?" Chubais—the man who had seven months earlier argued that Putin would make an ideal successor—was holding the microphone when the question sounded. He fidgeted and looked questioningly at a former Russian prime minister sitting to his right. The former minister, too, was clearly unwilling to respond. The panel's four members started looking back and forth at each other anxiously. After half a minute of this, the room exploded in laughter. The world's largest landmass, a land of oil, gas, and nuclear arms, had a new leader, and its business and political elites had no idea who he was. Very funny indeed.

One week later, Berezovsky commissioned three journalists from a newspaper he owned to write Putin's life story. One of them was a young blonde who had spent a couple of years in the Kremlin pool but had managed to remain unnoticed next to more colorful colleagues. Another was a young reporter who had won acclaim for his humorous reports but had never written about politics. The third member of the team was a star, a veteran political reporter who had spent the early eighties covering wars all over the world, and the late eighties writing about politics and, especially, about the KGB for *Moscow News*, perestroika's flagship publication. Natalia Gevorkyan was a reporter's reporter, the undisputed leader of the team, and the journalist Berezovsky knew best.

"Berezovsky would keep calling me and asking, 'Isn't he fucking amazing?'" she told me years later. "I would say, 'Borya, your problem is, you have never known a KGB colonel. He is not fucking amazing. He is perfectly ordinary.'"

"I was curious, of course, to know who this guy was who was now going to run the country," she told me. "So I got the sense he liked to talk and he liked to talk about himself. I've certainly spoken to many people who were more interesting. I had spent five years writing about the KGB: he was no better or worse than the rest of them; he was smarter than some and more cunning than some."

In addition to the forbidding task of putting together a book in a matter of days, Natalia Gevorkyan wanted to use her time with the acting president to help a friend. Andrei Babitsky, a reporter for the U.S.-funded Radio Free Europe/Radio Liberty, had disappeared in Chechnya in January. He had apparently been detained by Russian troops for violating their strict embedding policy: during the first war in Chechnya the media had been sharply and consistently critical of Moscow's actions, so this time around, the military banned journalists from traveling in the war zone unaccompanied by uniformed personnel. This policy not only hindered access to combatants on both sides but exposed journalists to danger: it is almost always safer, in a war zone, not to have a uniform on you or near you. The more enterprising reporters tried to circumvent the policy—and few were better at this than Babitsky, who had for years been reporting specifically on the North Caucasus.

For two weeks following his detention, Babitsky's family and friends heard nothing from him. Rumor soon spread in Moscow's journalist circles, however, that Babitsky had been seen in the infamous Russian prison of Chernokozovo in Chechnya. On February 3, the day after Gevorkyan and her colleagues began interviewing Putin for his biography, Russian officials announced that Babitsky had been exchanged for three Russian soldiers who had been held captive by Chechen combatants. The Russian officials claimed Babitsky had consented to the exchange, but this could hardly conceal the fact that Russian troops had treated a journalist—a Russian journalist—as an enemy combatant.

When Gevorkyan asked Putin about Babitsky, her question elicited what she later described as "undisguised hatred." The acting president's flattened affect momentarily broke, and he launched into a diatribe: "He was working directly for the enemy. He was not a neutral source of information. He worked for the outlaws. . . . He worked for the outlaws. So when the rebels said, 'We are willing to free a few of your soldiers in exchange for this correspondent,' our people asked him, 'Do you want to be exchanged?' He said, 'I do.' He does. . . . These were our soldiers. They were fighting for Russia. If we had not taken them back, they would have been executed. And they aren't going to do anything to Babitsky there, because he is one of them. . . . What Babitsky did is much more dangerous than firing a machine gun. . . . He had a map of getting around our checkpoints. Who asked him to stick his nose in there if he wasn't authorized by the official authorities? . . . So he was arrested and he became the object of an investigation. And he says, 'I don't trust you, I trust the Chechens, if they want to take me, you should give me to them. . . .' He got a response: 'Then go, get out of here!' . . . So you say he is a Russian citizen. Then he should have acted in accordance with the laws of your country, if you want to be protected by these laws."

Listening to this monologue, Gevorkyan grew convinced that the acting president had direct knowledge of Babitsky's case. So she decided to be direct too. "He's got a family, he has children," she said to Putin. "You have to stop this operation."

The head of state took the bait. "There will be a car arriving soon," he said. "It will deliver a cassette tape, and you will see that he is alive and well." Gevorkyan, who had maintained decorum throughout her many meetings with Putin, was momentarily shocked into rudeness. "Hello?" she almost screamed. "You handed him over to the outlaws. Is this what they told you?"

She excused herself to step outside the room to call a friend at Radio Liberty's Moscow bureau. "Tell his wife he is alive," she said.

"How do you know?" asked the friend.

"From the horse's mouth," Gevorkyan responded.

"Do you trust him?" the friend asked.

"Not really," Gevorkyan admitted.

But a few hours later the friend called her back. "You are not going to believe this," she said. "A car came, its license plate so dirty we couldn't make out the numbers. They offered to sell us a video-cassette tape and we paid two hundred dollars for it."

The video, which Radio Liberty immediately released to all media, was a grainy recording of Babitsky, looking pale, exhausted, and sleep-deprived, saying, "This is February 6, 2000. I am relatively all right. My only problem is time, since circumstances are stacking up in such a way that, unfortunately, I cannot make it home right away. Here my life is as normal as it can be in conditions of war. People who are near me try to help me in some way. The only problem is, I would really like to go home, I would really like all of this to end finally. Please don't worry about me. I hope to be home soon."

In fact, Babitsky was being held under lock and key in a residential house in a Chechen village. He was indeed sleep-deprived, exhausted, and, most of all, terrified. He did not know who was holding him prisoner; he knew only that they were armed Chechen men who had every reason to hate Russians and no clear reason to trust him. He was unable to sleep, fearing as he went to bed every night that he would be awakened to be taken to his execution, and he greeted every morning hating himself for not yet having devised a way to escape or gathered the courage to attempt to break free. Finally, on February 23, he was placed in the trunk of a car, driven to the neighboring republic of Dagestan, given crudely forged documents, and released there—only to be arrested a few hours later by Russian police, who transported him to Moscow, where he would face charges of forgery for the documents he was carrying.

It soon emerged that there had probably been no exchange: there was no documented trace of it, or of the soldiers who had supposedly been handed over by the Chechens. Babitsky's arrest, his televised handover to the enemy, and subsequent disappearance had all, it seems, been an effort to send a message to journalists. Defense Minister Igor Sergeyev told the media as much: Babitsky had been singled out, he said, because "the information he transmitted was not objective, to put it mildly." He added, "I would happily have given ten Babitskys for a single soldier." Putin had been in office for one month and already ministers were talking just like him—just as, it seems, they had been longing to talk for a while.

What Putin apparently did not expect was that what he viewed as meting out perfectly fair punishment would inspire outrage internationally. During his first month as acting president, Western leaders had acted much like the Russian people: they seemed so relieved that unpredictable, embarrassing Yeltsin was gone that they were willing to project their sweetest dreams onto Putin. The Americans and the British acted as though the outcome of the March election were a foregone conclusion. But now the Americans had no choice but to react: Babitsky was not simply a Russian journalist—he was a Russian journalist employed by a media outlet funded by an act of Congress. Secretary of State Madeleine Albright raised the issue in a meeting with Russian foreign minister Igor Ivanov on February 4, and five days later the State Department issued a statement condemning the "treatment of a noncombatant as a hostage or prisoner of war."

The unexpected scrutiny and outrage probably saved Babitsky's life. They also made Putin bitter and angry. He knew that what he was doing was just and that a man like Babitsky—someone who seemed not at all concerned about the Russian war effort and not at all ashamed to feel compassion for the enemy—did not deserve to live, or at least to live among Russian citizens. A conspiracy of bleeding-heart democrats had forced Putin to compromise. He had success-fully beaten these kinds of people back in Leningrad, and he would do it again now.

"The Babitsky story made my life easier," Gevorkyan later told me. "I realized that this was how [Putin] was going to rule. That this is how his fucking brain works. So I had no illusions. I knew this was how he understood the word *patriotism*—just the way he had been taught in all those KGB schools: the country is as great as the fear it inspires, and the media should be loyal."

Soon after this discovery, Gevorkyan left Moscow for Paris, where she still lives. Andrei Babitsky, as soon as he was able, left for Prague, where he continued to work for Radio Liberty. But in the year 2000, in the days leading up to the election, Gevorkyan said nothing publicly. Putin's biography was published as he wanted it; even the impassioned and telling passage about Babitsky was cut, though it had made it into an advance newspaper excerpt. With few exceptions, Russians were led to persist in placing their faith in Putin.

ON MARCH 24. two days before the presidential election, NTV, the television network founded and owned by Vladimir Gusinsky—the same oligarch who owned the magazine where I worked—aired an hourlong program, in talk-show format before a live audience, de-voted to the incident in the city of Ryazan the previous September when police responding to a call had found three bags of explosives under the stairway of an apartment building. Vigilant residents thought they had managed to foil a terrorist plan.

Just after nine that evening, September 22, Alexei Kartofelnikov, a bus driver for the local soccer team, was returning home to a twelve-story brick apartment building at Fourteen Novoselov Street. He saw a Russian-made car pull up to the building. A man and a woman got out and went in through a door leading to the cellar, while the driver—another man—stayed in the car. Kartofelnikov watched the man and the woman emerge a few minutes later. Then the car pulled right up to the cellar door, and all three unloaded heavy-looking sacks and carried them into the cellar. They all then returned to the car and left.

By this time, four buildings had been blown up in Moscow and two other cities; in at least one case, eyewitnesses later emerged saying they had seen sacks planted in a stairwell. So it is not surprising that Kartofelnikov tried to take down the license plate number of the car. But the part of the license plate signifying the region where the car was registered was covered with a piece of paper that had the number that stood for Ryazan on it. Kartofelnikov called the police.

The police arrived nearly forty-five minutes later. Two officers entered the cellar, where they found three fifty-kilogram sacks marked SUGAR stacked one atop another. Through a slit in the top sack, they could see wires and a clock. They ran out of the cellar to call for reinforcement and began evacuating residents from the seventy-seven apartments in the building while the bomb squad was on its way. They combed the building, knocking on all doors and ordering residents to exit immediately. People came outside in their pajamas, nightgowns, and bathrobes, not pausing to lock their doors: after weeks of watching news reports of apartment building explosions, everyone took the threat seriously. Several disabled people were wheeled outside in their wheelchairs, but several severely disabled people stayed inside their apartments, terrified. The rest of the residents would spend most of the night standing in the chilling wind outside their building. After a time, the manager of a nearby movie theater invited the residents to come in and even organized hot tea for them. In the morning, many of the residents went to work, though the police did not allow them to enter the building to wash up or get a change of clothes. At some point, many of the apartments were looted.

Even before all the residents had made it outside, the bomb squad had disabled the timer and analyzed the contents of the sacks. They concluded it was hexogen, a powerful explosive in use since World War II (in English-speaking countries it is more commonly known as RDX). It was also the substance used in at least one of the Moscow explosions, so the entire country had learned the word *hexogen* from an announcement made by the mayor of Moscow. The crudely made detonation mechanism contained a clock set for 5:30 in the morning. The terrorists' plan was apparently exactly the same as in the Moscow explosions: the amount of explosive would have destroyed the building entirely (and possibly damaged nearby structures), killing all residents in their sleep.

After the bomb squad concluded that the sacks contained explosives, the city's uniformed brass rushed to Fourteen Novoselov Street. The head of the local branch of the FSB addressed the residents, congratulating them on being born again. Alexei Kartofelnikov, the driver who had phoned in the suspicious people with their sacks, became an instant hero. Local officials praised him and the vigilance of ordinary people in general: "The more alert we are, the better we can fight the evil that has taken up residence in our country," the first deputy governor told news agencies.

The following day, all of Russia talked only of Ryazan. In the terrifying reality in which Russians had been living for nearly a month, this seemed like the first bit of relatively good news. If the people mobilized—if they watched out for themselves, it seemed to say—they might be able to save themselves. Not only that, the terrorists might actually be caught: the police knew the make and color of the car, and Kartofelnikov had seen the people who unloaded the sacks. On September 24, Interior Minister Vladimir Rushailo, looking gaunt and haunted, spoke at an interagency meeting devoted to the series of explosions. "There have been some positive developments," said Rushailo. "For example, the fact that an explosion was prevented in Ryazan yesterday."

But half an hour later, something entirely unexpected and perfectly inexplicable happened. The head of the FSB, Nikolai Patrushev, a former Leningrad hand whom Putin had brought in as his deputy at the secret police and then chose to replace himself when he became prime minister, spoke to reporters in the same building where the interagency meeting was taking place, and said that Rushailo was wrong. "First, there was no explosion," he said. "Second, nothing was prevented. And I don't think it was very well done. It was a training exercise, and the bags contained sugar. There were no explosives."

In the coming days, FSB officials would explain that the two men and one woman who had planted the sacks were FSB officers from Moscow, that the sacks contained perfectly harmless sugar, that the whole exercise had been intended to test the alertness of the ordinary people of Ryazan and the battle-readiness of Ryazan's law enforcement. Ryazan officials failed to cooperate at first but then confirmed the FSB story, explaining that the bomb squad had misidentified the sugar as explosives because its testing equipment had been contaminated through extensive use on real explosives in Chechnya. The explanations did little to calm fears or to convince anyone who knew anything about the way the FSB worked. It seemed unconscionable but not unimaginable that a couple of hundred people would be held outside, scared and cold, for an entire night for the sake of a training exercise: after all, the Russian secret police was not known for its considerate ways. What utterly defied explanation, though, was the fact that the local chapter of the FSB had not been informed of the exercise, or that the interior minister was allowed to embarrass himself in public a day and a half after the exercise—and after twelve hundred of his troops had been mobilized to catch the suspects as they fled Ryazan.

Over the course of six months, NTV journalists had pieced together the story, riddled as it was with inconsistencies, and now they presented it to the viewers. They tried to tread carefully. Niko-lai Nikolayev, the host, began with the premise that what had happened in Ryazan had indeed been a training exercise. When a member of the audience suggested that it was time to put together the entire chain of events and ask whether the FSB had been involved in the August and September explosions, Nikolayev practically shouted, "No, we are not going to do that, we are not going to go there. We are talking only about Ryazan." Still, the picture that emerged from the show was chilling.

Nikolayev had invited many of the residents of Fourteen Novo-selov Street, including Kartofelnikov, to be in the studio audience. None of them believed the training exercise story. Then an audience member identified himself as a resident of the Ryazan building and began saying he believed it was an exercise. The other residents turned to him incredulously and, within seconds, began shouting in unison that they did not know the man and he certainly did not live in their building. The rest of the FSB's case was as unconvincing and as shoddily executed as the act of planting a fake resident in the audience. The FSB representatives could not explain why the initial tests showed the substance was hexogen, or why the local chapter of the FSB was unaware of the supposed exercise.

Watching the program, I thought back to the conversation I had had with my editor half a year earlier. In just six months, the limits of the possible had shifted in my mind. I could now believe the FSB had most likely been behind the deadly bombings that shook Russia and helped make Putin its leader. When the agency suddenly found itself on the verge of being exposed—when twelve hundred Ryazan policemen had set out on a manhunt, armed with detailed descriptions of the FSB agents who had planted explosives—the FSB quickly came up with the training exercise story: unconvincing, but sufficient to prevent the arrest of secret police agents by regular police. The deadly chain of explosions halted at the same time.

IT TOOK Boris Berezovsky much longer to acknowledge that the unthinkable was possible and even likely. I asked him about it almost ten years later. By this time he had personally funded investigations, books, and a film that built on and extended Nikolayev's investigation, and had come to believe that it had been the FSB that terrorized Russia in September 1999. But he still had a very difficult time reconciling what he had thought was happening in 1999 with his later view of those events.

"I can tell you with absolute sincerity that at the time I was sure it was the Chechens," he told me. "It was when I came here [to London] and started looking back that I eventually came to the conclusion that the explosions were organized by the FSB. And this conclusion was based not only on logic—not even so much on logic as on facts. But at the time I did not see those facts, plus I did not trust NTV, which belonged to Gusinsky, who supported Primakov. So I did not even pay attention. And it never even occurred to me that there was a parallel game to ours—that someone else was doing what they thought was right to get Putin elected. Now I am convinced that was exactly what was going on." The "someone else" would have been the FSB, and the "parallel game" would have been the explosions, intended to unite Russians in fear and in a desperate desire for a new, decisive, even aggressive leader who would spare no enemy.

"But I am certain the idea itself was not Putin's," he suddenly said.

This made no sense to me. The explosions began just three weeks after Putin was appointed prime minister. That would suggest that preparations began while he was still head of the FSB. Berezovsky objected that this was not necessarily the case: "It was all organized in a very short time, and this was why there were so many obvious mistakes made." Even if Berezovsky was correct, however, Putin was succeeded at the FSB by his right-hand man, Patrushev, who would hardly have hidden the plan from Putin. And if Putin had firsthand knowledge of such a relatively minor operation as the detention of Andrei Babitsky, then it seemed absurd to imagine he had not known of the planned bombing spree.

Berezovsky agreed, although he still would not lay the entire enterprise at Putin's feet. He said he had come to believe that the idea had originated in Putin's inner circle but had not been intended to support Putin himself: it was designed to boost any successor of Yeltsin's choosing. I thought Berezovsky might have devised this theory to allow himself to go on believing he had been the kingmaker and not just a pawn in 1999. On the other hand, I had to admit he was probably right that the explosions could have been used to elect anyone: if enough blood was shed, any previously unknown, faceless, and unqualified candidate could become president. Even if he was chosen practically at random.

Official Moscow's position remains that all of the explosions were organized by an Islamic terrorist group based in the Caucasus.

Three

THE AUTOBIOGRAPHY
OF A THUG

The group Berezovsky had assembled to write Putin's biography had only three weeks to produce a book. Their list of sources was limited: they had Putin himself—six long sit-down interviews—his wife; his best friend; a former teacher; and a former secretary from St. Petersburg's city hall. They were not there to investigate the man; their job was to write down a legend. It turned out to be the legend of a postwar Leningrad thug.

St. Petersburg is a Russian city of grand history and glorious architecture. But the Soviet city of Leningrad into which Vladimir Putin was born in 1952 was, in the lived experience of its people, a city of hunger, poverty, destruction, aggression, and death. Just eight years had elapsed since the end of the Siege of Leningrad.

The siege had begun when Nazi troops completed their circle around the city, severing all connections to Leningrad, on September 8, 1941, and ended 872 days later. More than a million civilians died, killed by hunger or by artillery fire, which was unceasing for the duration of the blockade. Nearly half of these people died on their way out of the city. The lone route not controlled by the Germans bore the name the Road of Life, and hundreds of thousands of civilians died along this road, killed by bombs and famine. No city in modern times has seen famine and loss of life on this scale—and yet many survivors believed the authorities intentionally underestimated the number of casualties.

No one knows how long it takes a city to recover from violence so profound and grief so pervasive. "Imagine a soldier who is living a life of peacetime routine but is surrounded with the same walls and the same objects as were with him in the trenches," wrote, some years after the war, the authors of an oral history of the Siege of Leningrad, trying to conjure the extent to which the city was still living the siege. "The ceiling's antique molding bears the traces of shrapnel. The glossy surface of the piano bears the scratches left by broken glass. The shiny parquet floor has a burned-in stain where the wood-burning stove used to stand."

Burzhuikas—movable cast-iron wood-burning stoves—were what Leningrad residents used to heat their apartments during the siege. The city's furniture and books had gone into them. The black potbellied stoves were a symbol of despair and abandonment: the authorities, who had assured Soviet citizens they were well protected against all enemies—and that Germany was friend, not foe—had left the people of the country's second-largest city to starve and freeze to death. And then—when the siege was over—they had invested in restoring the glorious suburban palaces looted by the Germans but not in restoring the residential buildings in the city itself. Vladimir Putin was raised in an apartment that still had a wood-burning stove in every room.

His parents, Maria and Vladimir Putin, had survived the siege in the city. The elder Vladimir Putin had joined the army in the early days of the Soviet-German war and had been wounded seriously in battle not far from Leningrad. He was taken to a hospital inside the line of the siege, and Maria found him there. After several months in the hospital, he remained severely disabled: both of his legs were disfigured and caused him great physical pain for the rest of his life. The elder Putin was discharged from the military and returned home with Maria. Their only son, who must have been between eight and ten years old at the time, was staying at one of several homes for children organized in the city, apparently in the hope that institutions could provide better care than desperate and starving parents. The boy died there. Maria came close to death herself: by the time the siege was lifted, she was no longer strong enough to walk on her own.

These were the future president's parents: a disabled man, a woman who had come very close to dying from starvation and who had lost her children (a second son had died in infancy several years before the war). But by the measure of the postwar Soviet Union, the Putins were lucky: they had each other. Following the war, there were nearly twice as many women of child-bearing age as there were men. Statistics aside, the war had wrought tragedy in virtually every family, separating husbands and wives, destroying homes, and displacing millions. To have lived not only through the war but through the siege, and to still have your spouse—and your home— was, essentially, a miracle.

The younger Vladimir Putin's birth was another miracle, so un- likely that it has given life to the persistent rumor that the Putins adopted him. On the eve of Putin's first presidential election, a woman came forward in Georgia, in the Caucasus, claiming she had given him up for adoption when he was nine years old. A number of articles and a book or two advancing this story followed, and indeed even Natalia Gevorkyan was inclined to believe the story: she found his parents strikingly doting, and the fact that the team of biogra- phers found no one who remembered knowing the boy before he reached school age reinforced her suspicions. It is, however, not only impossible to prove or disprove the adoption theory but also unnecessary: the indisputable fact is, whether biological or adopted, Vladimir Putin, by the standards of his time, was a miracle child.

BECAUSE VLADIMIR PUTIN WAS CATAPULTED to power from obscurity, and because he spent his entire adult life within the confines of a secret and secretive institution, he has been able to exercise greater control over what is known about him than almost any other modern politician—certainly more than any modern Western politician. He has created his own mythology. This is a good thing, because, to a far greater extent than is usually possible for any man, Vladimir Putin has communicated to the world directly what he would like to be known about him and how he would like to be seen. What has emerged is very much the mythology of a child of post-siege Leningrad, a mean, hungry, impoverished place that bred mean, hungry, ferocious children. At least, they were the ones who survived.

One entered the building in which Putin grew up through the courtyard. St. Petersburg residents call these formations "well courtyards": enclosed on all sides by tall apartment buildings, they make a person feel as if he were standing at the bottom of a giant stone well. Like all such courtyards, this one was strewn with trash, potholed, and unlit. So was the building itself: the nineteenth-century stairs were crumbling, and the stairwell rarely had a working lightbulb. Chunks of the handrail were missing, and the rest of the construction wobbled wildly. The Putins lived on the top floor of the five-story building, and the journey up the dark stairs could be risky.

Like most apartments in central Leningrad, this was part of a flat once built with well-off renters in mind, then divided into two or three apartments, only to be split again among several families. The Putins' apartment did not have a proper kitchen, so a single gas stove and a sink were stationed in the narrow hallway one entered from the stairwell. Three families used the four-burner stove to prepare their meals. A makeshift but permanent toilet had been constructed by annexing part of the stairwell. The small space was unheated. To bathe, the residents would heat water on the gas stove and then wash themselves while perched over the toilet in the tiny cold room.

Vladimir Putin the younger was, naturally, the only child in the apartment. An older married couple lived in a windowless room that was eventually judged uninhabitable. An old observant Jewish couple and their grown daughter occupied a room on the other side of the hallway-cum-kitchen from the Putins. Conflicts flared regularly in the communal kitchen, but the adults apparently cooperated in shielding the boy from their quarrels. Putin often spent time playing in the Jewish family's room—and, speaking to his biographers, he made a striking assertion, claiming he did not differentiate between his parents and the old Jews.

The Putins had the largest room in the flat: around twenty square meters, or roughly twelve feet by fifteen. By the standards of the time, this was an almost palatial abode for a family of three. Almost incredibly, the Putins also had a television set, a telephone, and a dacha, a cabin outside the city. The elder Vladimir Putin worked as a skilled laborer at a train car factory; Maria took backbreaking unskilled jobs that allowed her to spend time with her son: she worked as a night watchman, a cleaning woman, a loader. But if one examines the fine shades of postwar Soviet poverty, the Putins emerge as practically rich. Given their unceasing doting on their son, this sometimes produced noteworthy results, such as first-grader Vladimir's sporting a wristwatch, a rare, expensive, and prestigious accessory for any age group in that time and place.

The school was just a few steps from the building where the Putins lived. The education offered was, from what one can gather, unremarkable. The teacher for the first four grades was a very young woman who was finishing her college education by going to night school. Not that education was a priority in 1960, when Vladimir Putin entered first grade at the age of almost eight. His father was, by all accounts, concerned primarily with discipline, not with the quality of schooling his son received. Nor was education part of the younger Putin's idea of success; he has placed a great emphasis on portraying himself as a thug, and in this he has had the complete cooperation of his childhood friends. By far the largest amount of biographical information available about him—that is, the bulk of the information made available to his biographers—concerns the many fistfights of his childhood and youth.

THE COURTYARD is a central fixture of postwar Soviet life, and Vladimir Putin's personal mythology is very much rooted in it. With adults working a six-day week and child care generally nonexistent, Soviet children tended to grow up in the communal spaces outside their overcrowded apartment buildings. In Putin's case, this meant growing up at the bottom of the well—in the well courtyard, that is, strewn with litter and populated by toughs. "Some courtyard this was," his former classmate and longtime friend Viktor Borisenko told a biographer. "Thugs all. Unwashed, unshaven guys with cigarettes and bottles of cheap wine. Constant drinking, cursing, fistfights. And there was Putin in the middle of all this. . . . When we were older, we would see the thugs from his courtyard, and they had drunk themselves into the ground, they were hitting bottom. Many of them had been to jail. In other words, they did not manage to get good lives for themselves."

Putin, younger than the thugs and slight of build, tried to hold his own with them. "If anyone ever insulted him in any way," his friend recalled, "Volodya would immediately jump on the guy, scratch him, bite him, rip his hair out by the clump—do anything at all never to allow anyone to humiliate him in any way."

Putin brought his fighting ways to grade school with him. References to fistfights abound in the recollections of his former schoolmates, but the following description gives a telling snapshot of the future president's temperament: "The labor [shop] teacher dragged Putin by the collar, from his classroom to ours. We had been making dustpans in his class and Vladimir had done something wrong. . . . It took him a long time to calm down. The process itself was interesting. It would start to look like he was feeling better, like it was all over. And then he would flare up again and start expressing his outrage. He did this several times over."

The school punished Putin by excluding him from the Young Pioneers organization—a rare, almost exotic form of punishment, generally reserved for children who were held back repeatedly and essentially deemed hopeless. Putin was a marked boy: for three years, he was the only child in the school who did not wear a red kerchief around his neck, symbolizing membership in the Communist organization for ten-to-fourteen-year-olds. Putin's outcast status was all the more peculiar considering how well-off he was compared with the other children at his school, most of whom were statistically unlikely to be living with two parents.

But to Putin, his thug credentials represented true status, flaunted in his responses to his biographers in 2000:

> "Why did you not get inducted into the Young Pioneers until sixth grade? Were things really so bad?"
>
> "Of course. I was no Pioneer; I was a hooligan."
>
> "Are you putting on airs?"
>
> "You are trying to insult me. I was a real thug."

Putin's social, political, and academic standing changed when he was thirteen: as a sixth-grader, he began to apply himself academically and was rewarded not only with induction into the Young Pioneers but, immediately after, by election to the post of class chairman. The fighting continued unabated, however: Putin's friends told his biographers a series of fighting stories, the same plot repeating itself year after year.

"We were playing a game of chase out in the street," a grade school classmate recalled. "Volodya was passing by, and he saw that a boy much older and bigger than me is chasing me and I am running as hard as I can. He jumped in, trying to protect me. A fight ensued. Then we sorted it out, of course."

"We were in eighth grade when we were standing at a tram stop, waiting," recounted another friend. "A tram pulled up, but it was not going where we needed to go. Two huge drunken men got off and started trying to pick a fight with somebody. They were cursing and pushing people around. Vovka calmly handed his bag over to me, and then I saw that he has just sent one of the men flying into a snowbank, face-first. The second one turned around and started at Volodya, screaming, 'What was that?' A couple of seconds later he knew exactly what it was, because he was lying there next to his buddy. That was just when our tram pulled up. If there is anything I can say about Vovka, it's that he never let bastards and rascals who insult people and bug them get away with it."

As a young KGB officer, Putin reenacted his earlier fights.

"He once invited me to witness the Procession of the Cross at Easter," recalls still another friend. "He was on duty, helping cordon off the procession. And he asked me if I wanted to come see the altar in the church. I said yes, of course: it was such a boyish thing to do—no one was allowed there, but we could just go in. So after the Procession of the Cross we were on our way home. And we were standing at a bus stop. Some people came up to us. They didn't look like criminals, more like college students who had had a bit to drink. They say, 'You got a smoke?' Vovka says, 'No.' And they say, 'What are you doing, answering like that?' And he says, 'Nothing.' And I didn't even have time to see what happened after. One of them must have hit him or pushed him. I just saw someone's stocking feet slide past me. The guy went flying somewhere. And Volod'ka says to me, all calm, 'Let's get out of here.' And we left. I really liked the way he threw that guy who tried to pick on him. One second—and his feet were up in the air."

The same friend recalled that a few years later, when Putin was attending spy school in Moscow, he came home to Leningrad for a few days, only to get into a fight on the subway. "Someone picked on him and he took care of the thug," the friend told Putin's biographers. "Volodya was very upset. 'They are not going to be understanding about this in Moscow,' he said. 'There will be consequences.' And I guess he did get into some kind of trouble, though he never told me any details. It all worked out in the end."

Putin, it would appear, reacted to the barest provocation by getting into a street brawl—risking his KGB career, which would have been derailed had he been detained for the fight or even so much as noticed by the police. Whether or not the stories are exactly true, it is notable that Putin has painted himself—and allowed himself to be painted by others—as a consistently rash, physically violent man with a barely containable temper. The image he has chosen to present is all the more remarkable because it seems inconsistent with a discipline to which Putin devoted his teenage years.

At the age of ten or eleven, Putin went shopping for a place where he could learn skills to supplement his sheer will to fight. Boxing proved too painful: he had his nose broken during one of his first training sessions. Then he found Sambo. Sambo, an acronym for the Russian phrase that translates as "self-defense without weapons," is a Soviet martial art, a hodgepodge of judo, karate, and folk wrestling moves. His parents were opposed to the boy's new hobby. Maria called it "foolishness" and seemed to fear for her child's safety, and the elder Vladimir forbade the lessons. The coach had to pay several visits to the Putins' room before the boy was allowed consistently to attend the daily training sessions.

Sambo, with its discipline, became part of Putin's transformation from a grade school thug into a goal-directed and hardworking adolescent. It was also linked to what had become an overriding ambition: Putin had apparently heard that the KGB expected new recruits to be skilled in hand-to-hand combat.

"IMAGINE A BOY who dreams of being a KGB officer when everyone else wants to be a cosmonaut," Gevorkyan said to me, trying to explain how odd Putin's passion seemed to her. I did not find it quite so far-fetched: in the 1960s, Soviet cultural authorities invested heavily in creating a romantic, even glamorous image of the secret police. When Vladimir Putin was twelve, a novel called *The Shield and the Sword* became a bestseller. Its protagonist was a Soviet intelligence officer working in Germany. When Putin was fifteen, the novel was made into a wildly popular miniseries. Forty-three years later, as prime minister, Putin would meet with eleven Russian spies deported from the United States—and together, in a show of camaraderie and nostalgia, they would sing the theme song from the miniseries.

"When I was in ninth grade, I was influenced by films and books, and I developed a desire to work for the KGB," Putin told his biographer. "There is nothing special about that." The protestation begs the question: Was there something else, besides books and movies, that formed what became Putin's single-minded passion? It seems there was, and Putin hid it in plain sight, as the best spies do.

We all want our children to grow up to be a better, more successful version of ourselves. Vladimir Putin, the miraculous late son of two people maimed and crippled by World War II, was born to be a Soviet spy; in fact, he was born to be a Soviet spy in Germany. During World War II, the senior Vladimir Putin had been assigned to so-called subversive troops, small detachments formed to act behind enemy lines. These troops reported to the NKVD, as the Soviet secret police was then called, and were formed largely from the ranks of the NKVD. They were on a suicide mission: no more than 15 percent of them survived the first six months of the war. Vladimir Putin's detachment was typical: twenty-eight soldiers were air-dropped into a forest behind enemy lines about a hundred miles from Leningrad. They had had about enough time to get their bearings and blow up one train when they ran out of food supplies. They asked the locals for food; the villagers fed them and then turned them in to the Germans. Several of the men managed to break out. The Germans gave chase, and Vladimir Putin hid in a swamp, submerging his head and breathing through a reed until the search party had given up. He was one of only four survivors of that mission.

Wars give birth to bizarre stories, and the legend with which the younger Vladimir Putin grew up is as likely to have been true as any other tale of miraculous survival and spontaneous heroism. It may also very well explain why he signed up for a German-language elective in fourth grade, when he was still a notoriously poor student. It certainly explains why, as a schoolboy, Putin had a portrait of the founding father of Soviet spyhood propped up on his desk at the dacha. His closest childhood friend recalled it was "some intelligence officer for sure, because Volod'ka told me it was," and Putin supplied his biographers with the name of his idol. Yan Berzin, hero of the Revolution, founder of Soviet military intelligence, creator of spy outposts in all European countries, was, like many early Bolsheviks, arrested and shot in the late 1930s for an imagined anti-Stalin plot.

His name was restored to honor in 1956 but has remained obscure ever since. You would have had to be a true KGB geek not only to know the name but to have secured the portrait.

It is not clear whether the elder Vladimir Putin had worked for the secret police before the war or continued to work for the NKVD after. It seems probable enough that he remained part of the so-called active reserve, a giant group of secret police officers who held regular jobs while also informing for—and drawing a salary from—the KGB. This may explain why the Putins lived so comparatively well: the dacha, the television set, and the telephone—especially the telephone.

At the age of sixteen, a year before finishing secondary school, Vladimir Putin went to the KGB headquarters in Leningrad to try to sign up. "A man came out," he recalled for a biographer. "He did not know who I was. And I never saw him again after that. I told him I go to school and in the future I would like to work for the state security services. I asked if it was possible and what I would have to do to achieve it. The man said they don't usually sign up volunteers, but the best way for me would be to go to college or serve in the military. I asked him which college. He said a law college or the law department of the university would be best."

"He surprised everyone by saying he would be applying to the university," his class teacher—the equivalent of a homeroom teacher in the United States—told his biographers. "I asked, 'How?' He said, 'I'll handle it myself.'" Leningrad University was one of the two or three most prestigious institutions of higher learning in the Soviet Union, certainly by far the most competitive in the city. How a mediocre student from a family that could by no means be considered well connected—even if I am correct in assuming that the elder Putin worked for the secret police—planned to gain admission was a mystery. His parents apparently protested, as did his coach: all of them favored a college to which Putin would be more likely to be accepted, which, in turn, would keep him out of mandatory military service and close to home.

Putin graduated from secondary school with the grades of "excellent" in history, German, and gym; "good" in geography, Russian, and literature; and "satisfactory" (the equivalent of a C) in physics, chemistry, algebra, and geometry. Leningrad University reportedly had forty people applying for a single spot. How did Putin get in? It is just possible that his determination was great enough that he could prepare himself for the grueling exams, at the expense of his high school work—a strategy that would have taken advantage of the fact that the university based admissions decisions solely on a series of written and oral exams, not on transcripts. It is also possible that the KGB ensured he would get in.

AT UNIVERSITY Putin kept to himself—as he had in the last couple of years of secondary school—staying out of community and Komsomol activities. He kept his grades up and spent his free time training in judo (his coach and teammates had traded in Sambo for an Olympic martial art) and driving around in his car. Putin was, more than likely, the only student at Leningrad University who owned a car. In the early 1970s a car in the Soviet Union was a rarity: mass car production was in gestation—even twenty years later, the number of cars per thousand people in the USSR barely reached sixty (compared with 781 in the United States). A car cost roughly as much as a dacha. The Putins won the car, a late-model two-door with a motorcycle engine, in a lottery, and rather than take the money—which would have been enough to get them out of the communal apartment and into a separate flat in a newly constructed building on the outskirts—gave the car to their son. That they gave the younger Putin this lavish gift, and that he accepted it, are further examples of the

Putins' extraordinarily doting relationship with their son, or their incongruous riches—or both.

Whatever the reason, Putin's relationship to money—extravagant and strikingly selfish for his social context—appears to have taken shape during his university years. Like other students, he spent his summers working on far-flung construction sites, where the pay was very good: the state compensated laborers well for the danger and hardship of working in the Far North. Putin made a thousand rubles one summer and five hundred the following year—enough to, say, put a new roof on the dacha. Any other young Soviet man in his position—an only son, living with and entirely financially dependent on his parents, both of them past retirement age—would have been expected to give all or most of that money to his family. But the first summer Putin joined two classmates in traveling straight from the Far North to the Soviet south, the town of Gagry on the Black Sea in Georgia, where he managed to spend all his money in a few days. The following year, he returned to Leningrad after working on a construction site, and spent the money he had made on an overcoat for himself—and a frosted cake for his mother.

"ALL THROUGH my university years I kept waiting for that man I spoke to at KGB headquarters to remember me," Putin told his biographers. "But they had forgotten all about me, because I had been a schoolboy when I came. . . . But I remembered they do not sign up volunteers, so I made no moves myself. Four years went by. Silence. I decided the issue was closed and started looking around for other possible job assignments. . . . But when I was in my fourth year, I was contacted by a man who said he wanted to meet with me. He did not say who he was, but somehow I knew right away. Because he said, 'We will be talking about your future job assignment, that is what I would like to discuss with you. I am not going to be any more specific for now.'

That's when I figured it out. If he does not want to say where he works, that means he works *there*."

The KGB officer met with Putin four or five times and concluded that he was "not particularly outgoing but energetic, flexible, and brave. Most important, he was good at connecting with people fast—a key quality for a KGB officer, especially if he plans to work in intelligence."

The day Putin learned he would be working for the KGB, he came to see Viktor Borisenko, who had remained his best friend since grade school. "He says, 'Let's go.' I say, 'Where are we going, why?' He doesn't answer. We get in his car and go," Borisenko told an interviewer. "We pull up at a Caucasian food place. I'm intrigued. I'm trying to figure out what's going on. But I never did. It was just clear that something extremely important had happened. But Putin isn't telling me what. He is not even giving any hints. But he was all very celebratory. Something very important had happened in his life. Only later did I understand that this was how my friend was celebrating, with me, his going to work for the KGB."

Later, Putin made no secret of his work for the KGB. He told a cellist named Sergei Roldugin, who would become his best friend, almost as soon as the two met. Roldugin, who had traveled abroad with his orchestra and had seen KGB handlers at work, says he was apprehensive and curious at once. "Once I tried to get him to talk about some operation that had gone down, and I failed," he told Putin's biographers. "Another time I said to him, 'I am a cellist, and that means I play the cello. I'll never be a surgeon. What's your job? I mean, I know you are an intelligence officer. But what does that mean? Who are you? What can you do?' And he said, 'I am an expert in human relations.' That was the end of the conversation. He really thought he knew something about people. . . . And I was impressed. I was proud and very much treasured the fact that he was an expert in human relations." (The skeptical note in Roldugin's "He really thought he knew something . . ." is as clear and unmistakable in the original Russian as it is in the English translation, but it seems that both Roldugin and Putin, who certainly vetted the quote, missed it.)

Putin's own descriptions of his relationships paint him as a strikingly inept communicator. He had one significant relationship with a woman before meeting his future wife; he left her at the altar. "That's how it happened," he told his biographers, explaining nothing. "It was really hard." He was no more articulate on the subject of the woman he actually married—nor, it seems, was he successful at communicating his feelings to her during their courtship. They dated for more than three years—an extraordinarily long time by Soviet or Russian standards, and at a very advanced age: Putin was almost thirty-one when they married, which made him a member of a tiny minority—less than ten percent—of Russians who remained unmarried past the age of thirty. The future Mrs. Putin was a domestic flight attendant from the Baltic Sea city of Kaliningrad; they had met through an acquaintance. She has gone on record saying it was by no means love at first sight, for at first sight Putin seemed unremarkable and poorly dressed; he has never said anything publicly about his love for her. In their courtship, it seems, she was both the more emotional and the more insistent one. Her description of the day he finally proposed paints a picture of a failure to communicate so profound that it is surprising these people actually managed to get married and have two children.

"One evening we were sitting in his apartment, and he says, 'Little friend, by now you know what I'm like. I am basically not a very convenient person.' And then he went on to describe himself: not a talker, can be pretty harsh, can hurt your feelings, and so on. Not a good person to spend your life with. And he goes on. 'Over the course of three and a half years you've probably made up your mind.' I realized we were probably breaking up. So I said, 'Well, yes, I've made up my mind.' And he said, with doubt in his voice, 'Really?'

That's when I knew we were definitely breaking up. 'In that case,' he said, 'I love you and I propose we get married on such and such a day.' And that was completely unexpected."

They were married three months later. Ludmila quit her job and moved to Leningrad to live with Putin in the smaller of two rooms in an apartment he now shared with his parents. The apartment, in a new concrete-block monstrosity about forty minutes by subway from the center of town, had been the Putins' since 1977: the younger Vladimir Putin had a room of his own for the first time at the age of twenty-five. It was about 130 square feet, and it had a single window placed so oddly high that one had to be standing to be able to look out of it. The newlyweds' living conditions, in other words, were roughly similar to those of millions of other Soviet couples.

Ludmila enrolled at Leningrad University, where she studied philology. She became pregnant with their first child about a year after the wedding. While she was pregnant, and for a few months after she had Maria, her husband was in Moscow, enrolled in a year-long course that would prepare him for service in the foreign intelligence corps. She had known he worked for the KGB long before the wedding, even though initially he told her he was a police detective: such was his cover.

THAT PUTIN SEEMS not to have been conscientious about using his cover is probably an indication that he was not sure what exactly he was covering up. His ambition—or, more accurately, his dream—had been to have secret powers of sorts. "I was most amazed by how a small force, a single person, really, can accomplish something an entire army cannot," he told his biographers. "A single intelligence officer could rule over the fates of thousands of people. At least, that's how I saw it."

Putin wanted to rule the world, or a part of it, from the shadows. That is very much the role he ultimately achieved, but when he first joined the KGB, his prospects of ever having anything significant or remotely interesting to do seemed far from certain.

In the middle to late 1970s, when Putin joined the KGB, the secret police, like all Soviet institutions, was undergoing a phase of extreme bloating. Its growing number of directorates and departments were producing mountains of information that had no clear purpose, application, or meaning. An entire army of men and a few women spent their lives compiling newspaper clippings, transcripts of tapped telephone conversations, reports of people followed and trivia learned, and all of this made its way to the top of the KGB pyramid, and then to the leadership of the Communist Party, largely unprocessed and virtually unanalyzed. "Only the Central Committee of the Communist Party had the right to think in broad political categories," wrote the last chairman of the KGB, whose task it was to dismantle the institution. "The KGB was relegated to collecting primary information and carrying out decisions made elsewhere. This structure excluded the possibility of developing a tradition of strategic political thinking within the KGB itself. But it was unparalleled in its ability to supply information of the sort and in the amount in which it was ordered." In other words, the KGB took the concept of carrying out orders to its logical extreme: its agents saw what they were told to see, heard what they were told to hear, and reported back exactly what was expected of them.

The internal ideology of the KGB, as of any police organization, rested on a clear concept of the enemy. The institution thrived on a siege mentality, which had driven the massive manhunts and purges of the Stalin era. But Putin entered the service not only in the post-Stalin era but also during one of the very few, very brief periods of peace in Soviet history: after Vietnam and before Afghanistan, the country was involved in no ongoing armed conflict, covertly or openly. The only active enemies were the dissidents, a handful of brave souls who drew a disproportionate amount of KGB force. A new law, Article 190' of the Penal Code, made it a crime to "spread rumors or information detrimental to the Soviet societal and governmental structure," giving the KGB virtually unlimited power in hunting down and fighting those who dared to think differently. Dissidents, suspected dissidents, and those leaning toward activity that might be considered dissident were the objects of constant surveillance and harassment. Putin claims not to have taken part in anti-dissident work but has shown in interviews that he was thoroughly familiar with the way it was organized, probably because he was lying about not having done it. A perfectly laudatory memoir of Putin written by a former colleague who defected to the West in the late 1980s mentions matter-of-factly that in Leningrad, Putin worked for the Fifth Directorate, created to fight the dissidents.

After university, Putin spent half a year pushing papers at the KGB offices in Leningrad. Then he spent six months going to KGB officer school. "It was an entirely unremarkable school in Leningrad," he told his biographers—one of dozens across the country where university graduates got their secret-police qualifications. After graduation, Putin was assigned to the counterintelligence unit in Leningrad. It was a backwater of backwater assignments. Counterintelligence officers in Moscow spent their time trailing suspected or known foreign intelligence agents, almost all of whom worked at foreign embassies in the city. There were no embassies in Leningrad, and no one, really, to trail.

After six months in the counterintelligence unit, Putin was sent to Moscow for a one-year training course, and then returned to Leningrad, now assigned to the intelligence unit. It was another dreary assignment, and Putin was stuck in it, like hundreds, possibly thousands, of unremarkable young men who had once dreamed of being spies and who now waited for someone to notice them. But they had been drafted by the bloated KGB for no particular reason and no particular purpose, so their waiting could be long and even endless. Putin waited for four and a half years.

His break came in 1984, when he was finally sent to spy school in Moscow for a year. There the thirty-two-year-old KGB major seems to have done everything possible to show just how much he needed this job. He wore a three-piece suit in sweltering heat, for example, to demonstrate respect and discipline. It was a wise strategy: spy school was, in essence, a very long, involved, and labor-intensive placement service—the students were studied carefully by the faculty, who would be making recommendations on their future.

One of Putin's instructors criticized Putin for his "lowered sense of danger"—a serious flaw for a potential spy. His Mastery of Intelligence instructor—in essence, the communication coach—said Putin was a closed, not very social person. Overall, however, he was a good student, entirely devoted to his work at the school. He was even appointed class foreman—his first leadership position since he was elected class chairman in sixth grade—and apparently did his job well.

Barring an unexpected disaster, Putin knew he would be assigned to work in Germany: much of his work at spy school had focused on improving his language skills. (He would eventually become fluent in German, but he never managed to lose his thick Russian accent.) The big question at graduation, then, was whether he would be going to East or West Germany. The former, while unquestionably appealing because it was a foreign assignment, was not at all what Putin had been dreaming of for nearly twenty years by now: it would not be espionage work. For that, he would have to be assigned to West Germany.

WHAT ULTIMATELY happened fell just short of failure. Following a year at spy school, Putin would be going to Germany, but not to West Germany, and not even to Berlin: he was assigned to the industrial

city of Dresden. At the age of thirty-three, Putin, with Ludmila—
who was once again pregnant—and one-year-old Maria, traveled to
another backwater assignment. This was the job for which he had
worked and waited for twenty years, and he would not even be
undercover. The Putins, like five other Russian families, were given
an apartment in a large apartment block in a little Stasi world: secret-
police staff lived here, worked in a building a five-minute walk away,
and sent their children to nursery school in the same compound.
They walked home for lunch and spent evenings at home or visiting
colleagues in the same building. Their job was to collect information
about "the enemy," which was the West, meaning West Germany and,
especially, United States military bases in West Germany, which were
hardly more accessible from Dresden than they would have been
from Leningrad. Putin and his colleagues were reduced mainly to
collecting press clippings, thus contributing to the growing mountains of useless information produced by the KGB.

Ludmila Putina liked Germany and the Germans. Compared
with the Soviet Union, East Germany was a land of plenty. It was also
a land of cleanliness and orderliness: she liked the way her German
neighbors hung their identical-looking laundry on parallel clothes-
lines at the same time every morning. Their neighbors, it seemed to
her, lived better than the Putins were used to. So the Putins saved,
buying nothing for their temporary apartment, hoping to go home
with enough money to buy a car.

The Putins had a second daughter and named her Ekaterina.
Putin drank beer and got fat. He stopped training, or exercising at
all, and he gained over twenty pounds—a disastrous addition to his
short and fairly narrow frame. From all appearances, he was seriously
depressed. His wife, who has described their early years together as
harmonious and joyful, has pointedly refrained from saying anything
about their family life after spy school. She has said only that her
husband never talked to her about work.

Not that there was much to tell. The staff of the KGB outpost in Dresden were divided among various KGB directorates; Putin was assigned to Directorate S, the illegal intelligence-gathering unit (this was the KGB's own terminology, denoting agents using assumed identities and falsified documents—as opposed to "legal intelligence gathering," carried out by people who did not hide their affiliation with the Soviet state). This might have been his dream posting—except that it was in Dresden. The job Putin had once coveted, working to draft future undercover agents, turned out to be not only tedious but fruitless. Putin and his two colleagues from the illegal-intelligence unit, aided by a retired Dresden policeman who also drew a salary from the unit, tracked down foreign students enrolled at Dresden University of Technology—there were a number of students from Latin America who, the KGB hoped, would eventually be able to go undercover in the United States—and spent months gaining their confidence, often only to find that they did not have enough money to entice the young people to work for them.

Money was a source of constant worry, hurt, and envy. Soviet citizens viewed long-term foreign postings as an incomparable source of income, often enough to lay the foundation for a lifetime of good living back home. East Germany, however, was viewed as not quite foreign enough, by ordinary people as well as by Soviet authorities: salaries and perks there could hardly be compared with those in a "real" foreign land, which is to say, a capitalist country. Shortly before the Putins arrived in Dresden, the government finally authorized small monthly hard-currency payments (the equivalent of about a hundred dollars) as part of the salaries of Soviet citizens working in Socialist bloc countries. Still, KGB staff in Dresden had to scrimp and save to ensure that at the end of their posting they would have something to show for it. Over the years, certain conventions of frugality had set in—using newspapers instead of curtains to cover the windows, for example. But while all the Soviet agents lived in the same sort of squalor, Stasi agents who had apartments in the same building enjoyed a much higher standard of living: they made a lot more money.

Still, it was in the West—so close and so unreachable for someone like Putin (some other Soviet citizens posted in Germany had the right to go to West Berlin)—that people had the things Putin really coveted. He made his wishes known to the very few Westerners with whom he came in contact—members of the radical group Red Army Faction, who took some of their orders from the KGB and occasionally came to Dresden for training sessions. "He always wanted to have things," a former RAF member told me of Putin. "He mentioned to several people wishes that he wanted from the West." This particular man claims to have personally presented Putin with a Grundig Satellit, a state-of-the-art shortwave radio, and a Blaupunkt stereo for his car; he bought the former and pilfered the latter from one of the many cars the RAF had stolen for its purposes. The West German radicals always came bearing gifts when they went east, the former radical told me, but there was a difference between the way Stasi agents received the goods and the way Putin approached it: "The East Germans did not expect us to pay for it, so they would at least make an effort to say, 'What do I owe you?' And we would say, 'Nothing.' And Vova never even started asking, 'What do I owe you?'"

Handing out assignments to RAF radicals, who were responsible for more than two dozen assassinations and terrorist attacks between 1970 and 1998, is exactly the sort of work Putin had once dreamed of, but there is no evidence he was directly connected to it. Instead, he spent most of his days sitting at his desk, in a room he shared with one other agent (every other officer in the Dresden building had his own office). His day began with a morning staff meeting, continued with a meeting with his local agent, the retired police officer, and finished with writing: every agent had to give a complete accounting of his activities, including Russian translations of any information he had obtained. Former agents estimate they spent three-quarters of their time writing reports. Putin's biggest success in his stay in Dresden appears to have been in drafting a Colombian university student, who in turn connected the Soviet agents with a Colombian student at a school in West Berlin, who in turn introduced them to a Colombian-born U.S. Army sergeant, who sold them an unclassified Army manual for 800 marks. Putin and his colleagues had high hopes for the sergeant, but by the time they obtained the manual, Putin's time in Germany was coming to an end.

JUST WHEN THE PUTINS LEFT the Soviet Union, that country began to change drastically and irrevocably. Mikhail Gorbachev came to power in March 1985. Two years later, he had released all Soviet dissidents from prison and was beginning to loosen the reins on Soviet bloc countries. The KGB leadership as well as its rank and file perceived Gorbachev's actions as disastrous. Over the next few years, a chasm would open up between the Party and the KGB, culminating with the failed coup in August 1991.

Watching the changes from afar, surrounded by other secret police officers—and no one else—Putin must have felt a hopeless, helpless fury. Back home, KGB leadership was pledging loyalty to the secretary general and his planned reforms. In June 1989, the head of the KGB in Leningrad issued a public statement condemning secret-police crimes committed under Stalin. In East Germany, as in the Soviet Union, people were beginning to come out into the streets to protest, and the unthinkable was quickly beginning to look proba-ble: the two Germanys might be reunited—the land Vladimir Putin had been sent here to guard would just be handed over to the enemy. Everything Putin had worked for was now in doubt; every-thing he had believed was being mocked. This is the sort of insult that would have prompted the agile little boy and young man that Putin had been to jump the offender and pound him until his fury had subsided. Middle-aged, out-of-shape Putin sat idle and silent as his dreams and hopes for the future were destroyed.

In the late spring and early summer of 1989, Dresden faced its first unsanctioned gatherings: handfuls of people collecting in public squares, first protesting the rigging of local elections in May and then, like the rest of Germany, demanding the right to emigrate to the West. In August, tens of thousands of East Germans actually traveled east—taking advantage of the lifting of travel restrictions within the Soviet bloc—only to descend on West German embassies in Prague, Budapest, and Warsaw. A series of Monday-night protests began across the cities of East Germany, growing bigger every week. East Germany shut its borders, but it was too late to stem the tide of both emigrants and protesters, and an agreement was ultimately brokered to transport the Germans from east to west. They would travel by train, and the trains would pass through Dresden, the East German city closest to Prague. Indeed, first the empty trains would travel through Dresden on their way to pick up the nearly eight thousand East Germans who were occupying the West German embassy in Prague. In the early days of October, thousands of people began to gather at the train station in Dresden—some of them carrying heavy luggage, hoping somehow to hitch a ride to the West, others simply there to witness the most astonishing event in the city's postwar history.

The crowds met with all the law enforcement Dresden could gather: regular police were joined by various auxiliary security forces, and together they threatened, beat, and detained as many people as they could. Unrest continued for several days. On October 7, Vladimir Putin's thirty-seventh birthday, East Germany celebrated the official fortieth anniversary of its formation, and riots broke out in Berlin; more than a thousand people were arrested. Two days later, hundreds of thousands came out across the country for another Monday-night demonstration, and their numbers more than doubled two weeks later. On November 9, the Berlin Wall fell, but demonstrations in East Germany continued until the first free elections in March.

On January 15, 1990, a crowd formed outside the Stasi headquarters in Berlin to protest the reported destruction of documents by the secret police. The protesters managed to overcome the security forces and enter the building. Elsewhere in East Germany, protesters began storming Ministry of State Security buildings even earlier.

Putin told his biographers that he had been in the crowd and watched people storm the Stasi building in Dresden. "One of the women was screaming, 'Look for the entrance to the tunnel under the Elbe River! They have inmates there, standing up to their knees in water.' What inmates was she talking about? Why did she think they were under the Elbe? There were some detention cells there, but, of course, they were not under the Elbe." Putin generally found the protesters' rage excessive and bewildering. It was his friends and neighbors under attack, the very people with whom he had lived and socialized—exclusively—for the last four years, and he could not imagine any of them were as evil as the crowd claimed: they were just ordinary paper-pushers, like Putin himself.

When the protesters descended on the building where he worked, he was outraged. "I accept the Germans' crashing their own Ministry of State Security headquarters," he told his biographers a dozen years later. "That's their internal affair. But we were not their internal affair. It was a serious threat. And we had documents in our building. And no one seemed to care enough to protect us." The guards at the KGB building must have fired warning shots—Putin said only that they demonstrated their will to do whatever was necessary to protect the building—and the protesters quieted down for a time. When they grew riotous again, Putin claimed, he himself stepped outside. "I asked them what they wanted. I explained that this was a Soviet organization. And someone in the crowd asks, 'Why do you have cars with German license plates? What are you doing here, anyway?' Like they knew exactly what we were doing there. I said that our contract allowed us to use German license plates. 'And who are you? Your German is too good,' they started screaming. I told them I was an interpreter. These people were very aggressive. I phoned our military representatives and told them what was going on. And they said, 'We cannot do anything until we have orders from Moscow. And Moscow is silent.' A few hours later, our military did come and the crowd dispersed. But I remembered that: 'Moscow is silent.' I realized that the Soviet Union was ill. It was a fatal illness called paralysis. A paralysis of power."

His country, which he had served as well as he could, patiently accepting whatever role it saw fit to assign him, had abandoned Putin. He had been scared and powerless to protect himself, and Moscow had been silent. He spent the several hours before the military arrived inside the besieged building, shoving papers into a wood-burning stove until the stove split from the excessive heat. He destroyed everything he and his colleagues had worked to collect: all the contacts, personnel files, surveillance reports, and, probably, endless press clippings.

Even before the protesters had chased the Stasi out of their buildings, East Germany began the grueling and painful process of purging the Stasi from its society. All of the Putins' neighbors not only lost their jobs but were banned from working in law enforcement, the government, or teaching. "My neighbor with whom I had become friends spent a week crying," Ludmila Putina told her husband's biographers. "She cried for the dream she had lost, for the collapse of everything she had ever believed. Everything had been crushed: their lives, their careers. . . . Katya [Ekaterina, the Putins'

younger daughter] had a teacher at her preschool, a wonderful
teacher—and she was now banned from working with children. All
because she had worked for the Ministry of State Security." Twelve
years later, the incoming first lady of post-Soviet Russia still found
the logic of lustration incomprehensible and inhumane.

The Putins returned to Leningrad. They carried a twenty-year-
old washing machine given to them by their former neighbors—who,
even having lost their jobs, enjoyed a higher standard of living than
the Putins could hope to attain back in the USSR—and a sum of
money in U.S. dollars, sufficient to buy the best Soviet-made car
available. This was all they had to show for four and a half years of
living abroad—and for Vladimir Putin's unconsummated spy career.
The four of them would be returning to the smaller of the two rooms
in the elder Putins' apartment. Ludmila Putina would be reduced to
spending most of her time scouring empty store shelves or standing
in line to buy basic necessities: this was how most Soviet women
spent their time, but after four and a half years of a relatively comfortable life in Germany, it was not only humiliating but frightening.
"I was scared to go into stores," she told interviewers later. "I would
try to spend as little time as possible inside, just enough to get the
bare necessities—and then I would run home. It was terrible."

Could there have been a worse way to return to the Soviet
Union? Sergei Roldugin, Putin's cellist friend, remembered him saying, "They cannot do this. How could they? I see that I can make
mistakes, but how can these people, whom we think of as the best
professionals, make mistakes?" He said he would leave the KGB.
"Once a spy, always a spy," his friend responded; this was a common
Soviet saying. Vladimir Putin felt betrayed by his country and his
corporation—the only important affiliation he had ever known, outside his judo club—but the corporation was filled with people who
increasingly felt betrayed, misled, and abandoned; it would be fair to
say this was the KGB's corporate spirit in 1990.

Four

ONCE A SPY

All of Russian history happens in St. Petersburg. The city was the capital of a prosperous empire depleted by World War I, at the start of which it lost its name: Germanic St. Petersburg became the more Russian-sounding Petrograd. The empire was destroyed by the one-two punch of the revolutions of 1917, for both of which Petrograd provided the stage. Soon the city lost its capital status, as the seat of power was moved to Moscow. Petrograd, with its poets and artists, remained the capital of Russian culture—even as the city lost its name yet again, becoming Leningrad the day the first of the Soviet tyrants died. The literary, artistic, academic, political, and business elites of the city would be gradually decimated by purges, arrests, and executions throughout the 1930s. That miserable decade closed with the Soviet-Finnish War, a disastrously ill-conceived act of Soviet aggression that segued into World War II. During the siege and after World War II, Leningrad, to which Putin's parents had returned, was the city of ghosts. Its buildings, once majestic, stood ravaged: the window glass had been blown out by the bombing and shelling; the window frames had been used for firewood, as had the furniture. Processions of rats, hundreds and thousands strong, would march past the buildings' pockmarked walls, taking up the entire width of the sidewalk, pushing aside the shadowy human survivors.

In the postwar decades, the city swelled with new people and their work. Leningrad became the military-industrial capital of the Soviet Union; hundreds of thousands of people from other parts of the empire settled in identical gray building blocks, which could not be erected fast enough to keep up with the influx. By the mid-1980s, the city's population was pushing five million—far exceeding capacity even by the modest living standards set in the Soviet Union. The heart of the city, its historic center, had meanwhile been all but abandoned by the city's builders; those families, like Putin's, who had survived the hell of the first half of the twentieth century were living in huge, rambling communal apartments in buildings that had once been grand but now, after decades of disrepair, had entered the stage of irreversible decay.

Yet the city to which Putin returned in 1990 had changed more in the four years he had been absent than it had changed in the forty years before that. The very people Putin and his colleagues had kept in check and in fear—the dissidents, the almost-dissidents, and the friends of friends of dissidents—now acted as if they owned the city.

ON MARCH 16, 1987, a massive explosion occurred in St. Isaac's Square in Leningrad. The blast brought down the Angleterre Hotel, whose grand façade had framed part of the city's most beautiful square for more than a hundred fifty years and whose history was the stuff of legend and St. Petersburg's cultural legacy. The great poet Sergei Yesenin had committed suicide in Room 5, which got the hotel men-

tioned in the work of at least half a dozen other poets. In a country
and a city where the facts of history were most often whispered and
the sites of history were frequently concealed, destroyed, or faked,
the Angleterre was a rare instance of an actual artifact—which is
probably why many citizens of Peter the Great's city, much of which
was literally crumbling, experienced the loss of this particular hotel
as almost a personal injury.

The demolition of the hotel was planned; what was not planned
was the birth, at the site of the destruction, of a movement that
would play a key role in bringing down the Soviet regime.

Mikhail Gorbachev had become the leader of the Soviet state in
March 1985. He had spent the first year of his reign solidifying his
base in the Politburo. In his second year in office, he floated the term
perestroika—restructuring—though no one, not even Gorbachev himself, quite knew what he meant. In December 1986, Gorbachev allowed the Soviet Union's best-known dissident, Nobel Peace Prize
winner Andrei Sakharov, to return to his home in Moscow from the
city of Gorky, where he had lived in internal exile for almost seven
years. In January 1987, Gorbachev advanced another new term, *glasnost*, or openness—which did not, for the then foreseeable future,
mean that censorship would be abolished, but it seemed to mean that
censorship would change: for example, libraries across the country
began loosening access to materials that had been kept under lock
and key. In February 1987, Gorbachev commuted the sentences of
140 dissidents who had been serving time in Soviet prisons and labor
colonies.

To be sure, Gorbachev did not intend to dissolve the Soviet
Union, or to end the Communist Party's rule, or, really, to change the
regime in a radical way—though he himself was fond of using the
word *radical*. Rather, he dreamed of modernizing the Soviet economy and Soviet society in discreet ways, without undermining their

basic structures. But the processes he set in motion led inevitably—
and, in retrospect, very rapidly—to the total collapse of the Soviet
system.

Five years before the tectonic shift, subtle subterranean tremors
began. Gorbachev had dangled the carrot of possible change—and
so people began to talk about change as if it were possible. Cautiously, people began to allow these conversations to spill out of their
kitchens and into other people's living rooms. Loose alliances began
to take shape. For the first time in decades, people were seriously
discussing politics and pressing social issues neither as members of a
dissident movement nor within the confines of formal Communist
Party structures—which is how those who took part in these conversations became known as the "informals." A majority of the informals
belonged to a specific generation: those born during the Khrushchev
thaw, the brief period in the late 1950s and early 1960s, when Stalinist terror had lifted and Brezhnev's stagnation had not yet set in. The
informals had no common political platform, or a common language
for the discussion of politics, or even a common understanding of the
place of such a discussion, but they shared two things: a distaste for
the ways of the Soviet state, and an abiding desire to protect and
preserve what little was left of their beloved historic city.

"The people of our generation saw only a dead end ahead: if you
did not escape, you'd face degradation," Yelena Zelinskaya recalled
twenty years later. Zelinskaya put out one of several samizdat publications that united the informals. "We could no longer breathe among
the lies, the hypocrisy, and the stupidity. There was no fear. And as
soon as the first rays of light seemed to break through—as soon as
people whose hands had been tied were allowed to move at least a
few fingers—people started to move. People weren't thinking about
money, or about improving their standing in life; all anyone thought
about was freedom. Freedom to conduct your private life as you
wish, freedom to travel and see the world. Freedom from hypocrisy

and the freedom not to listen to hypocrisy; freedom from libel, freedom from feeling ashamed for one's parents, freedom from the viscous lies in which all of us were submerged as if in molasses."

But whatever the informals were saying in the privacy of their homes, the state machine of mindless destruction kept moving. On March 16, 1987, a rumor spread through the city: The Angleterre Hotel was about to be razed. Informals of every stripe began to gather in front of the building. The leader of an informal preservation society, Alexei Kovalev, went inside the city government building, conveniently located in the same city square, and attempted to negotiate with a high-level bureaucrat there. She assured him the building was safe and implored him to "stop misinforming people and spreading panic." Barely half an hour later, the blast sounded, and the building the size of a city block turned into a huge cloud of coarse dust.

This was when something entirely unprecedented happened. "It seems, after the dust and smoke settled where the hotel had been, all that should have remained were memories," recalled Alexander Vinnikov, a physicist turned city activist. "That is what happened, but the memories were outstanding. Never before this moment could people have imagined that they could protest the actions of authorities and remain intact, not end up behind bars or at least out of work. We carried away the memory of an amazing sense of being right, the sense that comes to a person who stands among like-minded people in a public space, listening to a speaker giving voice, convincingly and precisely, to everyone's shared thoughts. And most important, we felt the full humiliation of the authorities' utter disregard for our opinion, and a sense of personal dignity began to well up, a desire to affirm our right to be heard and to have an impact."

So the crowd did not disperse. By the following afternoon, several hundred people were gathered in front of what used to be the Angleterre. The fence surrounding the demolition site was covered with homemade posters, fliers, poems written right on the fence, and simply the names of people who had taken part in the protest—and had bravely chosen to make their names known.

"We all found one another in St. Isaac's Square," read a prescient article written by Zelinskaya, then thirty-three years old, and posted on the fence. "We have set out on a difficult path. . . . We will probably make a lot of mistakes. Some of us will probably lose our voices. We will probably fail to accomplish everything we will set out to do, just as we failed to save the Angleterre. There really is a lot we do not know how to do. Can people whose opinion no one ever asked really be expected to argue well? Can people who have long been kept out of any sort of public activity be expected to have honed their fighting skills while sitting in their basements? Can people whose decisions and actions have never had tangible consequences even for their own lives be expected to calculate the trajectory of their activities?"

Hundreds of people continued to rally at the site for three days. The protest that would not end became known as the Battle of the Angleterre. And even after that, the fence, with its many posters and articles, remained, and so did an ongoing small gathering in front of it. People would now come to the Angleterre to find out what was happening in their city and their country, or to tell others; the site became known as the Information Point. The kitchen and living room discussions had come out, and the fence turned into a living page on which scores of samizdat publications were emerging from the underground.

Elsewhere in the city, other discussion venues were taking shape. In April, a group of young Leningrad economists formed a club. At their gatherings at the Palace of Youth, they took up unprecedented topics, such as the possibility of privatization. Before the year was out, one of them would float the idea of privatizing state enterprise by issuing stock vouchers to every Soviet adult. The concept was not well received at the time, but years later, this is exactly what would happen, and most of the club's participants would go on to play key roles in shaping post-Communist economic policy.

To those on the inside, Soviet society seemed to be changing at breathtaking speed. But the motion was two steps forward, one step back. In May, Soviet authorities stopped the jamming of most Western radio programs; on May 31, Leningrad city authorities shut down the Information Point in front of the Angleterre. In June, the local council elections contained a small but revolutionary experiment: in 4 percent of the districts, instead of the usual single name, two appeared on the ballot; for the first time in decades, a few voters were allowed to choose between candidates, even if both were advanced by the Communist Party. On December 10, Leningrad saw its first political rally that was not broken up by police. At least two of the speakers were men who had served time in the camps for opposing the Soviet regime.

THE PROCESS CONTINUED the following year. More discussion groups gradually formed, and their activities became more structured. Over time, actual leaders—people well-known and trusted outside their small social circles—emerged. In a couple of years, they would become the first post-Soviet politicians.

In the spring, some Leningrad residents announced they were launching what they called "Hyde Park" in the Mikhailov Gardens in the center of the city. One afternoon a week, anyone could make a public speech. "The rules were, anybody could speak for five minutes on any topic, excepting the propaganda of war, violence, and xenophobia of any sort," recalled Ivan Soshnikov, who was a thirty-two-year-old taxi driver at the time, and one of the masterminds behind the outdoor debating space. "You want to talk about human rights?

Go right ahead! One man brought the 1949 Declaration of Human Rights with him. Myself, I had already read it in samizdat, but people who had never seen it before were just beside themselves. And this went on for four hours every Saturday, from twelve to four. It was open mike. I should mention that this was before there was freedom of the press. So a lot of journalists would come and listen, but they could not publish what they heard."

After a few months, the police kicked "Hyde Park" out of the Mikhailov Gardens. The organizers took their show to the Kazansky Cathedral, a grand structure on Nevsky Prospekt, the city's main avenue. No longer shaded by the trees or shielded by a fence, the speakers and the listeners became even more visible than they had been in the original location. Rather than chase them away again, city authorities apparently decided to drown them out with sound. One Saturday, "Hyde Park" participants showed up in front of the cathedral, only to discover a brass band playing in front of it. The band came complete with its own audience, whose members shouted at the debaters: "Look, the band is here so that people can relax, this is no time or place for your speeches." During a break in the music, Ivan Soshnikov tried to chat up the conductor, who immediately volunteered that the band had been stationed in front of the cathedral by some sort of authority.

Ekaterina Podoltseva, a brilliant forty-year-old mathematician who had become one of the city's most visible—and most eccentric— pro-democracy activists, produced a recipe for fighting the brass band. She asked all the regular "Hyde Park" participants to bring lemons with them the following Saturday. As soon as the band began playing, all the activists were to start eating their lemons, or to imitate the process of eating if they found the reality of it too bitter. Podoltseva had read or heard somewhere that when people see someone eating a lemon, they begin, empathetically, producing copious amounts of saliva—which happens to be incompatible with playing a wind instrument. It worked: the music stopped, and the speeches continued.

On June 13, 1988, the Supreme Court of the USSR reversed the more than fifty-year-old guilty verdicts that had launched Stalin's Great Terror. The following day, a rally in memory of victims of political repression took place in Leningrad—the first such legal large-scale gathering in the history of the Soviet Union.

But the most important stories of 1988—not only in Leningrad but in all of the USSR—were the formation of an organization called the People's Front and the conflict between Armenia and Azerbaijan. The People's Front came into being more or less simultaneously and, it seemed, spontaneously in more than thirty cities all over the Soviet Union. Its avowed goal was to support perestroika, which was battling a growing backlash within the Party. But the People's Front's most important function was, probably, to conduct an experiment of unprecedented scope and scale: in a society that had almost no experience with social change or, for that matter, any other citizen activity that was not directed from the top, to form an organization, even a network of organizations, that was truly democratic in nature and structure.

"An organization that aims to democratize society must itself be democratic," proclaimed a founding document of the Leningrad organization. "This is why the bylaws of the People's Front will incorporate an effective firewall against bureaucratic and authoritarian tendencies. To this end, the coordinating council shall be elected by secret vote and may be reconstituted at any general meeting of the People's Front. To this end, the coordinating council does not have a permanent chairman but all of its members shall serve as chairman by turn. To this end, no member of the People's Front shall represent the organization's position on any issue if the issue has not been discussed at a general meeting of the People's Front. It is expected that all decisions taken by the coordinating council or by the general meeting shall be recommendations: members who are in the minority should not be obligated to participate in a decision with which they disagree but neither shall they have the right to counteract the actions of the majority in any way other than through the power of conviction." In other words, the main purpose of the People's Front was not to be the Communist Party.

Incredibly, it worked. Twenty years later, a mathematician who became an activist in the late 1980s recounted discovering the People's Front: "They would gather at the Food Industry Workers' House of Culture. Anyone could come. Some of those who came were not particularly mentally healthy people. The first impression was that of a complete madhouse: some of the speeches were totally nonsensical. This would go on for an hour or an hour and a half, discussions of god knows what, and then other people would start taking the mike—I later found out they were some of the leaders of the group. In the end, when they actually took a vote on some question or another, the resulting text of the resolution would be quite reasonable; it would have a definite political component and be written in good Russian. So it turned out that the people who were leading the organization at the time were people with whom one could really discuss things." The ability to discuss things was still the most highly valued commodity in the Soviet Union.

A woman quickly emerged as the evident leader and most trusted de facto spokesperson for the Leningrad People's Front. Marina Salye was unlike any politician the Soviet Union had ever known. In fact, she had little in common with any politician anywhere in the world. In her fifties, unmarried (she had long lived with a woman she called her sister), she had spent much of her adult life in the farthest reaches of the Soviet Union, studying rocks: she had a Ph.D. in geology. It was a path taken by many a member of the intelligentsia: find a profession that is not ideologically charged and get as far as possible away from the Soviet center of command. Never having joined the Communist Party, Salye was not part of any institution that had been discredited. At the same time, she had impeccable St. Petersburg credentials. Her great-great-grandfather was one of the most prominent residents in the history of St. Petersburg: Paul Buhre, watchmaker to the czar, made timepieces that are still working and highly valued in the twenty-first century. Two of her great-grandfathers had come to St. Petersburg in the nineteenth century, from France and Germany. Brilliant, well-spoken in the way of those who never mince words, Salye elicited instant trust and a desire to follow. "With a cigarette dangling from her lips, she could lead a crowd up and down Nevsky, stopping traffic," a political opponent of hers recalled twenty years later. "I saw her do it once, and it made a very strong impression. No one had a chance competing with her."

IN FEBRUARY 1988. conflict erupted between Azerbaijan and Armenia—the first of what would be many ethnic conflicts in the Soviet Caucasus. In relatively wealthy, overwhelmingly Muslim Azerbaijan, a region called Nagorno-Karabakh, populated mostly by ethnic Armenians, declared its intention to secede and join Armenia, a small, poor, mostly Christian republic of the USSR. With the exception of a few visionary dissidents, no one at the time could imagine that the Soviet empire would break apart—much less break apart soon. The events in Nagorno-Karabakh showed that the unthinkable was possible. Not only that, they showed exactly how it was going to happen: The USSR would break apart along ethnic lines, and the process would be painful and violent. But now pro-independence demonstrators came out into the streets of Nagorno-Karabakh in large numbers, and just days later, pogroms erupted in Sumgait, an Azerbaijan city with a sizable ethnic Armenian population. More than thirty people died; hundreds more were injured.

The Soviet intelligentsia watched in dismay as ethnic and religious enmities rose to the surface. In June, after Nagorno-Karabakh's regional government officially declared the region's intention to secede, more than three hundred people came out into a Leningrad square to demonstrate solidarity with the Armenian people. Toward the end of the summer, Leningrad pro-democracy activists arranged for Armenian children from Sumgait to travel to summer camps outside Leningrad. A Leningrad anthropologist named Galina Starovoitova—the one whose murder I would be covering ten years later—became the nation's most visible spokesperson for Armenian issues. On December 10, 1988, most members of the pro-secession Karabakh Committee in Nagorno-Karabakh were placed under arrest.

Two days later, a wave of police apartment searches swept through Leningrad. The five people whose apartments were raided were all radical pro-democracy activists; they included former political prisoner Yuli Rybakov and Ekaterina Podoltseva, the mathematician who had come up with the idea of eating lemons to silence the brass band. All five were listed in criminal proceedings initiated under Article 70 of the Soviet Penal Code, which provided for six months' to seven years' imprisonment for spreading anti-Soviet propaganda (more for repeat offenders). This would be the last Article 70 case in the history of the country.

The transformation of Soviet society, in other words, maintained its two-steps-forward, one-step-back mode: public rallies, which would have been unthinkable just two years earlier, were followed by search warrants, and the wrong kind of talk could still land one in prison for years. Censorship was lifting gradually: Boris Pasternak's *Dr. Zhivago* was finally published in the USSR that year, but Alexander Solzhenitsyn was still off-limits. Andrei Sakharov, though now allowed to live his private life in peace, faced often insurmountable hurdles in his public life. In the summer of 1988, the dissident and Nobel Prize winner visited Leningrad; the city's best-known tele-

vision journalist taped an interview with Sakharov, but the censors
kept it from the air. A producer decided to sneak it into the broadcast
of a pioneering late-night public affairs program that was rapidly
gaining popularity. She kept Sakharov's name out of the script that
had to be vetted by the censors, and they readily signed off on what
seemed, on paper, like innocuous banter: "Tonight on our program
you will see this." "You don't say!" "And this!" "Impossible! Seriously?"
"It's the honest truth!" "Can it be?" What the censors did not realize
was that images of Sakharov would be flashing on screen as this dialogue went on, not only leaving no doubt as to what the producers
planned to show but also giving viewers enough time to call everyone
they knew to tell them to turn on the television.

No one was fired for fooling the censors, and this was perhaps
one of the strongest indications that the changes under way in the
Soviet Union were profound and possibly irreversible—and that they
would transform not only the media but also the country's seemingly
intransigent political institutions. On December 1, 1988, a new election law went into effect, effectively ending the Communist Party's
monopoly on state power.

The year 1989 began with pro-democracy activists meeting in
Leningrad to organize what had seemed unthinkable just months
ago: an election campaign. A committee called Election-89 formed,
led by Marina Salye, among others; it printed out fliers that explained
how to vote: "There will be two, three, or four names on the ballot.
These are candidates who are competing with one another. You need
to choose *only one* name and cross out the rest." It was, in fact, a
convoluted system: 2,250 representatives were to be elected all over
the Soviet Union, including 750 to be elected from territorial districts, 750 to be elected from administrative districts, and 750 to be
elected by the Communist Party or institutions it controlled. Still, it
was the first time voters in most areas could actually choose between
two or more candidates.

In Leningrad, Communist Party functionaries were trounced. Galina Sarovoitova, the Leningrad anthropologist, was elected to represent Armenia in the Supreme Soviet. She joined a minority of the newly elected representatives—about three hundred of them—in forming a pro-democracy faction led by Sakharov. Once in parliament, the former dissident made it his goal to end the rule of the Communist Party, repealing the constitutional provision that guaranteed its primacy in Soviet politics. Other prominent members of the interregional group included rogue apparatchik Boris Yeltsin and Anatoly Sobchak, an extremely handsome and well-spoken law professor from Leningrad.

During the head-spinningly brief election campaign—less than four months passed between the passage of the revolutionary law on elections and the actual vote—Sobchak had made a name for himself as an outstanding public speaker. During one of his first appearances before potential voters, sensing that the audience was tired and bored, he set aside his prepared talk on city and national issues and made a conscious decision to dazzle the listeners with oratory. "I have a dream," he actually said, "that the next election will be organized not by the Communist Party but by voters themselves, and that these voters will be free to unite and form organizations. That campaign rallies will be open to all who want to listen, with no special passes required to enter. That any citizen will have the right to nominate himself or another person for office, and that the candidacy will not have to go through a multistep approval process but simply will be placed on the ballot provided there are sufficient signatures collected in support of the candidate." It was a decidedly utopian vision.

THE PEOPLE'S DEPUTIES, as members of the Soviet quasi-parliament were officially called, gathered for their first congress at the end of May 1989. The country's streets emptied out for two weeks: every family sat immobile in front of a television set, watching political debate out in the open for the first time in their lives, watching history being made. The huge, unwieldy gathering quickly turned into a standoff between two people: Gorbachev, the head of state, and Sakharov, the ultimate moral authority of his time. Youthful, energetic, and now certain of his position and his popularity, Gorbachev projected confidence. Sakharov—stooped, soft-spoken, prone to stumble when he talked as well as when he walked—looked out of place and ineffective. He seemed to be making his greatest mistake when, on the last day of the congress, he took the floor and launched into a long and complicated speech. He was calling for the repeal of Article 6 of the Soviet Constitution, which granted the Communist Party rule over the Soviet state. He was speaking of the impending collapse of the empire—both the Soviet Union proper and the Eastern Bloc—and imploring the congress to adopt a resolution on the need for reform. The huge hall was growing restless and increasingly rude: the people's deputies began stomping their feet and trying to shout Sakharov down. The old dissident at the microphone, straining to make himself heard, exclaimed: "I am addressing the world!"

Mikhail Gorbachev, sitting up on stage a few steps from where Sakharov was trying to give his speech, looked furious—both, it seemed, at the substance of Sakharov's words and at the pandemonium that broke out in the hall in response. Suddenly the old man went silent: Gorbachev had turned off his microphone. Sakharov gathered the pages of his talk from the lectern, took the few steps toward the secretary general, and extended his shaking hand with the sheets of paper. Gorbachev looked disgusted. "Get that away from me," he sputtered.

By humiliating Sakharov on television, Gorbachev went too far. Six months later, when the dissident died of a heart attack on the second day of the next Congress of People's Deputies—having, in the interim, seen the Berlin Wall come down and the Eastern Bloc come apart, just as he had predicted—Sakharov was widely perceived as a martyr, and Gorbachev as his tormentor. Tens, possibly hundreds, of thousands turned out for his funeral in Moscow. City authorities tried, habitually and ineffectually, to prevent a mass gathering by shutting down subway stations near the graveyard and posting police cordons around the perimeter; people walked for miles in the freezing cold and then proceeded coolly to break through the cordons.

In Leningrad, about twenty thousand people gathered for a memorial rally in the afternoon of the day Sakharov was buried. The organizers' bid to hold the event in the center of the city was rejected, so the rally began in one of those vast deserted areas that crop up around Socialist cities; this one was an amorphous space in front of the Lenin Concert Hall. A succession of speakers took the podium to speak about Sakharov. Despite the freezing cold, the crowd kept growing even as the brief winter sun disappeared. At dusk, the crowd made what seemed to be a spontaneous decision to march to the center of the city. Thousands of people fell into formation, as though directed by an invisible hand, and began a long, difficult walk.

People took turns walking in front, carrying a portrait of Sakharov and a lit candle. The entire way, Marina Salye marched behind the portrait, signifying, on the one hand, her willingness to follow in the great dissident's footsteps, and on the other to take responsibility for leading an illegal march. Less than six weeks earlier, Salye and her supporters had attended a different march, the annual November 7 celebration commemorating an anniversary of the October Revolution. Roughly thirty thousand people had joined the pro-democracy contingent during that parade. The police had tried to push the pro-democracy column away from the television cameras, but once it was level with the podium on which the first secretary of the Leningrad Regional Party Committee stood, waving to the crowd, the pro-democracy contingent stopped, and started chanting, "The People's Front! The People's Front!" Marchers in the official Communist contingent attempted to silence the chanters without breaking their own step. The Party secretary kept smiling and waving as though nothing out of the ordinary were going on. It was his last time up on the podium, greeting a November 7 crowd.

On November 7, the pro-democracy marchers had confronted the orderly, officially sanctioned Communist marchers; now they were simply claiming the city as their own. The march would take several hours. The crowd would overcome police efforts to break it up. They would stop to hold rallies at several symbolic locations along their route. Candles would appear in their hands. Thousands more would join them as they walked. For Salye, fifty-five and over-weight, the march was grueling exercise. She had come out that day wearing a heavy fur coat that was a bit too small, so she marched with it open in front, feeling exposed and inappropriate. At one point she slipped and fell, and though she did not hurt herself, she felt ashamed. Over the many hours of the march, she kept getting news from the back of the column that the police were once again trying to break up the procession.

"The following day," Salye recalled many years later, "we were at my house working on the People's Front platform because we were planning a congress, when a police colonel showed up to serve me a warrant for organizing an illegal march. He was amazing, the police-man: he said, 'You know, I could have come and not found you at home.' He was lovely. But I said, 'No, go right ahead.' And I accepted the warrant and we started calling lawyers and the media. The next morning I reported to the police station. . . . They kept trying to get me to say who had organized the march. I kept saying, 'How should I know? I don't remember. There were so many people there.'" In fact, one of Salye's People's Front comrades had been the master-mind behind the march.

"They kept demanding an answer," she continued. "A telegram was delivered while I was there: some well-known democratic leaders from Moscow were speaking up in my defense. Then I was told I'd be taken to court. I grabbed on to the desk with my bare hands as hard as I could and said, 'You'll have to carry me to court. I'm not going anywhere until my lawyer gets here.' I spent all day there at the police station. They kept making phone calls, trying to get instructions on what to do with me. In the end they took away all my documents, took me to a room with barred windows, and locked me there. And then it was all over, and I was allowed to leave the station to the joyous screams of my friends, who had gathered there."

The following day, Leningrad newspapers came out with front-page headlines reading "Arrested for Mourning Sakharov," and Marina Salye, already one of the most popular people in the city, became its indisputable political leader. In two months, Leningrad would hold a city council election and Salye would sail in. Years later she claimed she had had no intention of running for office—she had planned to coordinate the campaign for the People's Front candidates without running herself—but after her arrest for the Sakharov memorial march, she needed immunity from prosecution.

THIS WOULD BE the first elected city council in Leningrad history and, really, the first popularly elected governing body in the Soviet Union. Like all cities, Leningrad had been run by the local chapter of the Communist Party. New politicians, and new rules, proposed to relegate the Communist Party to the status of—well, a political party—and to rule the city through representative democracy. The transition was fast, painful, and sometimes hilarious. In the March election, pro-democracy candidates trounced the Communist Party, taking about two-thirds of the four hundred seats; 120 seats went to the People's Front. Following the vote, an organizing committee of sixty deputies-elect convened to discuss the future workings of the city

council. Leningrad's Party boss, Boris Gidaspov, invited the committee to see him at the Smolny Institute, a historic college building
that housed the regional Party headquarters. The deputies-elect politely suggested Gidaspov come see them himself, at the Mariinsky
Palace, the grand building facing St. Isaac's Square, where the old
Communist-run city council had held its sessions—where the activists of the Battle of the Angleterre had gone to try to negotiate with
city officials—and where the new democratic council would be
housed.

Gidaspov, the old guard personified, had spent his entire professional life in Leningrad's military-industrial complex, rising through
the ranks fast and running vast institutes before being appointed to
run the city Party organization in 1989. He walked into the conference room in the Mariinsky and headed straight for the head of the
table. No sooner had he sat down than one of the deputies-elect said,
"That is not your seat." This was the changing of the guard.

A similarly symbolic scene took place in the Mariinsky's main
hall days later, when the new city council convened for its first session.
The four hundred newly elected deputies took their seats in the grand
amphitheater, looking down on a small walnut desk at which two men
were already seated. Both were old-time Party bureaucrats, cast in the
same mold as Gidaspov: heavyset, square-shouldered, gray-suited,
with layered faces that never looked clean-shaven. One of them rose
and began reading a standard speech, which opened with words of
congratulations to the deputies on their election. One of those being
congratulated approached the desk to ask, "Who told you you were
running the meeting?" The bureaucrat trailed off, confused, and
Alexei Kovalev, the preservationist known as "the hero of the Battle
of the Angleterre," appeared at the front of the hall and suggested the
two visitors stop getting in the way of the session. The men got up,
and Kovalev and Salye took the two seats at the desk in order to run

the first meeting of the first democratically elected governing body in the Soviet Union.

The session began, as planned by the coordinating committee, with three of its members making procedural announcements. When they came to the front, the hall erupted with laughter, because all three sported the standard-issue intelligentsia look—turtleneck sweaters and beards. "It was fantastical," recalled a sociologist who was present at the session. "It was a total change of atmosphere: the suits with their mugs were out, and the informals were in."

Keeping with what one of them later termed "an acute sense of democracy" that brought them to the Mariinsky, the new deputies, in one of their first rulings, decided to remove all guards from the palace so that any citizen could gain access to any office or meeting hall. "The Mariinsky took on the look of a railroad station during the [Russian] Civil War," one of the city council members wrote later. "Dozens of homeless men would stand at the entrance to the main assembly hall, grabbing deputies and trying to push typed papers into their hands. I remember a bearded man who kept trying to get the deputies to consider some brilliant invention of his. We had voted to remove the guards from the palace—and it was literally the next day that we were forced to calculate the cost of bronze details of the building's interior that had gone missing."

The guard was soon reestablished, but the people kept coming. "People had so longed to be heard," another city council member recalled later. "When voters came to see us, we felt somewhat like priests administering confession. We would say, 'I cannot provide you with a new apartment; that would extend beyond the scope of my authority,' and they would respond, 'Just hear me out.' And we would listen, attentively and patiently. And people would leave satisfied."

The realization that voters expected not only to be heard but also to be protected and fed would come a few months later.

IN ACCORDANCE WITH THE PRINCIPLES of radical democracy, the city council had no formal leader. This, however, proved impractical and even impolitic: as members of the new city council struggled to invent parliamentary procedure more or less from scratch, testing and reasserting rules of order in real time—and often on the air of the local television channel—Leningrad voters began to grow impatient. The city, the country, and life itself seemed to be falling apart all around them while the democrats practiced democracy without getting anything done.

Marina Salye, still the city's most popular politician, decided not to run for chairman of the council. Twenty years later, she was hard-pressed to explain that decision: "I wish someone could tell me the answer," she said. "Was it my stupidity, my inexperience, my shyness, or my naiveté? I don't know, but the fact is, I didn't do it. And it was a mistake."

With Salye recusing herself, city council activists decided to reach out to one of the city's other two perestroika heroes: Anatoly Sobchak, the law professor who had earned a reputation in Moscow as the democrat from Leningrad. Sobchak was different from the bearded, sweater-wearing informals: in contrast to their contemplative, usually unassuming air, he was an ostentatiously sharp dresser—the Communists liked to criticize him for his "bourgeois" outfits, and his trademark checkered blazer still comes up in political reminiscences over twenty years later—and a forceful speaker. He seemed to love the sound of his own voice. As one of his former colleagues recalled, Sobchak "could derail a working meeting by delivering an impromptu forty-minute speech on the benefits of building an imaginary bridge" and mesmerize listeners while saying nothing of substance.

Though Sobchak belonged to Sakharov's Interregional Group in the Supreme Soviet, he was actually far more conservative than the informals who were calling him back to Leningrad. A law professor who had taught at the police academy, he was in many ways part of the outgoing Soviet establishment. He had recently joined the Communist Party, clearly believing that, with all of Gorbachev's reforms, the Party would continue to run the country. And in a divided city whose new democratic politicians were increasingly using its historic designation, St. Petersburg, he opposed changing the name of the city, arguing that the name Leningrad better reflected its military valor.

Sobchak was also much more of a politician than any of the informals knew how to be. He had far-reaching ambition: it would not be long before he started telling everyone he would be the next president of Russia. Meanwhile, at the city level, he apparently wanted to preside over the entire city council without being beholden to the democrats who had called him to the throne. To that end, he did some advance—and highly secretive—lobbying among the minority Communist Party faction of the council, and the Communists surprised everyone by voting in favor of Sobchak. A few minutes later Sobchak, in turn, upset expectations by not nominating Salye or one of the other prominent democrats to be his deputy. Instead, he named Vyacheslav Shcherbakov, a Communist Party member and a rear admiral. The democrats, taken aback, nonetheless honored their agreement with Sobchak and voted to confirm Shcherbakov as his deputy.

Sobchak then addressed the city council. He spelled out how he saw his mission: he was there to be the boss, not the leader. He viewed the city council as being bogged down in "democratic procedure for the sake of democratic procedure," as he put it, and he wanted to get on with the business of actually running the city. His voice growing more confident with every passing minute, Sobchak informed the city council that things were about to change.

"We realized our mistake as soon as we had voted for him," recalled one of the city council members later. Sobchak was intent on destroying what a majority of city council members saw as the greatest accomplishment of the two months that had passed since their own election: the invention of a non-Soviet way of doing business. The informals went home shocked and dejected.

Sobchak went to the airport to fly to a legal conference in the United States.

"HIS ST. PETERSBURG PERIOD WAS MURKIEST." Gevorkyan said of the campaign biography she and her colleagues wrote. "I never did figure out how he hooked up with Sobchak."

Back in Leningrad, Putin's KGB colleagues seemed to be seeking ways not to fight the new political reality but to adapt to it, and initially it seemed that this was what Putin would have to do as well: rather than leave the KGB in a huff, stay with it in a sulk and look around for new friends, new mentors, and perhaps new ways of wielding influence from the shadows.

The saying "Once a spy, always a spy" was factually correct: the KGB never let its officers off the leash. But where did all those used-up spies go? The KGB actually had a name and a structure of sorts for its bloat—"active reserve." These were the nearly uncountable and possibly uncounted numbers of KGB officers planted throughout the civilian institutions of the USSR.

Just over a year later, when a liberal Gorbachev appointee named Vadim Bakatin took over the KGB with the goal of dismantling the institution, it was the active reserve that he found most puzzling and intractable. "These were officers of the KGB who were officially employed by all state and civic organizations of any significance," he wrote. "Most often, many if not all staff within the organization were aware that these people worked for the KGB. Active reserve officers performed a variety of functions: some of them managed the systems of security clearances while others concentrated on monitoring the moods and conversations within the organizations and taking what they considered to be appropriate actions in regards to any dissidents. . . . Certainly, there exist situations when a secret police organization needs to have a person planted within some organization or another, but one would expect this kind of arrangement to be secret. What kind of a secret service has staff that everyone can identify?"

Bakatin answered his own question: "The KGB, as it existed, could not be termed a secret service. It was an organization formed to control and suppress everything and anything. It seemed to be created especially for organizing conspiracies and coups, and it possessed everything necessary to carry them out: its own specially trained armed forces, the capacity to track and control communications, its own people inside all essential organizations, a monopoly on information, and many other things." It was a monster that had its tentacles everywhere in Soviet society. Vladimir Putin decided to take his place at the end of one of those tentacles.

Putin told his friend the cellist that he was thinking of moving to Moscow to join the vast KGB bureaucracy in the capital. But then he decided to stay in Leningrad and, perhaps because he was always drawn to the familiar, turned to the only institution outside the KGB with which he had ever been linked: Leningrad State University. Putin's new job title was assistant chancellor for foreign relations. Like all organizations in the USSR, Leningrad State University was just beginning to recognize that the possibility of foreign relations existed. Its instructors and graduate students were starting to travel abroad to study and take part in conferences: they still had to overcome major bureaucratic hurdles, but the option of foreign travel, which had been reserved for a very select few, was now accessible to many. Students and instructors were also starting to come in from abroad: once again, an option that had been open only to students from Socialist bloc countries and a few handpicked graduate students from the West was now accessible to pretty much anyone. Like thousands of other Soviet organizations, Leningrad State University saw its state funding drastically cut and hoped that foreign relations, whatever form they might take, would bring in much-needed hard currency. It was a perfect job for a member of the active reserve: not only had such postings been traditionally reserved for KGB appointees, but everyone generally believed they really were better than anyone else at seeking and shoring up relations with foreigners; they were, after all, the only ones with experience.

Putin has said he planned to start writing a dissertation and perhaps stay at the university indefinitely. But in fact, like so many other things in the Soviet Union at the time, this job had an air of transition about it. He stayed at Leningrad State University less than three months.

THE STORY of how Putin came to work for Anatoly Sobchak during his tenure as chairman of the Leningrad City Council is well-known, often recounted, and most certainly untrue in many or all of its best-publicized details.

In the apocryphal version, Sobchak, the law professor and celebrity politician, was walking down the hall at the university, saw Putin, and asked him to come to work for him at the city council. In Putin's own version, a former classmate at the law faculty arranged a meeting in Sobchak's office. In Putin's version, he had attended Sobchak's lectures at the law faculty in the 1970s but had no personal relationship with him.

"I remember the scene well," Putin told his biographers. "I entered, introduced myself, and told him everything. He was an impulsive person, so he immediately said, 'I'll speak with the chancellor. You start work on Monday. That's it. I'll make all the arrangements and you'll be transferred.'" In the Soviet system of job assignments, office workers were indeed often transferred like serfs, by agreement of their owners. "I couldn't not say, 'Anatoly Alexandrovich, it would be my pleasure to come to work for you. I am interested. I even want the job. But there is a fact that will probably be an obstacle to this transfer.' He asks, 'What's that?' I say, 'I have to tell you that I am not just an assistant to the chancellor. I am a staff officer at the KGB.' He got to thinking, since this was a truly unexpected turn for him. He thought for a bit and then said, 'Well, screw it!'"

The dialogue is certainly fiction, and mediocre fiction at that. Why does Putin claim to have "told him everything" if he did not tell Sobchak about his KGB affiliation until after Sobchak extended the job offer? Why does Putin make Sobchak out to be both an ignorant fool—everyone at Leningrad State University knew Putin was a KGB officer—and a vulgarian? Probably because this was not a well-rehearsed lie when he told it to his biographers, whom he had likely expected to sidestep the delicate and too-obvious question of how a career KGB officer came to work for one of Russia's most prominent pro-democracy politicians.

Sobchak himself told a different fiction. "Putin was most certainly not assigned to me by the KGB," he said in a newspaper interview the same week that Putin was speaking to his own biographers—and this explains the discrepancy. "I found Putin myself and asked him to come and work for me because I had known him before. I remembered him very well as a student for his work at the law faculty. Why did he become my deputy? I ran into him, entirely by accident, in the hallway of the university. I recognized him, said hello, and started asking him what he had been up to. It turned out he had worked in Germany for a long time and was now working as an assistant to the chancellor. He had been a very good student, though he has this trait: he does not like to stand out. In this sense he is a person devoid of vanity, of any external ambition, but inside he is a leader."

Anatoly Sobchak certainly knew that Putin was a KGB officer. Moreover, that is exactly why he sought him out. This was the sort of politician Sobchak was: he talked a colorful pro-democracy line, but he liked to have a solid conservative base from which to do it. This was also why he chose a Communist and a rear admiral to be his deputy on the city council. Not only did Sobchak feel more secure surrounded by men who had emerged from various armed services, he felt more much more comfortable with these men than with the overeducated, excessively talkative, process-oriented pro-democracy activists like Salye and her ilk. He had taught law at the police academy in Leningrad; he had taught men who were just like what he perceived Putin to be: dependable but not brilliant, not outwardly ambitious, and ever mindful of the chain of command. In addition, he needed Putin for the exact same reason the university had needed him: he was one of the very few people in the city who had ever worked abroad—and the city needed foreign help and foreign money. Finally, Sobchak—who had risen through the ranks both at the university, where he was now a full professor, and in the Communist Party—knew that it was wiser to pick your KGB handler yourself than to have one picked for you.

Whether Sobchak was right in believing he was picking his own handler, however, is an open question. A former colleague of Putin's in East Germany told me that in February 1990, Putin had a meeting with Major General Yuri Drozdov, head of the KGB illegal-intelligence directorate, when the major general visited Berlin. "The only possible purpose of the meeting could have been giving Putin his next assignment," Sergei Bezrukov, who defected to Germany in 1991, told me. "Why else would the head of the directorate be meeting with an agent who was scheduled to be going home? That sort of thing just did not happen." Bezrukov and other officers wondered what Putin's new job would be and what made it important enough for the top brass to be involved. When Putin went to work for Sob-

chak, Bezrukov believed he had his answer: his old friend had been
called back in order to infiltrate the inner circle of one of the country's leading pro-democracy politicians. The university job had been
a stepping-stone.

Putin informed the Leningrad KGB that he was about to change
jobs. "I told them, 'I have received an offer from Anatoly Alexandrovich [Sobchak] to transfer from the university and work for him. If
this is impossible, I am willing to resign.' They responded, 'No, why
should you? Go work at the new job, no problem.'" The dialogue
seems to be another absurd fiction, even in the very unlikely event
that he had not been steered to Sobchak by the KGB itself. Putin
would have had no reason to suspect that the opportunity to plant
him alongside the city's most prominent democrat would be greeted
with anything but enthusiasm in the KGB.

By this time the new democrats had become the KGB's main
focus. The previous year, Gorbachev had created the Committee for
Constitutional Oversight, a law enforcement body intended to bring
Soviet governing practices in line with the country's own constitution. In 1990, the committee began its fight against covert KGB
operations, banning any actions based on secret internal instructions—
and the KGB ignored it. Instead, it conducted round-the-clock surveillance of Boris Yeltsin and other prominent democrats. It tapped
their phones, including ones in hotel rooms they rented. It also
tapped the phones of their friends, relatives, hairdressers, and sports
coaches. So it is extremely unlikely that Putin told his biographers
the truth when he claimed not to report to the KGB on his work
with Sobchak, all the while drawing a larger salary from the secret
police than he did at the city council.

How, if, and when Putin finally severed his connection with the
KGB is, astoundingly, not only not a matter of public record but not
even the subject of coherent mythmaking. Putin has said that within
a few months after he came to work for Sobchak, a member of the

city council began blackmailing him, threatening to expose him as a KGB officer. Putin realized he had to leave. "It was a very difficult decision. It had been nearly a year since I de facto stopped working for the security service, but my entire life still revolved around it. It was 1990: the USSR had not yet fallen apart, the August coup had not yet happened, so there was no final clarity as to which way the country would go. Sobchak was certainly an outstanding person and a prominent politician, but it seemed risky to tie my own future to his. Everything could have been reversed in a minute. And I could not imagine what I would do if I lost my job at city hall. I was thinking I might go back to the university, write a dissertation, and take odd jobs. I had a stable position within the KGB, and I was treated well. I was successful within that system, yet I decided to leave. Why? What for? I was literally suffering. I had to make the most difficult decision in my life. I thought for a long time, trying to collect my thoughts, then gathered myself together, sat down, and wrote the resignation letter on my first attempt, without writing a draft."

This monologue, pronounced ten years later, is in fact a remarkable document. If Putin did leave the most feared and frightening organization in the Soviet Union, he never—not even retrospectively—framed his decision in ideological, political, or moral terms. Ten years later, as he prepared to lead a new Russia, he readily admitted that he had been willing to serve any master. Most of all, he would have liked to hedge his bets and serve them all.

Hedge his bets he did. The KGB lost his letter of resignation—whether by clever arrangement or by virtue of being an organization chronically incapable of managing its own paperwork. Either way, Vladimir Putin was still an officer of the KGB in August 1991, when the KGB finally undertook the state coup for which it seemed to have been designed.

Five

A COUP AND A CRUSADE

I t took me two years to get Marina Salye to talk to me. And then it took me about twelve hours of tough driving, including half an hour of nearly impossible driving—my instructions were to "drive as far as you can and walk the rest of the way"—to get to Salye's house. At the end of the road I was to look for the tricolor Russian flag flying high over a wooden house. It would have been hard to miss: Russians are not in the habit of flying the flag over their homes.

Salye was now living in a village, if you can call it that: twenty-six houses and only six people. Like so many Russian villages, this one, hundreds of miles from the nearest big city and about twenty miles from the nearest food shop, was an empty nest, forgotten, futureless. Seventy-five-year-old Salye lived there, with the woman she called her sister, because no one could find them there.

The other woman, who was a few years younger and seemed to be in better health, brought out the boxes of papers Salye had taken with her when she disappeared from view. Here were the results of months of ceaseless digging she had undertaken—after uncovering the story of the missing meat.

IN 1990, the world was going to hell. Or at least the Soviet Union was. On January 13, 1990, pogroms broke out in the streets of the Azerbaijan capital, Baku, historically the most diverse of all the cities in the Russian empire. Forty-eight ethnic Armenians were killed and nearly thirty thousand—the city's entire remaining Armenian population—fled the city. World chess champion Garry Kasparov, a Baku Armenian, chartered a plane to evacuate family, friends, and their friends. On January 19, Soviet troops stormed Baku, ostensibly to restore order, and left more than a hundred civilians—mostly ethnic Azeris—dead.

The Soviet empire was splitting at the seams. The center was helpless to hold it together; its army was brutal and ineffectual.

The Soviet economy, too, was nearing collapse. Shortages of food and everyday products had reached catastrophic proportions. If Moscow was still able, albeit barely, to mobilize the resources of the entire huge country to get basic goods onto at least some of its store shelves, then Leningrad, the country's second-largest city, reflected the full extent of the disaster. In June 1989, Leningrad authorities had begun rationing tea and soap. In October 1990, sugar, vodka, and cigarettes joined the list of rationed products. In November 1990 the democratic city council felt compelled to take the terrifyingly unpopular step of introducing actual ration cards—inevitably reminiscent of the ration cards used during the siege of the city in World War II. Every Leningrad resident now had the right to procure three pounds of meat per month, two pounds of processed meats, ten eggs, one pound of butter, half a pound of vegetable oil, one pound of flour, and two pounds of grains or dry pasta. In introducing the ration cards, the city councillors hoped not only to stave off hunger—the word, in all its obscenity, was no longer perceived as belonging to history or to far-away lands—but also to prevent public unrest.

The city came perilously close to mass violence twice that year: during the tobacco riot of August 1990 and the sugar riot a few weeks later. Cigarettes had been scarce for some time, but the big stores in central Leningrad generally had at least one brand for sale. One day in late August 1990, though, even the stores along Nevsky Prospekt had no smokes. A crowd gathered in front of one of the stores in the morning, in anticipation of a delivery that never came. The store closed for lunch, to reopen an hour later, its shelves still empty. By three in the afternoon, a mob of several thousand enraged smokers had blocked traffic on Nevsky and was getting ready to start crashing store windows. Police leadership called the city council in a panic: if violence broke out, they would be unable to prevent either injury or property damage. Some of the deputies, led by Sobchak, rushed over to Nevsky to try to calm the crowd.

The politicians arrived just in time. The protesters had already uprooted a huge sidewalk planter and dislodged a long piece of fence from a nearby yard and were constructing barricades across the city's main avenue. Traffic was at a standstill. Police special forces, formed just a couple of years earlier and already known for their brutality in breaking up rallies—their batons were nicknamed "the democratizers"—had arrived at the scene and were getting ready to storm the protesting smokers and their barricades. Unlike the regular police, these troops in riot gear did not seem at a loss: they were certain there would be blood. Sobchak and several other well-known deputies tried to reason with different groups within the crowd, picking out people who seemed to recognize them and striking up conversations. Former dissident and political prisoner Yuli Rybakov, now also a city council member, walked over to the special forces to assure their brass that a truckload of cigarettes would be arriving any minute and the protest would be resolved peacefully.

Another city council team, led by Salye, was combing the city's warehouses, looking for a stash of cigarettes. They found some and delivered them to the protesters on Nevsky well after dark. The smokers lit up and dispersed, leaving the city council members to disassemble their makeshift barricades and consider the prospects of future riots that might not be resolved with such relative ease, because eventually, it seemed, the city would run out of everything.

A few weeks later, at the height of late-summer preserves-making season, sugar disappeared from store shelves. Fearing a repeat of the tobacco riot, a group of city councillors began investigating. They uncovered what they believed was a Communist Party conspiracy to discredit the city's new democratic regime. Taking advantage of the fact that no one really knew any longer who held what authority in the city, Communist Party functionaries had apparently pulled some old levers in order to prevent the unloading of freight trains that had transported sugar to Leningrad. Marina Salye called an emergency meeting of some city council members and dispatched them personally to monitor the arrival, unloading, and delivery of sugar to stores. A riot was thus averted.

By this time Marina Salye, the geologist, had been elected to chair the city council's committee on food supplies. Somehow it seemed that a woman who had never had anything to do with food or retail, who had never been much of a professional organizer or anyone's boss, but who appeared inherently uncorrupted and incorruptible would do the best possible job of preventing hunger in Leningrad. The city's most trusted politician was logically given the city's most important and most difficult job.

IN MAY 1991, Salye, in her capacity as chairwoman of the Leningrad City Council's committee on food supplies, traveled to Berlin to sign contracts for the importing of several trainloads of meat and potatoes

to Leningrad. Negotiations had more or less been completed: Salye
and a trusted colleague from the city administration were really there
just to sign the papers.

"And we get there," Salye told me years later, still outraged, "and
this Frau Rudolf with whom we were supposed to meet, she tells us
she can't see us because she is involved in urgent negotiations with
the City of Leningrad on the subject of meat imports. Our eyes are
popping out. Because we are the City of Leningrad, and we are there
on the subject of meat imports!"

Salye and her colleague rushed to call the food supplies committee of the Leningrad city administration, a counterpart to her own
committee: the only explanation they could imagine was that the
executive branch had, inexplicably, elbowed in on the contract. But
the chairman of the committee knew nothing of the negotiations. "So
I call Sobchak," Salye remembered. "I say, Anatoly Alexandrovich, I
have just found out—and by now I have been given figures—that
Leningrad is buying sixty tons of meat. Sobchak calls the External
Economic Bank while I am hanging on—I can hear him speaking—and
he names the firm and the bank confirms that, yes, a credit line for
ninety million deutsche marks has been opened for this firm. And he
doesn't tell me anything else: he says, 'I have no idea what is going on.'"

Salye went home empty-handed, only half hoping that the sixty
tons of meat supposedly bought by the city would actually material-
ize. It did not, which meant she hardly had time to pursue the mystery meat story, which kept nagging at her. Three months later,
however, it was subsumed by another event, much more frightening
and no less mystifying—and, in Salye's mind, inextricably connected
with her German misadventure.

THE MOST IMPORTANT JUNCTURE in modern Russian history, the country's most fateful moment, is, strangely, not the subject of any coher-

ent narrative. There is no national consensus on the nature of the events that defined the country, and this very lack of consensus is, arguably, modern Russia's greatest failing as a nation.

In August 1991, a group of Soviet federal ministers, led by Gorbachev's vice president, attempted to remove Gorbachev from office, with the ostensible goal of saving the USSR from destruction. The coup failed, the USSR fell apart, and Gorbachev lost power anyway. Twenty years later, there is no universally or even widely believed story of the events. What motivated the ministers? Why did their takeover fail as quickly and miserably as it did? Finally, who won, exactly?

The expectation of a hard-line backlash had been in the air since the beginning of the year. Some people even claimed to know the date of the planned coup ahead of time; I know at least one entrepreneur, one of the very first Russian rich, who left the country because he had been tipped off about the coup. Nor did one need to have an inside track to the KGB or an overactive imagination in order to expect the coup: a sense of dread and of a fatal kind of instability was palpable. Armed ethnic conflicts were flaring up all over the country. The Baltic republics—Latvia, Lithuania, and Estonia—decided to sever their ties with the Soviet Union, and Boris Yeltsin, chairman of the Russian Supreme Soviet, supported them in this. Gorbachev sent tanks into Vilnius, the Lithuanian capital, to suppress the uprising there. That was in January. In March, there were tanks in the streets of Moscow when Gorbachev, either driven to despair by the sense that the country was out of control or caving in to hard-liners within his own administration, or both, tried to ban all public demonstrations in Moscow; that was when I first saw Galina Starovoitova leading hundreds of thousands of Muscovites who had defied the decree and the tanks. Also in March, Gorbachev organized a referendum on whether to maintain the Soviet Union as an entity; the people in nine of the fifteen constituent republics voted in favor, but six republics boycotted the vote. At the end of the month, Georgia conducted its own referendum and voted to secede from the USSR.

The republics stopped paying dues to the federal center, exacerbating a budget crisis that was already massive. Shortages of food and basic goods grew worse even when it seemed worse was not possible. In April, the government tried gingerly to loosen price controls; prices went up but supplies did not. In June, Ukraine declared its independence from the USSR, as did Chechnya, which was actually a part of the Russian Republic of the USSR. Russia held presidential elections in June, electing Yeltsin. Moscow and Leningrad both established the office of mayor, which had not existed in Soviet times, and in June, Sobchak was elected mayor of Leningrad. It was a job that suited him better than being chairman of the city council: he had, after all, always acted the executive. Putin became deputy mayor for international relations.

OVER TWO YEARS of constant political change and tumultuous civic debate, Soviet citizens had grown dependent on their television sets. On August 19, 1991, those who rose early woke up to find them silent. Or not quite silent: *Swan Lake*, the ballet, was being broadcast over and over. Starting at six in the morning, state radio began airing a series of political decrees and addresses. An hour later, the same documents began to be read on the television as well.

"Countrymen! Citizens of the Soviet Union!" began the most eloquent of the documents, all of which were broadcast repeatedly. "We speak to you at a critical juncture for our fatherland and for all of our people! Our great motherland is in grave danger! The politics of reform, launched by M. S. Gorbachev, intended to guarantee the dynamic development of the country and the democratization of our society, has led us to a dead end. What began with enthusiasm and hope has ended in loss of faith, apathy, and despair. The government at all levels has lost the trust of the citizenry. Politicking has taken over public life, forcing out genuine care for the fate of the fatherland and the citizen. An evil mockery has been made of state institutions. The country has, in essence, become ungovernable."

The junta, which included the chairman of the KGB, the prime minister, the interior minister, the deputy chairman of the security council, the defense minister, the vice president, the chairman of the Supreme Soviet, and the heads of the trade and agricultural unions, went on to make promises to the people:

"Pride and honor of the Soviet man shall be restored fully."

"The country's growth should not be built on a falling standard of living of its population. In a healthy society, a constant growth of wealth will be the norm."

"Our foremost task will be finding solutions to the problems of food and housing shortages. All forces will be mobilized to satisfy these, the most important of the people's needs."

To that end, proclaimed a different document, "taking into account the needs of the population, which has demanded that decisive measures be taken to prevent the slipping of the society toward a national catastrophe, that law and order be secured, a state of emergency shall be declared in several locations in the USSR for a period of six months, beginning at four o'clock in the morning Moscow time, 19 August 1991." The junta, accordingly, called itself the State Committee for the State of Emergency in the USSR (GKChP SSSR). They told the people over and over that Gorbachev was ill, unfit to hold office. In fact, he was under house arrest at a vacation home in the Black Sea resort of Foros.

THE SECOND HALF OF AUGUST is dead season in Russian cities. City councils were out of session; many politicians, activists, and other citizens were out of town. When people who were in town heard the news, they began gathering at their workplaces, hoping to get some direction or some information, or simply to experience grief and dread together with other human beings.

The first three members of the Leningrad City Council arrived at the Mariinsky Palace just after seven in the morning. They decided to convene a session of the council, so they began making phone calls. By ten, they still did not have a quorum. But this was when those present saw General Viktor Samsonov, head of the Leningrad Military District, come on television, identify himself as the regional representative of the GKChP and declare a state of emergency in the city. In the absence of a quorum, Igor Artemyev, a deputy chairman of the city council, decided to call at least a working meeting to order. The bearded, soft-spoken Artemyev, a thirty-year-old Ph.D. in biology, inexperienced in running meetings, was entirely unprepared for what came next. He gave the floor to the first person who asked for it; it happened to be an appointed representative of the GKChP, Rear Admiral Viktor Khramtsov. He had barely begun to speak when Vitaly Skoybeda, a thirty-year-old city council member known for his propensity to get into fights, stormed the floor, shouting that Khramtsov should be arrested—and slugging him.

City Council chairman Alexander Belyaev, who had been out of town, walked in at this key juncture. Calling the proceedings to order, he quickly approached the rear admiral, who was still prone on the hall's spectacular parquet floor, and asked him whether there was a document establishing a state of emergency in the city. There was not. In that case, Belyaev resolved, there was no state of emergency. Marina Salye called the GKChP a "military coup"—a not yet obvious definition that struck those present as very exact. The councillors began discussing a plan of resistance, forming a coordinating committee, and drafting a statement in opposition to the coup. The question now was how to get the message to the people of Leningrad.

Mayor Sobchak, too, was out of town, and no one knew how to

reach him. He called the city council on the phone in the late morning or early afternoon, just when the councillors had completed their discussion. "We told him that we are planning to go to the television station in order to inform the city as soon as possible that this is a military coup," Salye told me years later. "He said, 'Don't do it, it will just cause panic. Wait for me to get there.'" Several of the city councillors, including Salye, tried to get to the television station anyway, but they were not allowed in. The waiting for Sobchak commenced.

Sobchak had spent the morning at Boris Yeltsin's dacha outside Moscow. The Russian president had summoned all the leading democrats then in Moscow. It was a scared and confused group of men. By any logic anyone could understand, Yeltsin should have been arrested; no one could figure out why he had not been. In fact, a warrant for his arrest had been signed overnight, and he should have been taken when he flew into Moscow that morning. But for some reason no one could explain then or later, the arrest did not take place. KGB agents were then directed to encircle Yeltsin's dacha. They saw him enter the house and later leave it, but they never received a final order to place him under arrest; as it turned out later, two deputy commanders of the unit in charge of the operation had objected and ultimately blocked the warrant. The KGB agents sat armed and idle outside his house as Yeltsin sped off toward the seat of the Russian government in central Moscow.

Others present, including Sobchak, traveled to the airport to fly to their respective cities to coordinate local resistance efforts. But before leaving Moscow, Sobchak called Leningrad and directed police special forces to block all entrances and exits to the Leningrad television station. Whether he did this before or after placing the call to the city council is not clear. What is clear is that this was why Salye and others were not allowed to enter.

They waited. Sobchak should have landed long ago. He had, but before coming to the city council—as all of Leningrad seemed to expect him to do: a crowd was gathering in front of the Mariinsky, growing larger every hour—Sobchak went to Leningrad district military headquarters to speak with General Samsonov. "Why did I do so?" he wrote later in a memoir. "I still cannot explain my actions. It must have been intuition, because when I arrived at the district headquarters in Palace Square, a GKChP working meeting was just getting under way in Samsonov's office. . . . Our conversation ended with Samsonov giving me his word that, barring any extreme or extraordinary events, there would be no troops in the city, and my promising to maintain safety in the city."

In fact, what Sobchak did was choose a course of action distinctly different from that of his colleagues in Moscow and many other cities: once again, he decided to hedge his bets by creating a situation in which he would be safe if the hard-liners won but get to keep his democrat's credentials if they lost.

MOSCOW'S CITY COUNCIL also convened at ten in the morning and also resolved to oppose the coup. Unlike their Leningrad colleagues, Moscow city councillors had the unequivocal support of the city's mayor, Gavriil Popov, who, among other things, ordered city services to cut off water, power, and telephone connections to any buildings from which GKChP supporters were operating, and city banks to stop issuing funds to GKChP and affiliated organizations. The city council and the mayor's office together formed a task force to coordinate resistance efforts. As troops were entering the city from different directions throughout the day of August 19, so were volunteers gathering around the Moscow "White House," the high-rise that was home to the Russian government. When GKChP representatives called Moscow's deputy mayor, Yuri Luzhkov, to try to negotiate, Luzhkov, who had always been more of a bureaucrat than a democrat, cursed them and hung up the phone.

Sobchak, meanwhile, completed his negotiations with General Samsonov and finally went to his office at the Mariinsky Palace, where Putin had posted and was personally supervising a heavy guard. By the middle of the day, tens of thousands of people had gathered in front of the Mariinsky Palace, hoping for news—or an opportunity to act. Sobchak eventually appeared in the window of his office and read a statement—not his own, but that of Russian president Boris Yeltsin and other members of his government. "We call on the people of Russia to respond appropriately to the putschists and to demand that the country be allowed to return to its normal course of constitutional development." After nine in the evening, joined by his deputy the rear admiral, he finally traveled to the Leningrad TV station, where he read his own address—inspired and eloquent as ever. The speech was particularly important because Leningrad television broadcast to many cities all over the country, and though the GKChP apparently tried to stop the broadcast as soon as Sobchak started to speak, Leningrad persisted. Sobchak called on the city's residents to come to a rally the following day. He sounded defiant, but he was not: he had previously cleared the plan with General Samsonov, promising to keep the demonstrators confined to a clearly circumscribed space. After he finished speaking, Sobchak, and Putin with him, went into hiding: he would spend the next two days in a bunker beneath Leningrad's largest industrial plant, emerging only once to appear at a press conference. He was terrified.

On the second day of the coup, the strangest thing happened. Marina Salye was manning the phones at the city council's makeshift resistance headquarters when Yeltsin's vice president, General Alexander Rutskoy, called and started screaming into the phone: "What the hell did he do? He read a decree? What the hell did he read?" It took a few minutes for Salye to figure out what Rutskoy was talking about, and it took her much longer than that to understand what it meant. Rutskoy had issued a decree removing General Samsonov

from his post as the head of the Leningrad Military District and replacing him with Rear Admiral Shcherbakov, Sobchak's deputy.
Replacing a hard-liner loyal to the GKChP with someone loyal to
the democratic mayor seemed like a logical step, and one that Sobchak should have welcomed. Except it upset Sobchak's carefully
constructed hedge and would in essence have forced him to take
Yeltsin's side not only in his speeches, which he had done, but also
in his actions. So Sobchak, the lawyer, fudged the language in Rutskoy's decree, which he read at his press conference, rendering the
document invalid.

There was a barrage of decrees, statements, addresses, and orders coming from both sides of the barricades. It was a war of nerves
rather than a legal battle, for any organization, or any person, obeyed
only the decrees issued by the authority he recognized. This was why
Yeltsin could not just call Samsonov and order him to clear out of
his office: Samsonov reported to the GKChP, not to Yeltsin. So the
democratic government in Moscow had hoped that Sobchak, by
reading the decree aloud, with all his eloquence and all his authority,
would invest the document with enough power that the troops stationed in Leningrad would believe Rear Admiral Shcherbakov to be
their new commander. But when Sobchak read the decree, he replaced the job title now assigned to Shcherbakov with something
called "top military chief," a term no one recognized, a fictitious job
from some parallel world that cast no doubt on General Samsonov's
authority. This was Sobchak's way of keeping his own situation un-
defined and stable.

AND THEN THE COUP CRUMPLED. After a two-day standoff in the center of Moscow, most of the troops failed to move on the White
House, and the few armored personnel carriers that did were stopped
by a handful of unarmed volunteers and the barricades they had

constructed from sidewalk stones and overturned electric buses. Three people died.

Gorbachev returned to Moscow. The incredibly fast process of taking apart the Soviet Union commenced. At the same time, the Russian and Soviet governments launched the process of taking apart the Soviet Union's most powerful institution, the KGB, although this effort would prove much more complicated and much less efficient.

On August 22, the Russian Supreme Soviet passed a resolution establishing a white, blue, and red flag as the new flag of Russia, replacing the Soviet-era red flag with its hammer and sickle. A group of city council members, led by Vitaly Skoybeda—the one who had slugged the hard-liner three days earlier—set off to replace the flag in Leningrad. "The flag was on a corner of Nevsky Prospekt, over the Party headquarters," Yelena Zelinskaya, the samizdat publisher, recalled in an interview years later. "It was the most noticeable place in the city. They started taking it down, a group of people including journalists and city council members. An orchestra showed up for some reason; it was the brass band of the military school. And a television crew was there filming. They lowered the red flag carefully. As the orchestra played, they raised the tricolor. The man who took down the flag was standing right there among us, on Nevsky. So there we were, a group of people, standing in the street, with an orchestra playing, and this man with a red flag in his hands, and we were suddenly totally lost as to what to do. Here we had a flag that for eighty years had been the symbol of the state; we had all hated it but we had also all feared it. And then one of our staff members says, 'I know what to do: we are going to give it back to them.' The district Party headquarters was across the street. And he grabbed the flag and ran across the Nevsky, without looking left or right. Cars stop. The orchestra is playing a march, and he is running across the very wide Nevsky, and just when the orchestra is playing the last note, he tosses the flag as hard as he can against the Party headquarters doors. There is a pause. And then the door opens slowly just a crack; a hand reaches out and quickly yanks the flag inside. The door closes. This was the highlight of my entire life. I saw the Russian flag raised over Nevsky."

Five days after the coup began, Moscow held a funeral for the three young men who died trying to stop the troops. Three Leningrad politicians, including Salye, flew in for the ceremony. They joined Nikolai Gonchar, chairman of the Moscow City Council and a prominent democrat, at the head of the funeral procession. "The procession kept starting and stopping," Salye told me later. "And every time we stopped, Gonchar turned to me and said, 'Marina Yevgeniyevna, what was it?' He said it about ten times." By the end of the day, Gonchar had Salye convinced that the coup was not what it had seemed.

So what was it? Why did the coup, so many months in the making, fall apart so easily? Indeed, why did it never really take off? Why were the democratic politicians, with the exception of Gorbachev, allowed to move around the country freely and have telephone contact? Why were none of them arrested? Why, in the three days that they ostensibly held power in the Soviet Union, did the hard-liners fail to capture the main communication or transportation hubs? And why did they fold without a fight? Was the coup simply a mediocre attempt by a group of disorganized failures? Or was there something more complicated and more sinister going on? Was there, as Salye ultimately came to believe, a carefully engineered arrangement that allowed Yeltsin to remove Gorbachev and broker the peaceful demise of the Soviet Union but also placed him forever in debt to the KGB?

I happen to think it was neither—and both. Even while it was going on, on either side of the barricades, different people were telling themselves different stories about the coup. When it ended, the nominal winners—the people who fought for democracy in Russia—failed to shape or advance a story that would have become the common truth of the new Russia. Everyone was thus left with his or her individual narrative. In the end, for some people those three days in August 1991 remained a story of heroism and the victory of democracy. For others, they remained—or became—the story of a cynical conspiracy. Which story is right depends on which of them belongs to the people who hold power in Russia. So the question becomes: What is the story that Vladimir Putin tells himself about the coup?

OVER THOSE THREE DAYS IN AUGUST, Putin was even less visible than usual. He stayed by Sobchak's side at all times. It was Sobchak's other deputy, Shcherbakov, who had the visible role, who acted as both spokesman and point man: he stayed behind in the mayor's office, night and day and night again, as Sobchak, accompanied by Putin, hid in the bunker. We know that Sobchak was playing both sides of the barricades; in fact, the barricades may have bisected his inner circle. Early in the crisis, Shcherbakov discovered that someone had placed a tiny tracking device on his lapel. On the morning of August 21, Shcherbakov remembered, "I had pushed five chairs together in my office and lain down to sleep on them. I woke up because I sensed someone looking at me. Anatoly Alexandrovich [Sobchak] had returned. 'Go back to sleep, Vyacheslav Nikolayevich,' he said. 'Everything is fine and good. Congratulations.' I immediately reached for my lapel to feel for the bug—and it was no longer there. So someone in my immediate circle had placed it and then removed it so it would not be found. Someone who was working for the other side."

Nine years later, Putin answered his biographers' questions about the coup. "It was dangerous to leave the city council building in those days," he reminisced. "But we did many things, we were active: we went to the Kirov industrial plant, spoke to the workers there, and went to other factories, even though we did not feel particularly safe doing so." This is mostly a lie: many independent eyewitnesses describe Sobchak, and Putin with him, going into hiding in the bunker at the Kirov industrial plant, where Sobchak may or may not have given a speech before literally going underground. There is no indication they went to any other factories or did anything during the last two days of the crisis but emerge for that single press conference.

"What if the hard-liners had won?" the biographers asked. "You were a KGB officer. You and Sobchak would certainly have been put on trial."

"But I was not a KGB officer anymore," Putin responded. "As soon as the coup began, I made up my mind as to which side I'm on. I knew for a fact that I would never do anything as directed by the coup organizers and would never be on their side. And I knew full well that this would be considered at least a violation. So on August 20 I wrote my second letter of resignation from the KGB."

This makes no sense. If Putin knew that his first letter of resignation, supposedly written a year earlier, was lost, why did he not write a second one immediately—especially if, as he claimed, he had initially decided to resign under threat of blackmail? In addition, how would he have known that the letter was lost? Presumably, there was only one way: he continued to draw a salary from the KGB, meaning he was very much a KGB officer when the coup began.

But now, he claimed, he mobilized all efforts to break with the organization. "I told Sobchak, 'Anatoly Alexandrovich, I wrote a letter of resignation once but it "died" somewhere along the way.' So Sobchak immediately called [KGB chief and one of the coup leaders Vladimir] Kryuchkov and then the head of my district. And the following day, I was told that my letter of resignation had been signed."

This part of the story seems to be pure fiction. "I do not think the phone call he describes could have taken place on August 20," said Arseniy Roginsky, a Moscow human-rights activist and historian who spent about a year after the coup combing through KGB archives and studying that institution. "Kryuchkov simply would not have handled a personnel question, especially one that concerned a not particularly senior officer, that day." Nor is it easy to imagine Sobchak, who was so busy playing both sides, acting essentially to sever his own ties to the KGB. In addition, it is not clear how Putin managed to deliver a physical letter—the one that was supposedly signed the next day—to KGB headquarters that day, especially if he never left Sobchak's side. Finally, even if some of what Putin said were true, it would mean that his resignation was accepted on the last day of the coup, when it was all but clear that the hard-liners had failed.

Most likely, Putin, like his boss, spent the days of the coup on the fence and, if he resigned from the KGB at all, did so only once the coup was over. Unlike Sobchak and many other people, he had not even taken Yeltsin's lead a few months earlier and resigned from the Communist Party: Putin's membership expired two weeks after the failed coup, when Yeltsin issued a decree dissolving the Party. So the question is still: What is the story that Putin told himself during the coup? Is there a chance he was the person or one of the people in Sobchak's inner circle who actively supported the hard-liners? The answer is yes.

THE NINETY MILLION DEUTSCHE MARKS' worth of meat that Marina Salye had caught wind of in May had never materialized in Leningrad, but she did not forget about it in the dramatic events that followed. Insulted and mystified by what had happened in Germany, Salye continued to try to get to the bottom of the story. After the failed coup, when access to records of all sorts briefly got easier, she was finally able to get her hands on some documents, and by March 1992 she had pieced together the story.

In May 1991, Soviet prime minister Valentin Pavlov granted a Leningrad company called Kontinent the right to negotiate trade contracts on behalf of the Soviet government. Within weeks, Kontinent had signed the meat contract with the German firm. The meat was delivered—but to Moscow rather than Leningrad. The reason was plain: The future GKChP, of which Pavlov was a leader, was trying to stock Moscow food warehouses in order to flood store shelves once they seized power.

The name of the man who had negotiated with the Germans on behalf of Kontinent? Vladimir Putin.

Once Salye thought she knew what had happened, she tried to take action. In March 1992 she traveled to Moscow to see an old acquaintance from the Leningrad pro-democracy movement. Yuri Boldyrev, a handsome, moustachioed young economist, had been elected to the Supreme Soviet alongside Sobchak; now he was working as the chief comptroller in the Yeltsin administration. Salye hand-delivered a letter describing the initial results of her investigation: the peculiar story of the meat that had apparently traveled from Germany to Moscow. Within days, Boldyrev had written a letter to another Leningrad economist, who was now the foreign trade minister, asking him to curtail Putin's powers. The letter was ignored. Putin had presumably created a base of wealth and influence from which he could not easily be shaken.

What exactly was Putin's role in the government of Russia's second-largest city? A woman who worked at the mayor's office at the same time recalls Putin as a man with an empty office save for a desk with a lone glass ashtray sitting atop it, and with similarly color-less glassy eyes looking out from behind the desk. In his early months in city government, Putin had struck some of his colleagues as eager, curious, and intellectually engaged. Now he cultivated an impervi-ous, emotionless exterior. The woman who worked as his secretary later recalled having to deliver a piece of upsetting personal news to her boss: "The Putins had a dog, a Caucasian shepherd named Malysh [Baby]. He lived at their dacha and was always digging holes under the fence, trying to get out. One time he did get out, and got run over by a car. Ludmila Alexandrovna grabbed the dog and drove him to the veterinary clinic. She called his office from there and asked me to tell her husband that the veterinarian had been unable to save the dog. I went into Vladimir Vladimirovich's office and said, 'You know, there is a situation. Malysh is dead.' I looked—and there was no emotion in his face, none. I was so surprised at his lack of reaction that I could not keep from asking, 'Did someone already tell you?' And he said calmly, 'No, you are the first person to tell me.' That's when I knew I had said the wrong thing."

The "wrong thing" in the story presumably refers to the question about whether Putin had already been informed of his dog's death. But the scene as a whole is remarkable for the palpable sense of uncertainty and even fear that it conveys.

When his biographers asked him about the nature of his work in St. Petersburg, Putin responded with the lack of subtlety that had come to characterize his answers to sensitive questions. He had tried to take over the casinos, he said. "I believed at the time that the casino business is an area where the state should have a monopoly," he said. "My position ran opposite to the law on monopolies, which had already been passed, but still I tried to make sure that the state, as embodied by the city, established control over the entire casino industry." To that end, he said, the city formed a holding company that acquired 51 percent of the stock of all the casinos in the city, in the hopes of collecting dividends. "But it was a mistake: the casinos funneled the money out in cash and reported losses every time," Putin complained. "Later, our political opponents tried to accuse us of corruption because we owned stock in the casinos. That was just ridiculous. . . . Sure, it may not have been the best idea from an economic standpoint. Judging from the fact that the setup turned out to be inefficient and we did not attain our goals, I have to admit it was not sufficiently thought through. But if I had stayed in Petersburg, I would have finished choking those casinos. I would have made them share. I would have given that money to elderly people, teachers, and doctors." In other words, said the incoming president of Russia, if the law got in the way of his ideas of how things should be done, that would be too bad for the law. He had little else to say about his years as Sobchak's deputy.

In early 1992, Marina Salye had set out to learn exactly what the little man with the empty office was actually doing. The city council launched a full-fledged investigation, the results of which— twenty-two single-spaced typed pages plus dozens of pages of appendices—Salye presented to her colleagues less than two months following her visit to Boldyrev. She discovered that Putin had entered into dozens of contracts on behalf of the city, many if not all of them of questionable legality.

Putin's department in the mayor's office was now called the Committee for Foreign Relations. Most of its activities ostensibly centered on providing for foodstuffs to be brought into the city from other countries. The city had no cash with which to buy the food: the ruble was not a convertible currency; Russia's monetary system, inherited from the Soviet Union, was out of balance, and efforts to right it immediately led to hyperinflation. But Russia had plenty of natural resources, which it could trade, directly or indirectly, for food. To that end, the government in Moscow allowed subjects of the federation to export natural resources.

Salye found that Putin's department had entered into a dozen export contracts, together worth $92 million. The city agreed to provide oil, timber, metals, cotton, and other natural resources granted to it by the Russian state; the companies named in the contracts undertook to export the natural resources and import foodstuffs. But Salye's investigation found that every single contract contained a flaw that made it legally invalid: all were missing seals or signatures, or contained major discrepancies. "Putin is a lawyer by training," she wrote later. "He had to know that these contracts could not be used in court." In addition, Putin had violated the rules of these import-export barter operations, set by the Russian government, by picking the exporting companies unilaterally rather than by holding an open competition.

The food that by contract was supposed to be brought into Leningrad never made it to the city. But the commodities mentioned in these dozen contracts apparently had been transported abroad; in fact, another irregularity to which Salye's investigation drew attention was the inordinate nature of the commissions written into the contracts: between 25 and 50 percent of the sum of each contract, for a total of $34 million in commissions. All evidence seemed to point to a simple kickback scheme: handpicked companies received lucrative contracts—and they did not even have to hold up their end.

Asked about the investigation by his biographers, Putin acknowledged that many of the firms with which he had signed contracts had failed to bring any food to the city. "I think the city did not do all it could, of course," he said. "We should have worked more closely with law enforcement, we should have beaten it out of their firms. But it made no sense to try to go to court: the firms would just disappear instantly, stop functioning, remove their goods. In essence, we had no claim against them. Remember that time: it was full of shady businesses, financial pyramids, that sort of thing." This was the same man who, just a day or two earlier, had emphasized to his biographers how vicious he could be if someone so much as seemed to cross him, the same man who flared up instantly and had a hard time winding down, the same man whom his friends remember all but scratching out his opponents' eyes when he was angered. Why would this man sit idly while one private company after another violated the terms of the contracts he had signed with them, leaving his city without the food supplies it so badly needed?

Because it was rigged to end that way from the beginning, Salye believes. "The point of the whole operation," she wrote later, "was this: to create a legally flawed contract with someone who could be trusted, to issue an export license to him, to make the customs office open the border on the basis of this license, to ship the goods abroad, sell them, and pocket the money. And that is what happened."

But that, Salye believed, was not all that happened. Moscow had actually given St. Petersburg permission to export a billion dollars' worth of commodities, so the twelve rigged contracts she found represented only a tenth of the wealth that should have traveled through Putin's office. What was the rest of the story? She eventually found evidence that all, or nearly all, of the commodities, including aluminum, oil, and cotton, had been exported, or, as she put it, "had vanished": there was simply no documentation. But her report to the city council focused only on the twelve contracts for which there was documentation; nearly a hundred million dollars' worth of commodities ostensibly bartered for food that never arrived.

The city council reviewed Salye's report and resolved to forward it to Mayor Sobchak with the recommendations that the report be submitted to the prosecutor's office and that Sobchak dismiss Putin and Putin's own deputy, whose signature was on many of the contracts. Sobchak ignored the recommendations and the report itself. The prosecutor's office would not launch an investigation without Sobchak's permission. Salye had already hand-delivered a three-page letter to Yeltsin outlining some of the biggest violations and asking that they be investigated. There had been no reaction. Only Boldyrev, Russia's chief comptroller, had reacted with understanding, immediately sending a letter to the foreign trade minister and pursuing the case.

Boldyrev reviewed the documents Salye had brought him. His findings were essentially the same as Salye's: someone had been stealing from the people of St. Petersburg. He summoned Sobchak to Moscow to respond. "Sobchak came and brought all of his deputies with him," Boldyrev recalled in an interview later. Putin came. "They wrote down their versions of the events. . . . I then reported the findings to Yeltsin."

And then nothing happened. The Russian president's office in Moscow forwarded some documents to the Russian president's representative office in St. Petersburg—and the story died.

"IT WAS JUST AN ORDINARY INVESTIGATION," Boldyrev explained many years later. "It uncovered significant violations, but they were not radically more serious than what was going on in the rest of Russia. They were standard-issue violations having to do with obtaining the right to export strategically important resources in exchange for foodstuffs that never materialized. It was just a typical case at the time."

Russia's new elite was busy redistributing wealth. This is not to say that all of them behaved like Putin—the scale and the brazen nature of the embezzlement uncovered by Salye is shocking even by early-1990s Russia standards, especially if we take into account how fast he acted—but all of the country's new rulers treated Russia like their personal property. Less than a year earlier, it had all belonged to other people: the Communist Party of the USSR and its leaders. Now the USSR no longer existed, and the Russian Communist Party was a handful of stubborn retirees. All that had been theirs was now nobody's. While economists tried to figure out how to turn state property into private property—a process that still is not completed twenty years later—the new bureaucrats were simply taking the old state edifice apart.

Sobchak was handing out apartments in the center of St. Petersburg. They went to friends, relatives, and valued colleagues. In a country where property rights had not really existed and where the Communist ruling elite had long enjoyed the status of royalty, Sob-

chak, who basked in his early popularity, saw nothing wrong with
what he was doing.

"And here are the papers on an entire city complex Sobchak
tried to give away to some development company," Salye told me all
these years later, fishing several more sheets of paper from her pile.
"This was a rare situation where we managed to get it reversed, but
what a fight it was."

"But wasn't he acting just like some regional party boss?" I
asked. "They were always giving away apartments."

"This was different," said Salye. "It was different because he
talked a good line. He knew he had to present a different exterior,
and he succeeded in doing this. He played the democrat when he
was really a demagogue."

Perhaps because Sobchak was so good at projecting the image
of a new kind of a politician, Salye and her colleagues seem to have
believed he would take action when presented with evidence of
Putin's wrongdoing. But why should he have? Why would he have
drawn a line between his own habits of handing out city property
and Putin's ways of pocketing profits from the sale of public resources? Why should he have listened to the democrats in the city
council at all? He could not stand them—and what irked him most
was precisely their militant idealism, their absurd insistence on doing
things as they should be done rather than as they had always been
done. This adherence to an imaginary ethical code invariably got in
the way of doing things at all.

So Sobchak did not get rid of Putin. Instead, he got rid of the
city council.

BY FALL 1993. Boris Yeltsin was fed up with the Russian legislature. It
was an oddly constituted body: over a thousand representatives who

had been elected, in a convoluted quasi-democratic procedure, to the Congress of People's Deputies, of whom 252 belonged to the Supreme Soviet, a two-chamber body that attempted to perform the functions of a representative branch of government in the effective absence of relevant law. The Russian Federation did not yet have a new, post-Soviet constitution, and it would be years before its civic and penal codes would be rewritten. Among other things, the law still criminalized possession of hard currency and a variety of acts that involved the possession and sale of property. In this situation, the Congress of People's Deputies granted Yeltsin the right to issue decrees on economic reform that violated the laws that were on the books—but the Supreme Soviet was charged with the job of reviewing these decrees, and granted veto power. In addition, the Supreme Soviet had a presidium constituted of more than thirty people who, in the Soviet system of government, functioned as a collective head of state; in the post-Soviet system, once the position of president had been established, the function of the presidium was unclear. In effect, though, the Supreme Soviet had the power to stall or block any action of the president. As Yeltsin's economic reforms drove prices higher and higher—even as food shortages stopped, as though by magic—his government grew less and less popular and the Supreme Soviet moved to oppose almost all of his initiatives.

On September 21, 1993, Yeltsin issued a decree dissolving the Supreme Soviet and calling for the election of a proper legislative body. The Supreme Soviet refused to disband, barricading itself inside the White House—the very same building where Yeltsin's people had set up camp during the coup two years earlier. This time troops did open fire and shelled the White House, forcing Supreme Soviet members out on October 4.

Leading democratic politicians, including former dissidents, supported what became known as "the execution of the Supreme Soviet," so exasperated were they with seeing the president stonewalled.

The idealistic St. Petersburg City Council was more or less alone in taking a stand against Yeltsin's actions. A few weeks after the "execution," just days before a new Russian constitution was published, heralding an era of relative legal stability, Sobchak traveled to Moscow and convinced Yeltsin to sign a decree dissolving the St. Petersburg City Council. A new election would not be held until the following December, leaving Russia's second-largest city in the hands of one man for an entire year.

Marina Salye decided to leave city politics. She became a professional political organizer, later moving to Moscow to work there.

SIX YEARS LATER, in the period leading up to Putin's election as president of Russia, perhaps the only critical voice belonged to Marina Salye. She published an article, "Putin Is the President of a Corrupt Oligarchy," in which she detailed and updated the findings of her St. Petersburg investigation. She tried in vain to talk her liberal colleagues out of supporting Putin in the election. She found herself increasingly marginalized: she recalled that, during a meeting of the right-liberal political coalition, she and Yeltsin's first prime minister, Yegor Gaidar, were the only two people—out of over a hundred—who did not vote in favor of supporting Putin.

A few months after the election, Salye went to see one of the few politicians whom she still believed to be an ally. They had talked of forming a new organization. Sergei Yushenkov was a career military man who had become a strong convert to liberalism during perestroika and held fast to his beliefs throughout the 1990s. The visit to Yushenkov scared Salye so much that even ten years later she refused to divulge the details.

"I got there, and there was a certain person in his office," she told me.

"What kind of person?"

"A certain person. We had a conversation that I wouldn't call constructive. I went home and told Natasha that I'm going to the country."

"Did he threaten you?"

"No one threatened me directly."

"So, why did you decide to leave?"

"Because I knew this person."

"And what did seeing him mean?"

"It meant that I should get as far away as possible."

"I'm sorry, I don't understand," I persisted, feeling I was on the verge of being thrown out of Salye's hideout.

"I knew what this person was capable of. Is that clearer?"

"Yes, thank you. But what was he doing in Yushenkov's office? Did they have something in common?"

"No. I did not know what he was doing there, and most of all I did not know why Yushenkov did not get him out of there when I came. It means he was unable to get rid of him, even though the conversation Yushenkov and I were about to have was not meant for anyone else's ears."

"I see."

"That is all I am going to say."

Salye gathered her things and moved to that house, a twelve-hour impossible drive from Moscow, where I found her ten years later. For years, rumors circulated that she was living abroad, perhaps in France (I assume it was her French surname that gave rise to that fantasy), and that she had received a threatening New Year's Eve postcard from Putin. I heard several people quote the imaginary post-card using exactly the same wording: "I wish you a Happy New Year and the health to enjoy it." Salye told me there was never any post-card; as I had suspected, the persistent rumor told me more about the image Putin had created for himself than about Salye's fate. But post-card or no postcard, Salye was terrified.

Sergei Yushenkov continued his political career. In 2002, he left the liberal faction of parliament in protest against his colleagues' persistent support for Putin's policies and what he called "a bureaucratic police regime." On the afternoon of April 17, 2003, while walking from his car to his apartment building in northern Moscow, Yushenkov was shot in the chest four times. Writing his obituary for the political analysis website I was then editing, I said, "Sometimes, when we journalists are afraid to say something under our own byline, we call people like Yushenkov, who, without looking over his shoulder, will say something clear and definitive, and all the more necessary for being predictable. There are very few people like that left."

Six

THE END OF
A REFORMER

Once Putin's biography was published in February 2000, he ceased being the young democratic reformer of Berezovsky's invention; he was now the hoodlum turned iron-handed ruler. I do not think his image-makers were even conscious of the shift.

One person who could not have imagined Putin's public transformation from democrat to strong hand was Sobchak. The two were united in their antipathy to democratic processes, but in the early 1990s, a public allegiance to democratic principles was the price of admission to public life—and to the good life.

In the early 1990s, members of the new business and political elites were hacking apart the old system all over Russia. They were, without a doubt—and, apparently, without pangs of conscience—appropriating and redistributing chunks of the system; at the same time, the most enterprising of them were also conjuring up a new system—and changing with it. People like Mikhail Khodorkovsky, a

Komsomol functionary turned banker turned oilman, and Mikhail Prokhorov, a clothing reseller turned metals mogul turned international investor, and Vladimir Gusinsky, an importer turned banker and media magnate, were self-invented entrepreneurs who started with shady moneymaking schemes but, as their worldview expanded and their ambitions grew accordingly, began to position themselves as not only businessmen but philanthropists, civic leaders, and visionaries. As their views evolved, they invested money and energy in constructing a new political system.

Sobchak abhorred this new system and so did Putin, and this is why he, unlike many of Sobchak's early allies, remained with the mayor after the 1991 failed coup and the 1992 corruption scandal and the 1993 dissolution of the city council. I am not sure why Sobchak, who had had a brief but intense love affair with democratic politics, developed such a hatred for the ways of democracy; I think, as a megalomaniac, he was deeply wounded every time he did not get his way—and by political competition itself, by the very possibility of dissent. In addition, he had Putin at his side at all times, always trying to get him to see the disadvantages of the democratic system. It was Putin, for example, who convinced Sobchak—and manipulated a number of city council members—to institute the office of mayor in the city: otherwise, Putin told his biographers years later, Sobchak "could be removed by those very same city council members anytime." Putin's own opposition to democratic reform was no less personal than Sobchak's, but ran much deeper.

Like most Soviet citizens of his generation, Putin was never a political idealist. His parents may or may not have believed in a Communist future for all the world, in the ultimate triumph of justice for the proletariat, or in any of the other ideological clichés that had been worn thin by the time Putin was growing up; he never even considered his relationship to these ideals. The way he has talked

about the Young Pioneers, from which he was kept as a child, or the
Komsomol, or the Communist Party, in which his membership simply expired along with the organization itself, makes it clear that he
never saw any substantive meaning in his belonging to these organizations. Like other members of his generation, Putin replaced belief
in communism, which no longer seemed plausible or even possible,
with faith in institutions. His loyalty was to the KGB and to the
empire it served and protected: the USSR.

In March 1994, Putin attended a European Union event in Hamburg that included a speech by Estonian president Lennart Meri. Estonia, like the two other Baltic republics, was annexed by the Soviet
Union at the start of World War II, then lost to the Germans, to be
retaken by the Soviets in 1944. The three Baltic states were the last
to be included in the Soviet empire and the first to emerge from it—
in no small part because they had a population that still remembered
a time before the Soviets. Meri, Estonia's first democratically elected
leader in half a century, had been active in the anti-Soviet liberation
movement. Now, speaking in Hamburg, he referred to the Soviet
Union as "occupiers." At this point Putin, who had been sitting in the
audience among Russian diplomats, rose and left the room. "It looked
very impressive," recalled a St. Petersburg colleague who would go on
to run the Russian federal election commission under President Putin.
"The meeting was held in Knights' Hall, which has ten-meter-tall
ceilings and a marble floor, and as he walked, in total silence, each step
of his echoed under the ceiling. To top it all off, the huge cast-iron
door slammed shut behind him with deafening thunder."

That Putin felt the need to break diplomatic protocol—to literally turn his back on the president of a neighboring country and a
very important trade partner for the city of St. Petersburg—shows
just how personally he took the matter: what he perceived as an attack on the Soviet Union hurt him as deeply as personal insults that

had sent him into a rage when he was younger. The breathless manner in which his colleague recounted the story for Putin's biographers shows how deep a vein of Soviet nostalgia Putin was tapping.

Putin loved the Soviet Union, and he loved its KGB, and when he had power of his own, effectively running the financial system of the country's second-largest city, he wanted to build a system just like them. It would be a closed system, a system built on total control—especially control over the flow of information and the flow of money. It would be a system that aimed to exclude dissent and would crush it if it appeared. But in one way, the system would be better than the KGB and the USSR had been: this one would not betray Putin. It would be too smart and too strong for that. So Putin worked diligently to centralize control not only over all foreign trade but also over business that was springing up domestically—hence his effort to take over casinos, which had appeared suddenly and grew extremely fast. He also eventually moved to manage the city's relationship with the media, both print and electronic, which he alternately isolated from city hall and strong-armed into covering particular stories in particular ways.

Sobchak had picked the right right-hand man: Putin hated the wishy-washy democrats even more than he did, and he was even better than Sobchak at working the politics of fear and greed.

POLITICIANS LIKE SOBCHAK are usually the last to learn their luster is gone. When Sobchak ran for reelection in 1996, the city hated him. Under his rule, St. Petersburg had been transformed in ways both tragic and farcical—though much of this was hardly Sobchak's fault. The city's economy was in shambles: more than a million of its five million residents had been employed by the military-industrial plants, which had slowed down or stopped altogether. As was the case elsewhere in Russia, a few people were getting very rich very fast, first by buying and selling anything and everything (for example, exporting Russian timber and importing Chinese umbrellas), then, gradually, by privatizing Soviet industrial plants and creating new institutions. Many Russians, however, got poorer—or at least felt a lot poorer: there were so many more goods in the stores now, but they could afford so little. Nearly everyone lost the one thing that had been in abundant supply during the Era of Stagnation: the unshakable belief that tomorrow will not be different from today. Uncertainty made people feel even poorer.

St. Petersburg's economic problems made much of the rest of Russia seem well-off in comparison. Three-quarters of the city's population lived below the poverty line. Its infrastructure, already weak in the late 1980s—which provided part of the impetus for the informal preservation movement—was now in ruins. Streets had not been repaved in so long that, whenever it rained or snowed—which in this northern seaside city was often—the streets turned into rivers of mud. Public transport was at a standstill: the city was not replacing buses that had to be retired. In a city composed entirely of large apartment buildings, working elevators were becoming extinct. Electricity in the center of town was flickering off and on. In studies of relative levels of standard of living, the country's second-largest city regularly ranked in the twenties among Russian cities.

Against this backdrop, Sobchak insisted on maintaining the persona of a worldly, sophisticated politician: always meticulously turned out, with his blond wife on his elbow, shuttled around in limousines, surrounded by bodyguards. Alexander Bogdanov, a young pro-democracy activist, remembered being snubbed by Sobchak in 1991, just two months after the failed coup, on the first Revolution Day in post-Communist Russia: "There was a concert in Palace Square. No one quite knew whether we should be celebrating or commemorating this day as a day of tragedy. So there was a rally in the afternoon and a dance at night. While Sobchak and [his wife

Ludmila] Narusova were holding a banquet in the Tavrichesky Palace, with an entrance fee of five hundred rubles! That was before hyperinflation hit, this was a huge sum of money. . . . So there we were, walking around the dance carrying banners with the words 'A Day of National Tragedy,' looking and feeling like idiots. And I said, 'You know what? Why are we wasting our time here? Let's go to the Tavrichesky Palace, where they are having a feast.' We arrived at the Tavrichesky just as they were all getting into their cars. Sobchak came out in tails, with Narusova wearing a beautiful dress and some sort of wraparound turbanlike hat. Sobchak had a bodyguard who would go on to be Putin's chief bodyguard. He had this stupid habit: he would go up to me and just about curse me out, saying, 'You are getting to me! Get out of here! Disappear, I am sick of you!' So I said to Sobchak, 'Why is your bodyguard always threatening me?' And Ludmila Borisovna [Narusova] said to me, 'Why are you always making a fool of yourself?' And Sobchak was all relaxed, all important, getting into his limousine, and he said to me, 'Shut up, the people elected me!' I remembered that for the rest of my life. That's the kind of snob he was."

As Sobchak's deputy mayor, Putin performed the jobs that Soviet tradition had reserved for KGB men in the "active reserve": in addition to being responsible for foreign trade, he also aimed to control the flow of information in and out of the government. Yuri Boldyrev, Yeltsin's chief comptroller who had unsuccessfully tried to follow up on Salye's allegations, served as a senator from St. Petersburg in 1994–1995. "Not once during this time was I allowed to go live on air on St. Petersburg television," he recalled later. "Only after I had stopped being a senator was I allowed to speak live—and even then the anchors kept interrupting me, so in the end I said nothing."

Whenever I went to St. Petersburg on a story, the first person I would go see was Anna Sharogradskaya: her office was on Nevsky Prospekt, just down the street from the railroad station, and she knew everything. She ran the Independent Press Center, which provided space for press conferences for anybody who wanted to hold one—including those who would be turned down by every other space in town. She knew everyone, and she feared no one. She was in her late fifties by the time the Soviet Union collapsed, and she remembered a time when things had been a lot more scary. One time Sharogradskaya organized a press conference that exposed the Sobchak administration's practice of bugging the offices of journalists and politicians, including his own employees. Many people had known or suspected this was the case, but only the local English-language newspaper, run and staffed by expats, dared run the story. Sharogradskaya was always convinced that Putin, who was largely responsible for the mayor's relationship with the media, organized the bugging.

In keeping with KGB practices, the information that Sobchak was allowed to receive was heavily edited. This was certainly part of the reason he never suspected how unpopular he had become. Some of St. Petersburg's television-viewing audience saw Sobchak making this unpleasant discovery. "There was a show called *Public Opinion,*" recalled Sharogradskaya. "It was a popular show during the 1996 election. When Sobchak saw that his popularity rating was six percent, he shouted, 'That's impossible!,' jumped up, and left the studio. The show was shut down. The host, Tamara Maksimova, was fired. Her husband, Vladimir, who was the director of the show, called me and said he wanted to hold a press conference. I said, 'No problem,' and scheduled it for noon the next day. Vladimir called the following morning, three or four hours before the scheduled press conference, and said it had to be canceled: 'We cannot do this, because we are being threatened: something might happen to our daughter.' I said, 'Please tell that to the journalists. I cannot not explain the reason for the cancellation.' They came and told everyone that they were being threatened and they were scared. Journalists tried to ask them questions, but they would not respond."

When Sharogradskaya told me stories like these in the 1990s, I heard them as tales from a different land. Russia was a messy, often illogical place in those years, but never had I felt unsafe working as a journalist—not until I started writing from and about St. Petersburg, that is. At Sharogradskaya's invitation, I taught a reporting course at the Independent Press Center, taking the train in on weekends to work with a group of university journalism majors. (I was teaching the same course at Moscow University, but St. Petersburg University wanted no part of it—which is why Sharogradskaya's organization ended up hosting it.) On election weekend, I sent the students out to take notes at polling stations in the center of town. The students returned with bloodied noses and black eyes; two young people needed medical attention. They had presented themselves as journalism students at two polling stations; the guards had radioed for instructions and had then roughed them up. This was how St. Petersburg politicians treated St. Petersburg journalists.

Realizing too late that he was about to lose the election, Sobchak made desperate attempts to fix the situation. He asked Alexander Yuriev, a political psychologist at St. Petersburg University who had tried to warn Sobchak he was desperately unpopular, to run his campaign. A few days after Yuriev agreed, he faced a brutal attempt on his life: someone rang his doorbell and then tossed sulfuric acid through the open door. Because the door opened inward, some of the acid settled on the door itself and some even ricocheted back at whoever had thrown it; this was probably why Yuriev did not get a lethal dose. He was then also shot—and survived that as well. It took him long months, and two skin transplants, to recover.

In the run-up to the election, Sobchak also tried to buy the loyalty of the city's press corps, giving out loans and grants, driving the city's budget ever deeper into debt. It was too late. The press hated him, other politicians hated him, and ordinary people hated him.

Sobchak lost the election. His campaign manager in the end was
Vladimir Putin.

FOR ITS NEXT MAYOR, St. Petersburg elected Sobchak's own public
works deputy, a man in every way his opposite: plain-looking, poorly
turned-out, Vladimir Yakovlev could barely put two words together.
But in a city where public transportation was at a standstill, buildings
were crumbling, and electricity was flickering on and off, he somehow inspired hope that he would try to fix the right things. Or, at the
very least, he would not lie about them. Yakovlev would not, in fact,
be successful at fixing what ailed St. Petersburg—the city continued
to get poorer, dirtier, and more dangerous—but four years later, Yakovlev easily won reelection because St. Petersburg was still battling
the hated ghost of Mayor Sobchak.

In losing the election, Sobchak lost not only power and influence but also immunity from prosecution—which, at this point, was
probably what he feared most. For almost a year, a special prosecutor's team of nearly forty investigators dispatched by the prosecutor
general's office in Moscow had been looking into allegations of corruption in the mayor's office. One person, a real estate developer, had
already been arrested and was testifying against city officials. This
part of the investigation concerned an apartment building in the
center of St. Petersburg that had allegedly undergone illegal recon-
struction, and city funds had allegedly been used in the process. Almost all the building's residents, including Sobchak's own niece, were
either highly placed city employees or their close relatives.

Now Sobchak, too, was likely to join the list of suspects. Most of
his allies had abandoned him, some before the election, like the deputy who replaced him in the mayor's office; others joined the new
regime after Sobchak lost the vote. Putin turned down a job offer in

the new administration—the display of loyalty that had placed him so high in Berezovsky's esteem—and soon decamped for Moscow, as though airlifted by an invisible hand. The way he told the story to his biographers, an old Leningrad apparatchik now working in the Kremlin remembered Putin and arranged a good post for him in the capital. Putin was now deputy head of the presidential property management office, which sounds very much like another "active reserve" posting. Whether this was the product of secret-police design, providence, or habit is probably unimportant: Putin once again had a job with little public responsibility but a lot of access.

Putin's new job and his old connections were clearly a boon to Sobchak, who was now living with the daily threat of arrest. The prosecutor's office was chasing Sobchak, trying to deliver a summons so he could be interrogated. Not until October 3, 1997, did Sobchak finally arrive at the prosecutor's office; he was accompanied by his wife, who was a parliament member. During the interrogation, Sobchak said he felt ill and Narusova demanded an ambulance. With television cameras looking on, Sobchak was taken straight from the prosecutor's office to the hospital, where he was reportedly diagnosed with a heart attack. Exactly a month later, Narusova informed the press that Sobchak was now well enough to be transferred to a different clinic, at the Military Academy Hospital, where he would be in the care of Yuri Shevchenko, a family friend of the Putins, who had personally treated Ludmila Putina following a serious car accident a few years earlier.

Around the time Sobchak was transferred into Shevchenko's care, Putin flew to St. Petersburg from Moscow. He visited his old boss at the hospital. Four days later, during a national holiday— November 7 was no longer called Revolution Day, but the country still got a day off—Sobchak was taken by ambulance to the airport, where a Finnish medevac plane was waiting to take him to Paris. The planning was brilliant: no one noticed that Sobchak was gone until the holiday weekend ended three days later. Russian correspondents immediately stormed the American Hospital in Paris, where Shevchenko said Sobchak was being treated—but hospital officials said they had no such patient. The same day, Narusova told the media that Sobchak had undergone an operation and was feeling better. Airport officials, meanwhile, told journalists that the former mayor had seemed perfectly well boarding the plane: the ambulance had driven straight onto the tarmac, and, contrary to their expectations, he had emerged on foot, all but running to the plane.

Sobchak commenced the life of an émigré in Paris: he roomed with a Russian acquaintance, walked around town a lot, occasionally lectured at the Sorbonne, and wrote a memoir in which he portrayed himself as a man betrayed many times over; the title was *A Dozen Knives at My Back*. Yuri Shevchenko became the Russian minister of health care in July 1999, as soon as Putin commenced his sudden ascent to state power.

What was Putin himself doing at the Kremlin? His new posting seems to have been something of a sinecure. He used the time to write and defend a dissertation, a goal he had set for himself when he went to work at Leningrad University seven years earlier. The dissertation, oddly, was not on international law, as he had originally planned, but on the economics of natural resources, and he defended it at St. Petersburg's little-known Mountain Institute rather than the university. Nine years later, a researcher at the Brookings Institution in Washington, D.C., decided to study the dissertation closely; he said he found about sixteen pages of text and no fewer than six charts taken verbatim from an American textbook. Putin never acknowledged the plagiarism charges.

Whatever Putin's actual responsibilities in the Kremlin, his influence would have been considerable: he was now as well placed and well connected as any person in Russia could be without at the same time being a public person. That may well be why the special prosecutor's team never turned up much against the former mayor and his close allies: the three officials who were charged in the case were all acquitted, and the prosecutors turned their attention elsewhere. It no doubt helped that the former mayor himself was out of their reach and not testifying.

ENCOURAGED BY his former deputy's meteoric rise, Sobchak decided to end his Paris exile and go back to Russia in the summer of 1999. He returned full of hope and even more full of ambition. As Sobchak was leaving Paris, Arkady Vaksberg, a forensics specialist turned investigative reporter and author with whom Sobchak had become friendly during his years in France, asked him whether he hoped to return to Paris as an ambassador. "Higher than that," replied Sobchak. Vaksberg was sure the former mayor was aiming for the foreign minister's seat: the rumor in Moscow's political circles was that Sobchak would head up the Constitutional Court, the most important court in the country.

With characteristic overconfidence, Sobchak immediately ran for parliament—and suffered an embarrassing loss. But once Putin launched his election campaign, he appointed his former boss his "empowered representative"—a job that basically entitled Sobchak to campaign for Putin (candidates may have dozens and even hundreds of "empowered representatives"). Campaign Sobchak did, seeming to forget that his political reputation had once rested on his democratic credentials. He called Putin "the new Stalin," promising potential voters not so much mass murder as an iron hand—"the only way to make the Russian people work," Sobchak said.

But Sobchak didn't stop at the rhetoric. He talked too much, as had always been his way. Just as Putin was dictating his new official life story to the three journalists, Sobchak was reminiscing, in response to questions asked by other journalists, and recounting key episodes of Putin's career in ways that contradicted the story told by his old protégé.

On February 17, Putin asked Sobchak to travel to Kaliningrad, a Russian exclave wedged between Poland and Lithuania, to campaign for him. The request was urgent: Sobchak had to fly out that day, frustrating his wife, who did not like to see him travel on his own. She claimed she had to watch that he took his medicine. Most acquaintances believed the squeaky-voiced peroxide blonde simply did not trust her husband out of her sight. It is also possible that she feared for his safety. But she was in parliament in Moscow that day, and could not join her husband on his emergency campaign jaunt. The former mayor traveled with two male assistants who doubled as bodyguards. On February 20, Sobchak died at a private hotel in a resort town outside Kaliningrad.

Local journalists soon picked up on some odd circumstances surrounding Sobchak's death. Chief among them was the fact that two different autopsies had been performed on the body—one in Kaliningrad and one in St. Petersburg, at the military hospital run by Yuri Shevchenko, the same doctor who had helped engineer Sobchak's escape to Paris; he was now Russia's minister of health, but he had not given up his post at the hospital. The official cause of death was a massive but natural heart attack.

Still, ten weeks following Sobchak's death, the prosecutor's office in Kaliningrad opened an investigation into a possible case of "premeditated murder with aggravating circumstances." Three months later, the investigation was closed without a finding.

At Sobchak's funeral, held in St. Petersburg on February 24, Putin, sitting with the wife and a daughter of the deceased, appeared genuinely bereft. He was as emotional as Russian television viewers would ever see him. In his only public statement that day, Putin said, "Sobchak's passing is not just a death but a violent death, the result of persecution." This was widely understood to mean that Sobchak,

unfairly accused of corruption, had succumbed to the stress before his former deputy could fully restore him to the grandeur he
deserved.

Back in Paris, Arkady Vaksberg decided to launch his own investigation into his acquaintance's death. He was never a close friend or
even a great fan of the imperious Russian politician, but he was an
investigative journalist with actual forensics experience and a great
nose for a story. It was Vaksberg who dug up the most puzzling detail of the circumstances of Sobchak's death: the two bodyguard-
assistants, both physically fit young men, had had to be treated for
mild symptoms of poisoning following Sobchak's death. This was a
hallmark of contract killings by poisoning: many a secretary or bodyguard had fallen similarly ill when their bosses were killed. In 2007,
Vaksberg published a book on the history of political poisonings in
the USSR and Russia. In it, he advanced the theory that Sobchak was
killed by a poison placed on the electrical bulb of the bedside lamp,
so that the substance was heated and vaporized when the lamp was
turned on. This was a technique developed in the USSR. A few
months after the book was published, Vaksberg's car was blown up
in his Moscow garage; Vaksberg was not in it.

Seven

THE DAY THE MEDIA DIED

I spent Election Day, March 26, 2000, in Chechnya. I wanted to avoid the entire question of going to the polls in an election I felt was a mockery, following a campaign best described as a travesty. In the course of less than three months since Yeltsin's resignation, Putin had not made any political pronouncements—and this, he and his spin people seemed to think, was a virtue: he felt that dancing for his votes was beneath him. His campaign had consisted essentially of the book that put forward his vision of himself as a thug, in addition to a turn at piloting a fighter plane amid much press attention, landing it at Grozny airport a week before the election. His entire political message seemed to be: "Don't mess with me."

So I accepted an invitation, extended by the military press office, to cover the voting from Chechnya. I knew I would have little opportunity to move around and that I would have Russian officers monitoring my every move, but I figured I would get some idea of the state of a place I had known fairly well; I had last been in Chechnya

about three years earlier, soon after the cease-fire agreement had
taken hold.

Grozny had been a city of nearly a million people before the
first war, at least half a million after it was over. I was reasonably
familiar with Grozny's geography: it was a manageable-size city, with
a few hills and identifiable neighborhoods, most with enough high-
rise buildings to allow one to get one's bearings. Soon after the bombing of the city during the first war, some European observers had
compared it to Dresden, the German city bombed into oblivion by
the British and Americans toward the end of World War II. I had felt
it was a fair comparison—and yet, Grozny had retained its basic
landscape.

Now it was gone. I could see no high-rise buildings. I could not
identify any monuments, though there had been many. Every part of
the city looked the same and smelled the same: burning flesh and
concrete dust. It was horribly, deafeningly quiet. I obsessively took in
the signs, the only reminder of human life and human communication
in the city: CAFÉ; INTERNET; AUTO PARTS; PEOPLE LIVE HERE. The last was
the wording of signs people had put up as they returned to their
homes after the last war, hoping to prevent looting and shooting.

A dozen loudspeakers had been mounted around what used to
be a city, as audible markers of polling stations or of soup kitchens set
up by the federal Ministry for Emergencies. People, mostly women,
walked the streets in twos and threes, silently moving toward the
sound coming from the nearest speaker, surely hoping to find a soup
kitchen rather than a polling station.

We journalists were escorted by our military guides to one of
the nine polling stations. We arrived around noon to find a crowd
of people, again mostly women, who had been there since sunrise.
They had come in hopes of receiving humanitarian aid: either someone had promised them food and clothing would be distributed at
polling stations, or it was simply a rumor that had brought them

there. DEMOCRACY IS DICTATORSHIP OF THE LAW, the sign over the entrance to the small building proclaimed, quoting an oxymoronic pronouncement of Putin's in direct violation of election law. There was no humanitarian aid in sight.

An old woman came up to me and asked me to write that she had been reduced to living in the street.

"Did you vote?" I asked her.

"I voted," she responded.

"Who did you vote for?"

"I don't know," she responded simply. "I can't read. I had a ballot and I put it in."

Hours later, at a polling station in a different part of town, I saw some people approaching from a distance. I ran to them before my handlers could stop me, in the hopes of catching some Grozny residents outside the polling station. They turned out to be three people, two of them very old, whom I had seen at the first polling place. All three were dragging empty carts behind them. They told me that after the bus with the journalists left, local officials told them there would be no humanitarian aid; they had spent hours walking back to what had been their homes.

Using my brief moments out of sight of the handlers, I tried to ask these people why they had returned to Grozny. The old couple directed the younger woman to tell me her story. She tried to resist, saying, "What is the point of talking about it?" but in the end did not dare disobey her elders. "We came back to get our relatives' bodies. They took us to them. They were all tied up with wire. But there is one head they never found." Eight members of her family had been among the thousands detained and then summarily executed by Russian troops. The woman and her immediate relatives had left Grozny months before, and stayed with relatives in a small village. The eight relatives had not had the money to leave the city: every time one passed through a checkpoint set up by the Russian troops, one had to pay. As we talked, another woman approached us with two of her nieces in tow, a pale eight-year-old and a surly teenager. "Their father was killed in the shelling," she said. "Their mother couldn't take it and died, and their grandmother died too. The girls buried them in the yard. We dug the father up yesterday, washed the body, but the men are scared to go outside to bury him, so he is just lying there at home." She asked the teenager to confirm her story, but the girl started crying and stepped away from our group.

These people told me they had voted for a human-rights activist whose final tally was in such low single digits that most media outlets did not even mention her. But I saw a lot of Putin voters among the Chechens too. "I'm sick of war," a middle-aged man in Grozny told me. "I am sick of being passed on, like a baton, from one gang of thugs to the next." I looked around: we were in an area of Grozny that had consisted mostly of private homes; now there were only metal fences separating one ghost property from another. "Wasn't it Putin who did this?" I asked.

"War has been going on for ten years," the man responded, exaggerating only slightly: the first armed uprisings in Chechnya dated back to 1991. "What could he have changed? We long for a strong power, power that is united. We are the kind of people who need an arbiter."

There was a Chechen man among the ten little-known candidates hopelessly competing with Putin in this election. A Moscow millionaire, a real estate developer, he had shipped tons of flour to Chechen refugee camps in advance of the election. "No point in voting for him," the Chechen deputy manager of one of these camps, in neighboring Ingushetia, told me. "I might vote for him, but nobody in Russia is going to." He was going to vote for Putin: "He is a good man. He didn't do this to us for himself: there were many others interested in starting this again."

The man's boss, a fifty-year-old wizened man named Hamzat,

told me, "They said to vote for Putin because he is going to be president anyway." Hamzat had spent twenty-nine days in Russian detention during the first Chechen war; he still bore two scars on his head
and a permanent dent over his shoulder blade where he had been hit
with the butt of a rifle. He showed me a picture of his son, a puffy-
lipped, curly-haired sixteen-year-old who was now in Russian detention himself. Hamzat found the camp where his boy was, but his
jailers demanded a thousand dollars ransom—a perfectly common
practice on both sides of the conflict. Hamzat did not tell me what
happened next, but other residents of the refugee camp did: they took
up a collection in the camp but managed to scrape together barely a
tenth of the required sum. The boy was still in captivity.

The camp was made up of a field full of surplus military tents
and a ten-car train that had been towed there. It was a common
enough solution to the lack of intact housing; I myself was staying in
a military train a few towns over. Hamzat's office was in a train car.
A sheet of paper was posted on the outside with sixty-one names,
written by hand, under the headline "Located in the Naursk Jail,
Later Transported to the Pyatigorsk Hospital." Ages from sixteen to
fifty-two were noted next to the names. These appeared to be inmates who had been moved to a hospital before a press visit to
Chechnya's most notorious jail. A fellow inmate had made the list
in hopes of helping relatives find their lost ones. Someone had written "killed" in blue ballpoint pen next to one of the names.

In accordance with the military's regulations, I was spending
most of my time in the company of Russians in uniform. I would
have much preferred to stay on the Chechen side—not so much because I found their cause more sympathetic, but because I found the
atmosphere of constant fear on the Russian side exhausting. With
soldiers getting ambushed every day, the young conscripts and their
commanding officers could not relax even when they tried to drink
themselves into oblivion, as they did every night, to drown out the

gunfire that never seemed to stop. There was fire all around us during the day, too, even on Election Day. When I tried to wander into a formerly densely populated neighborhood of Grozny, my two handlers begged me to stop. "There isn't anybody there anyway," one of them pleaded. "What do you need to go there for? We'll all get turned off." He meant killed. These troops—all of whom voted for Putin, as directed by their brass—were supposed to be in control of Grozny. But Russians would be losing people here every day for years to come.

A new Russian-appointed district head in Grozny sang Putin's praises on cue. "A golden man has come to power in Russia today," he said. "A firm man." Before the election, local organizers had combed the cellars in the neighborhood, making lists of voters. They came up with 3,400 and got as many ballots, but ran out by midday. "I told them there would be additional people," the district head complained, "and they wouldn't listen! But where did all these people come from? It's not like they emerged from under the ground!"

In fact, they had very much emerged from underground, not just in the sense that they had been living in the cellars of their demolished buildings, but in the sense that many of the people who came to vote—most of them older women—came to the polling station bearing two or three passports each, their own and those of their family members who, I presumed they hoped, were still alive. Those who had lost their passports could use a special form to cast their vote, although this also meant their own documents could be used to vote elsewhere. I tested my theory as I moved from precinct to precinct: everywhere I went, I was welcome to cast my vote, using my Moscow documents or nothing at all.

Before the start of the second war, Chechnya had an official population of 380,000. By the time of the election, its voter rolls swelled to 460,000, padded not only by Russian troops but by the dead souls whose real or imaginary passports were used. Just below 30 percent voted for Putin, his worst showing in all of Russia. Overall, however, the man without a face, who did not have a political platform and did not campaign, emerged with over 52 percent of the vote, eliminating the need for a second tour.

ON MAY 7, 2000, Vladimir Putin was inaugurated as president of Russia. Strictly speaking, this was the first such ceremony in history: Yeltsin had been elected to his first term when Russia was still a part of the Soviet Union. So Putin had the opportunity to shape a ritual. At his prompting, the ceremony, originally planned for the Kremlin's modernist State Palace, where the Communist Party had held its congresses and Yeltsin's administration had organized conferences, was moved to the Kremlin's historic Great Palace, where the czars had once lived. Putin walked through the hall, down a long red carpet, swinging his left arm and holding his right arm, slightly bent at the elbow, oddly immobile, a gait that would soon become familiar to Russian TV viewers and would give one American observer cause to speculate Putin had suffered a trauma at birth or perhaps a stroke in. utero. I am more inclined to think the gait is just what it looks like: the manner of a person who executes all his public acts mechanically and reluctantly, projecting both extreme guard and extreme aggression with every step. To Russians, his walk also looked like an adolescent affectation, as did the habit of wearing his watch on his right hand though he is right-handed; this fashion immediately caught on among bureaucrats at every level, and the country's leading watch factory, in Tatarstan, soon launched a new model, called the Kremlin Watch for the Left-handed, and s..ipped the first watch in the series to Moscow as a gift for Putin. He was never seen in public wearing the inexpensive, domestically manufactured watch, although he was photographed wearing several different timepieces over the next few years, most often a $60,000 white-gold Patek Philippe Perpetual Calendar.

There were fifteen hundred invited guests at the inauguration ceremony, an inordinate number of them in uniform. One guest deserved particular note: Vladimir Kryuchkov, the former head of the KGB and an organizer of the 1991 coup. A reporter at the scene described him as "an old man of short stature who had difficulty standing and rose only once, when the national anthem was played." Kryuchkov was easy to spot because he sat apart from the rest of the guests: he was not exactly a member of the contemporary Russian political elite. Yet no one dared object publicly to the presence of a man who had attempted to use arms to quash Russian democracy. He had spent seventeen months in jail and was pardoned by the parliament in 1994. Most newspaper reports of the inauguration ignored his presence altogether. *Kommersant*, the leading business daily, gave Kryuchkov paragraph twenty out of thirty-four. Had journalists had the gift of foresight, they probably would have featured him a lot more prominently, for Russia was commemorating not only the change of leader but a change of regime—one that Kryuchkov had come to welcome.

Just a few months earlier, on December 18, 1999—two weeks before becoming acting president—Putin had spoken at a banquet celebrating the day the Soviet secret police was founded, an obscure professional holiday that was destined to gain prominence in the coming years, with congratulatory banners adorning the streets, and television reports of the celebrations. "I would like to report," Putin said at the banquet, "that the group of FSB officers dispatched to work undercover in the federal government has been successful in fulfilling the first set of assignments." The roomful of secret police brass roared with laughter. Putin later tried to downplay it as a joke, but on the same day he had restored a memorial board on the FSB

building, reminding the world that Yuri Andropov, the only secret
police chief to have become general secretary of the Communist
Party, had worked there.

   Since the campaign to elect Putin and the man himself had
seemed to exist parallel to each other, Putin had taken few other public actions between December and the inauguration. He had chosen
his prime minister, a man whose imposing stature, booming bass
voice, and Hollywood-actor good looks and white-toothed smile be-
lied his lack of political ambition. Mikhail Kasyanov seemed to have
bureaucracy in his bones: he had come up through the ranks of Soviet
ministries, made a smooth transition to working for ministers in a
series of Yeltsin's cabinets, and recently become finance minister.

   "He called me in on January 2," just three days after Yeltsin had
tendered his resignation, Kasyanov told me. "He laid out his conditions for my appointment. He said, 'As long as you don't butt in on
my turf, we'll be fine.'" Kasyanov, entirely unaccustomed to street
language, was struck by Putin's wording much more than by the substance of what he was saying. The constitution gave the prime minister extensive authority over the uniformed services; Putin was telling
him he would have to forfeit these powers if he wanted to be prime
minister. Kasyanov assented easily, asking in return that Putin allow
him to press forward with planned economic reforms. Putin agreed
and appointed him his first deputy prime minister, promising to make
him the premier right after the inauguration.

   Kasyanov essentially took over running the government. Putin
set about preparing what he had called his "turf." His first decree as
acting president granted immunity from prosecution to Boris Yeltsin. His second established a new Russian military doctrine, aban-
doning the old no-first-strike policy regarding nuclear weapons and
emphasizing a right to use them against aggressors "if other means
of conflict resolution have been exhausted or deemed ineffective."
Soon another decree reestablished mandatory training exercises for

reservists (all Russian able-bodied men were considered reservists)—something that had been abolished, to the relief of Russian wives and mothers, after the country withdrew from Afghanistan. Two of the decree's six paragraphs were classified as secret, suggesting they might shed light on whether reservists should expect to be sent to Chechnya. A few days later, Putin issued an order granting forty government ministers and other officials the right to classify information as secret, in direct violation of the constitution. He also reestablished mandatory military training in secondary schools, both public and private: this subject, which for boys involved taking apart, cleaning, and putting back together a Kalashnikov, had been abolished during perestroika. In all, six of the eleven decrees Putin issued in his first two months as acting president concerned the military. On January 27, Kasyanov announced that defense spending would be increased by 50 percent—this in a country that was still failing to meet its international debt obligations and was seeing most of its population sink further and further into poverty.

If anyone in Russia or outside had cared to pay attention, all the clues to the nature of the new regime were there within weeks of Putin's ascent to his temporary throne. But the country was busy electing an imaginary president, and the rest of the Western world would not begin to doubt its choice for years to come.

WHEN PUTIN WAS INAUGURATED. I was in Chechnya again: in the face of what now passed for politics and political journalism, I badly needed to feel I was doing something meaningful. With the country's political system crumbling before my eyes, I felt particularly lucky to be able to research and publish the stories I felt were important. This time I had been traveling with military officers and self-organized volunteers who were looking for Russian soldiers missing in action in

Chechnya; they numbered about a thousand at the time, half of them missing since the last war.

I returned from Chechnya the weekend of the inauguration. My second day back in the office, which also happened to be Vladimir Putin's second day officially in the office of the president, police special forces descended on the corporate headquarters of Vladimir Gusinsky's Media-Most, the company to which my magazine belonged. Scores of men in camouflage, wearing black knit masks with slits for their eyes and armed with short-barrel automatic rifles, pushed their way into offices of the newly renovated building in the very center of Moscow, about a mile from the Kremlin, roughed up some of the staff, and threw piles of paper into cardboard boxes that they then loaded onto small trucks. The prosecutor's office, the presidential administration, and the tax police later made confused and confusing public statements explaining the raid: they said they suspected tax irregularities; they said they suspected misconduct on the part of Media-Most's internal security service; they even said they suspected the media company was spying on its own journalists. The nature of the raid was in fact familiar to anyone who had been involved in business or had even observed business in Russia in the 1990s: the raid was a threat. These kinds of raids were usually staged by organized-crime groups to show who was boss—and who had greater influence with the police. This raid was unusual, though, in several respects: its scale (scores of officers, several truckloads full of documents); its location (central Moscow); its timing (broad daylight); and its target (one of the country's seven most influential entrepreneurs). It was also unusual in its alleged initiator, whom Media-Most's outlets identified as Vladimir Putin. He himself claimed no knowledge of the event; during the raid he was in the Kremlin, meeting with Ted Turner, reminiscing about the Goodwill Games held in St. Petersburg in the 1990s, and discussing the future of media.

The months that followed the raid on the Media-Most head-quarters are the sort of period that is always difficult to recall and describe: the time between the diagnosis and the inevitable outcome, between the day when you learn how the story will end and the day it actually ends. I think it is fair to say that the roughly seventy people who worked at my magazine and the hundreds of people who worked at Gusinsky's daily newspaper and his television channel, NTV—the same channel that had aired the investigative piece on the apartment-block explosions—all knew on the day of the raid that this was the beginning of the end of Russia's largest private media company. Yet we continued to work almost as though nothing had happened, as though the story of the company's troubles were yet another story to cover.

I do not remember learning of Vladimir Gusinsky's arrest on June 13. I may have heard about it on the car radio, though this seems unlikely: the summer of 2000 was my second summer of bicycling in Moscow, which was then a novel form of transport in the city; I was even working on a story on city biking that June. I may have heard about the arrest from a colleague. I may have gotten a phone call from a friend telling me about it. However I got the news, the most important thing I heard was not even that one of the country's most influential men, who happened to pay my salary, had been arrested, but that he was arrested on charges stemming from the privatization of a company called Russkoye Video. This was my story to write.

RUSSKOYE VIDEO was a television production company that had belonged to Dmitry Rozhdestvensky, the St. Petersburg man who had been in prison for two years by now. His was a story I had followed for some time without understanding it, starting back when I went to St. Petersburg to write about Galina Starovoitova's murder.

My sources there—including Starovoitova's aide, who had survived the shooting—insisted on taking me to see an elderly couple living in a spacious, well-appointed apartment on the Griboyedov Channel. Over the course of several meetings spread over a few months, they told me the story of their son, Dmitry Rozhdestvensky, a well-educated forty-four-year-old television producer who had done fairly well for himself under Sobchak (whose reelection campaign he had helped run) and who was now in prison.

It seemed someone had set out to get Rozhdestvensky. First, in March 1997, he had been subjected to a tax audit. Then in May he received a letter from the local secret-police office informing him that the transmitter used by the television station of which he was part owner represented a threat to state security. Then Rozhdestvensky was interrogated repeatedly in connection with Sobchak's case. "They suspected Dmitry of laundering Sobchak's money," his mother told me. "But Dmitry was lucky: Sobchak never paid his company even the money they were owed for producing and airing his election ads." In March 1998, Dmitry Rozhdestvensky was finally charged with tax evasion. One night that month, the special prosecutor's team searched the apartments of forty-one people connected with Rozhdestvensky's company, including freelancers.

"That's when they really started in on him," the old woman told me. Her son was called in for questioning almost every day; his apartment, office, and dacha were searched repeatedly. In August 1998, Dmitry's wife had a stroke. "We were at the dacha then," said his mother. "He was going in for questioning daily and we were never sure whether he was coming back. I could handle that sort of thing—my own father was imprisoned three times under Stalin—but [Dmitry's wife] Natasha turned out to be the weaker one."

In September 1998, Dmitry Rozhdestvensky was charged with embezzlement and placed under arrest. I first met his parents two months later. Over the following twenty months, I visited the Rozhdestvenskys several times and they updated me on their son's case.

Dmitry was being moved from jail to jail, landing in Moscow and, later, at a secret-police prison outside St. Petersburg. Charges against him were shuffled: first he was accused of embezzling a car, then of embezzling advertising contract money, then of misappropriating funds to build a retreat. From what I could tell, his business and family affairs were so tightly and messily intertwined that the prosecutors could probably keep finding ways to keep him behind bars as long as they wanted. What I could not figure out was why someone wanted Rozhdestvensky in jail.

His parents told me it was Vladimir Yakovlev, the man who had replaced Sobchak, exacting his revenge for Rozhdestvensky's involvement in Sobchak's reelection campaign. But other people had supported Sobchak too. Was Rozhdestvensky being made the scapegoat because others, like Putin, were now too powerful to reach? Possibly. Or was it not Yakovlev at all who was after revenge, but one of Rozhdestvensky's former business partners, who included Putin and several other influential St. Petersburg men who had apparently founded a television production company linked to the city's casinos? Also possible. Or was it, as Starovoitova's aide thought, a macabre case of blackmail on the part of an entrepreneur who had unsuccessfully tried to pressure Rozhdestvensky into selling his company? Possible, too.

I kept going back to see the Rozhdestvenskys because I could not figure out how to write the story of their son. The more it developed, the less I understood. The entrepreneur who had been said to blackmail Rozhdestvensky was eventually arrested and charged with a number of contract killings, including one of a deputy mayor in charge of real estate development: he had been gunned down on Nevsky Prospekt in broad daylight in 1997. One thing was clear: Whatever was going on with Rozhdestvensky had little or nothing to do with the legal case against him and everything to do with the way business and politics were done in St. Petersburg.

Now this case and this company most Russians had never heard of had somehow landed Vladimir Gusinsky in prison. I sat down and started sorting through the half a file drawer's worth of papers I had collected on the case—mostly legal complaints and supporting documents—as I had done several times over the preceding two years. For the first time they started to make sense to me, even though I still could see no case there—just as the high-powered lawyers at Media-Most could not. "There are no charges," a smart middle-aged female corporate lawyer was telling me, genuinely confused. "I can't even understand what the crime is supposed to be. I can't figure out where they got the figures they cite here. Here they say the very company was created illegally, but they reference a law that contains nothing pertinent. And even if the company was created in violation of the law, Media-Most had nothing to do with it." The bigger company had bought Russkoye Video, along with dozens of other regional production and broadcasting companies, when it was forming a nationwide entertainment network. The St. Petersburg company was not even one of the larger advertising vehicles in the network: it was bought primarily for its huge library of B movies that the network could use to fill the airways while it worked to set up its own production.

"This would be funny if it weren't so sad," the lawyer said. "I wish Russian crime were really like this," meaning made up of borderline illegalities.

Russian crime did not look like that, but many Russian legal cases would come to look just like this one: slapped together, full of contradictions. I realized that my original theory about Dmitry Rozhdestvensky's case was correct: this was indeed someone's personal vendetta. But the culprit was neither the current governor of St. Petersburg, as some people maintained, nor a jailed mafia boss, as others believed.

Something, it seems, had gone terribly wrong between Dmitry Rozhdestvensky and Vladimir Putin, with whom he had worked on

Sobchak's failed reelection campaign. This explained why, after I had followed the case for nearly two years, the prosecutor in the case threatened me the last time I called him, on February 29, 2000. "Leave it alone," he said. "Believe me, Masha, you don't want to get any deeper into this. Or you'll be sorry." I had been writing about court cases in Russia for years, and no one—not even accused criminals and their often unsavory associates—had ever spoken to me in this manner. What was so important and frightening about this case? Only the fact that it was being pursued on behalf of the man who was now acting president of Russia. The prosecutor, Yuri Vanyushin, was a classmate of Putin's from the law faculty. He had gone to work for the prosecutor's office right out of university, just as Putin had gone to the KGB, but when Putin returned to Leningrad and went to work for Sobchak, Vanyushin joined him in city hall. When Putin left for Moscow six years later, Vanyushin returned to the prosecutor's office, becoming an investigator who specialized in "very important cases," an actual legal category. Rozhdestvensky's case did not meet the formal criteria for being a "very important case," but it was clearly very important to a very important person.

Another close associate of Putin's, Viktor Cherkesov, who had been appointed head of the St. Petersburg chapter of the FSB after much lobbying by Putin and much protest from former dissidents, had stepped in when the case against Rozhdestvensky seemed to be slow getting off the ground. After a tax audit failed to provide grounds for a criminal case, Cherkesov sent Rozhdestvensky a letter informing him that the transmitter Russkoye Video was using was a threat to national security. After Russkoye Video stopped using it, another television company took it over: it had apparently stopped being a threat. A year later, Cherkesov joined Putin in Moscow, becoming his first deputy at the FSB.

Rozhdestvensky's parents hoped their son would be released

from prison once his old friend Vladimir Putin became head of the secret police, then head of government, and, finally, head of state. Instead, Vanyushin kept the case alive even as charges kept falling apart and away; he just kept raking in other, similarly shaky premises for keeping him in jail. At the end of the summer of 2000, a court would finally take Rozhdestvensky's failing health into account and release him pending trial. Rozhdestvensky died in June 2002 at the age of forty-eight.

What I was now learning, as I went through the documents that I had kept for nearly two years, was the same thing Natalya Gevorkyan learned when she confronted Putin about the journalist Andrei Babitsky: "He is a small, vengeful man," was how she put it. The case against Gusinsky was, just like the case against Rozhdestvensky, a case of personal vendetta. Gusinsky had not supported Putin in the election. He was friendly and had significant business dealings with Moscow mayor Yuri Luzhkov, who was a leader of the anti-Family opposition coalition. It was Gusinsky's television channel that had aired the program about apartment building explosions two days before the election.

Gusinsky's arrest had no real connection to Russkoye Video; it just so happened that the man behind the arrest had detailed knowledge of the Russkoye Video case—which was as good as any other when all that was required was to get one of Russia's most powerful men behind bars. If there were any irregularities in the company's founding documents, Putin knew of those too: sifting through my files, I found a document authorizing the formation of the company, signed by Vladimir Putin.

Vladimir Gusinsky spent just three days in jail. As soon as he was released on his own recognizance, he left the country, becoming the first political refugee from Putin's regime—only five weeks after the inauguration.

UNLIKE THE OWNER of my company, I was still in Moscow. And, it seemed, I was in a lot of trouble, just as prosecutor Vanyushin had warned me I would be. I had written an article about the Russkoye Video case; it was published a few days after Gusinsky left the country, and it was illustrated with the document I had found—the one signed by Putin. Next thing I knew, there was a man on a ladder parked outside my apartment door—twenty-four hours a day. "What are you doing here?" I would ask every time I opened the door to find him there. "Fixing," he would growl.

A few days later, my home phone was turned off. The telephone company claimed to have had nothing to do with it, but it took days to get it turned back on. These were classic KGB tactics, intended to make me understand I was never safe and never alone: this approach had not changed since the 1970s, when the same sorts of goons would take up residence in people's stairways to let them know they were being watched. This knowledge did not make things any easier for me. The intrusion tactics worked just as well now as they had thirty years earlier: within a few days of this, I was going crazy with unidentifiable worry.

I used a reporting opportunity to leave the country for a couple of weeks. And I decided to look for another job. Mine had been the best job in the world, and while I worked it, I risked my life many times over, going to Chechnya, the former Yugoslavia, and other post-Soviet war zones. But I was not prepared to live under constant threat, no matter how unspecific it was. There was an opening for Moscow bureau chief at the American weekly magazine *U.S. News & World Report*, and I jumped at the opportunity.

Meanwhile, Gusinsky, shuttling between England and Spain, where he owned a home, was negotiating with the Russian state the fate of his media empire. Gusinsky personally owned 60 percent of his company; another 30 percent was held by the state gas monopoly, Gazprom, and 10 percent more belonged to private individuals, mostly top managers within the company. Gusinsky had borrowed heavily from a state-held bank to finance the setup of his satellite network. Less than a year earlier, he had still entertained well-founded hope that his debts would be forgiven: his once cozy relationship with Yeltsin and his role in his 1996 reelection campaign made this seem a reasonable expectation, at least to Gusinsky himself. Now some of the credits were overdue and the state was calling in the rest early, demanding stock instead of cash—aiming to enable the state gas monopoly to take control of the companies. Gusinsky was trying to restructure the debt in such a way that none of the stockholders would own a controlling share, which would guarantee the media outlets' editorial independence.

As negotiations grew more adversarial, someone—each side said it was the other—leaked to the press a document Gusinsky had signed before leaving the country. He seemed to have agreed, in writing, to cede a majority share of his company to Gazprom in exchange for his personal freedom. Most damningly, the document was signed not only by Gusinsky and the head of Gazprom's media arm—reconstituted especially for the occasion—but also by the press minister, Mikhail Lesin. In other words, this was a classic organized-crime contract, formalizing the exchange of one's business for one's personal safety, and the state was a party to it. Once the document was leaked, Gusinsky said publicly that the minister had personally threatened him, forcing him to sign over his business under duress, "virtually at gunpoint." He termed the entire process "state racketeering."

Putin refused to comment on the situation. Yet no one seemed to doubt that the order to wrestle the media company away from Gusinsky had come directly from him. His prime minister, the white-toothed Mikhail Kasyanov, appeared genuinely surprised and even shocked by the revelations and reprimanded Lesin publicly, before

television cameras. Three days later, Mikhail Gorbachev emerged
from nine years of de facto political retirement to meet with Putin
and ask him to set the Gusinsky situation right. The older man left
the meeting dejected, telling the media Putin refused to interfere. The
next day Prime Minister Kasyanov opened the cabinet meeting by
once again reprimanding his press minister, Lesin. Russian journalists
and political analysts took this as a clear sign that the prime minister
felt helpless in a situation orchestrated by the president himself.

Soon enough, this kind of takeover of private businesses large
and small would become commonplace. But the system Boris Yeltsin
had left behind was not quite ready to accommodate "state racketeering." Yeltsin's successive governments had not succeeded in turning the Russian courts into a functioning justice system, but they
had succeeded in planting the seeds of ambition in them. Now these
courts, mostly at the lower levels, would refuse some of Gazprom's
claims, with one city court even throwing out the case against Gusinsky altogether. In the end, it took the state monopoly almost a year
to gain control of Gusinsky's media empire. In April 2001, after a
nearly weeklong standoff when NTV staff maintained a live broadcast of the takeover, the old editorial staff was forced out. A week later,
my former colleagues at the magazine *Itogi* came to work to find the
doors locked and every last staff member fired.

I WAS ALREADY GONE, having taken the job at *U.S. News & World
Report* the previous summer. Before I started, I had flown to the
Black Sea for a short vacation. But after just a couple of days in the
sun, I had to fly back up north: a nuclear submarine was sinking in
the Barents Sea, taking 118 seamen with it.

Of all the heartbreaking stories I had ever had to cover and the
people of Russia had ever had to witness, the *Kursk* disaster was possibly the most devastating. For nine days, the mothers, wives, and

children of the sailors aboard the submarine—and the entire country along with them—maintained hope that some of them were still alive. The country kept vigil while the navy and the government flailed in their rescue efforts. Norwegian and British teams offered to help but were turned away, supposedly because of security concerns. Worst of all, the new president was silent: he was on vacation on the Black Sea coast.

The *Kursk* makes an easy metaphor for the post-Soviet condition. Its construction began in 1990 as the Soviet Union neared collapse; it was commissioned in 1994, easily the lowest point in Russian military history, but just as the Russians' superpower ambitions, temporarily set aside while the empire was being dismantled, began to reassert themselves. The nuclear submarine was huge, as those ambitions had once been—and would be again, with Putin in power, promising to rub the enemy out in the outhouse. The *Kursk*, which had barely been maintained since it was launched, served its first mission in the summer of 1999, when Putin came to power, and was to undertake its first significant training exercise in August 2000.

It would become clear later that neither the submarine nor its crew nor, really, the entire Russian Northern Fleet had been ready for the exercise. In fact, the training exercise was not officially called one, at least in part because the participating ships and their men would have been unable to fulfill all the legal and technical requirements of a full-fledged exercise. Instead, the submarine and other battleships going out to sea on August 12 were called to an "assembly march," a term that was nonexistent and therefore carried no clear requirements. The submarine went to sea with an unpracticed and undertrained crew that had been pulled together from several different vessels, so the men had no experience as a team. The submarine was equipped with training torpedoes, some of which were past their expiration dates, while the rest had not been properly serviced. Some torpedoes had visible rust holes; others had rubber connector rings that had been used more than once, in violation of safety regulations. "Death is on board with us," one of the crew told his mother six days before the accident, referring to the torpedoes.

It was one of these torpedoes that, evidently, caught fire and exploded. There were two blasts aboard the submarine, and most of the crew died instantly. Twenty-three survivors moved to an unaffected section of the vessel to await rescue. They had the equipment necessary to survive in the submarine for some time; they could reasonably expect to be saved—after all, they were engaged in a training exercise, there were several battleships in the near vicinity, and the accident should have been discovered almost instantly.

But while the tremors caused by the explosion were picked up by a Norwegian seismic station, Russian ships located much nearer to the submarine seemed to take no notice of its fate. It was nine hours before the fleet acknowledged there had been an accident; it was about this long again before the vacationing president was informed. Rescue efforts commenced, but the rescue crews apparently lacked the training necessary to do their jobs. They never even succeeded in docking to the sub.

Most of the twenty-three survivors could conceivably have climbed out themselves—the accident had occurred in relatively shallow waters—but this section of the submarine was, contrary to regulations, not equipped with a hose necessary to evacuate the crew. The twenty-three seamen sat in the dark until one of their air-regeneration plates caught fire, filling the compartment with noxious fumes that killed the men.

For the more than two days they survived underwater, the twenty-three men beat out their SOS, attempting to aid in rescue efforts that were first nonexistent, then useless. At the very end, their knocking grew haphazard and desperate. They never heard a response to their message: obeying an unwritten rule of the fleet, the rescuers kept silent, ostensibly to prevent enemy vessels from identifying their location. It was for the same essential reason that early offers from British and Norwegian divers to help with the rescue effort were turned down. When a Norwegian crew was finally allowed to enter Russian waters and descend to the *Kursk*, eight days after the accident, they easily managed to dock to the submarine on their first try. When they did not succeed in opening the hatch, they fashioned a suitable tool for the job and, nine days after the accident, were able to enter the submarine and confirm there were no survivors.

For ten days, the country stayed glued to its television sets, waiting for news from the *Kursk*. Or from the new president, the one who had promised to restore Russian military might. First he said nothing. Then, still on vacation, he made a vague comment that seemed to indicate that he considered salvaging the equipment on board the *Kursk* more important than rescuing the crew. On the seventh day of the disaster, he finally agreed to fly back to Moscow—and was duly cornered by a television crew in the Black Sea resort city of Yalta. "I did the right thing," Putin said, "because the arrival of nonspecialists from any field, the presence of high-placed officials in the disaster area, would not help and more often would hamper work. Everyone should keep to his place."

The remark made it clear Putin viewed himself as a bureaucrat—a very important and powerful bureaucrat, but a bureaucrat still. "I'd always thought if you became president, even if you were merely appointed to this role, you had to change," Marina Litvinovich, the smart young woman who had worked on Putin's preelection image, told me. "If the nation is crying, you have to cry along with it."

By the time of the *Kursk* disaster, Litvinovich, who was still in her twenties, had become a permanent member of what had become a permanent media directorate at the Kremlin. Once a week, the heads of the three major television networks and Litvinovich would meet with Putin's chief of staff, Alexander Voloshin, to discuss current affairs and plan their coverage. In August 2000, only three members of the group were present: Litvinovich, Voloshin, and the head of the state television and radio company; everyone else was on vacation, as Muscovites usually are in August. "I was screaming at Voloshin," Litvinovich remembered. "I screamed that he [Putin] had to go there. And finally Voloshin picked up the phone and called Putin and said, 'Some people here think you should go there.' And I was thinking, Putin should be the one calling and screaming, 'Where is my plane?' And I realized that if I had not gone to that meeting, he would not have gone to the Arctic.'"

THE CLUSTER of military towns that make up the home of Russia's Northern Fleet is a world unto itself, closed to outsiders and hostile to them, but generally resigned to and trusting of the authorities. Journalists were not allowed to enter Vidyayevo, the town that served as the *Kursk*'s home port. Families of crew members were loaded onto chartered buses that took them through checkpoints at breakneck speed. A few times, some of the relatives braved the three-mile trek (no transportation was available to them once they had been brought in) from their accommodations in Vidyayevo to the checkpoint, where journalists kept vigil. One group of women who came out of Vidyayevo wanted to record a video address demanding that rescue efforts continue. A woman asked journalists to drive a separate group to the local big city of Murmansk to buy memorial wreaths to deposit at sea.

Locals looked on these anxious women with a mixture of pity and fear. Here, in towns full of dilapidated five-story concrete buildings with missing windowpanes and, often, no central heating, everyone was used to danger and decay. "Accidents happen," seamen and their women told me over and over again. Meanwhile, women armed with brooms and buckets washed the sidewalks and public squares with soap and water, hoping to protect against radiation that might be leaking from the *Kursk*—even though the authorities posted bills assuring the public there was no radiation danger.

Ten days after the disaster, relatives of the crew were finally gathered in Vidyayevo's assembly hall, expecting to see Putin. While they waited—and they waited for hours—military fleet commander Admiral Vladimir Kuroyedov addressed the audience. The admiral, a big man with a rough, leathery face, used his finely honed skills to deflect all questions. Here is how one of the very few journalists allowed to witness the event, one of the coauthors of Putin's official biography, described the scene:

> "Do you believe that the guys are alive?" he was asked.
>
> And you know what he said?
>
> "That's a good question! I am going to respond to it as directly as you asked it. I still believe that my father, who died in 1991, is alive."
>
> Then he was asked another question—probably also a good one.
>
> "Why didn't you ask for foreign help right away?"
>
> "I see," he said, "that you watch Channel 4 more than you watch Channel 2."
>
> "When did you inform the authorities that you did not have the necessary equipment to save them?"
>
> "Three years ago," he said.
>
> I thought someone would hit him. But instead, they all just kind of wilted and lost interest in the conversation.

Kuroyedov left a frustrated audience. Vice Premier Ilya Klebanov, who had been placed in charge of the rescue efforts, was present; a woman jumped up onstage, grabbed Klebanov by the lapels, shook him, and screamed, "You bastard, you go there and save them!" When Putin finally arrived, four hours after the appointed time, wearing a black suit with a black shirt to signify mourning but looking, as a result, vaguely like a mafioso, the crowd attacked him too. Now his biographer was the only journalist allowed to remain in the room, and here is part of how he described the meeting in his article the next day:

"Cancel the mourning immediately!" someone interrupted him from the other end of the hall. [A national day of mourning had been declared for the following day.]

"Mourning?" Putin asked. "I was, like you, full of hope to the last, I still am, at least for a miracle. But there is a fact we know for certain: People have died."

"Shut up!" someone screamed.

"I am speaking of people who have definitely died. There are people like that in the submarine, for certain. That's who the mourning is for. That's all."

Someone tried to object, but he would not let them.

"Listen to me, listen to what I'm about to say. Just listen to me! There have always been tragedies at sea, including the time when we thought we were living in a very successful country. There have always been tragedies. But I never thought that things were in this kind of condition." . . .

"Why did you take so long in attracting foreign help?" a young woman asked.

She had a brother aboard the submarine. Putin took a long time explaining. He said that the construction of the submarine dated back to the end of the 1970s, and so did all the rescue equipment that the Northern Fleet had. He said that [defense minister] Sergeev called him on the 13th at seven in the morning, and until then Putin had known nothing. . . . He said that foreign aid had been offered on the 15th and had been accepted right away. . . .

"Don't we have those kinds of divers ourselves?" someone shouted out in despair.

"We don't have crap in this country!" the president answered furiously.

The article reported that Putin spent two hours and forty minutes with the families of the crew and managed, in the end, to bring them around—in large part because he devoted an hour to detailing compensation packages for them. He also agreed to cancel the day of mourning, which was in the end, in a twist of macabre irony, observed everywhere in Russia except Vidyayevo. But Putin emerged from the meeting battered and bitter, and unwilling ever again to expose himself to such an audience. After no other disaster—and there would be many in his tenure as president—would Putin allow himself to be pitted publicly against the suffering.

IN SHORT ORDER. two things happened to cement Putin's view of his visit to Vidyayevo as a disaster. On September 2—three weeks after the *Kursk* sank—Sergei Dorenko, the Channel One anchorman who had done most of the legwork in Berezovsky's television campaign to create Putin a year earlier, did a show criticizing Putin's handling of the submarine disaster. Dorenko obtained audiotapes of the meeting with relatives and aired excerpts that made the biographer's newspaper report seem laudatory in comparison. In one of the excerpts, Putin could be heard descending into a rant. "You saw it on television?" he screamed. "That means they are lying. They are lying! They are lying! There are people on television who have been working to destroy the army and the navy for ten years. They are talking now as though they are the biggest defenders of the military. All they really want to do is finish it off! They've stolen all this money and now they are buying everyone off and making whatever laws they want to make!" Putin ended with a high-pitched shout.

Dorenko, a charismatic, macho character with a deep baritone, spent nearly an hour dissecting Putin's behavior, replaying some of the president's least appropriate remarks, focusing on showing him still on vacation, tanned and relaxed in light-colored resort clothing, smiling and laughing with his holiday companions, most of them highly placed officials. Again and again, he showed Putin to have lied. The president claimed that the sea had been stormy for eight days, hampering rescue efforts. In fact, said Dorenko, the weather had been bad only during the first few days, but even that had no effect at the depth at which the *Kursk* was situated. Dorenko compared Putin to a schoolboy who is late for class. "We don't know what kind of teacher Putin's fibs are intended for, but we know what a teacher says in these kinds of cases: 'I don't care what you thought was right—I only care that you get here on time.'"

Dorenko cut to footage of a state television interview Putin had given the day after the Vidyayevo visit. Looking official and collected, the president said that it had barely been a hundred days since he accepted the burden of running the country. In fact, Dorenko pointed out, it had been 390 days since Putin was appointed prime minister and anointed Yeltsin's successor, and prior to that he had run the FSB, "which is supposed to keep an eye on the admirals."

"The regime does not respect us, and this is why it lies to us," Dorenko concluded.

I think it was then, a year after the beginning of his miraculous ascent, a hundred days after becoming president, that Putin realized that he now bore responsibility for the entire crumbling edifice of a former superpower. He was no longer entitled to seethe at the people who had destroyed Soviet military might and imperial pride: by dint of becoming president, to a great number of his compatriots he had now become one of those people. His transformation was not unlike that of a longtime opposition politician who suddenly assumes power—except Putin had never been a politician at all, so his anger had been private but his humiliation was now public. He may have felt that he had been tricked: the people against whom he had ranted when he lost his temper in Vidyayevo—the ones who had disgraced the military on television and had passed "whatever laws they wanted"—had brought him to power to make him the fall guy. And then they used their television networks to humiliate him further.

Six days after the Dorenko show, Putin appeared on CNN's *Larry King Live*. When King asked, "What happened?" Putin shrugged, smiled—impishly, it seemed—and said, "It sank." The line became infamous: it played as cynical, dismissive, and deeply offensive to all who were affected by the tragedy. Only reviewing the transcript of the show ten years later did I realize what Putin was trying to communicate. He was indicating that he would not press the line some hapless Russian spin doctor had invented—that the *Kursk* had collided with an American submarine. *Never mind that crazy conspiracy theory*, his shrug was intended to say. *It just sank.*

The world saw something entirely different, and Putin learned a key lesson. Television—the very same television that had created him, a president plucked out of thin air—could turn on him and destroy him just as fast and with the same evident ease.

So Putin summoned Berezovsky, the former kingmaker and the man still in charge of Channel One, and demanded that the oligarch hand over his shares in the television company. "I said no, in the presence of [chief of staff] Voloshin," Berezovsky told me. "So Putin changed his tone of voice then and said, 'See you later, then, Boris Abramovich,' and got up to leave. And I said, 'Volodya, this is goodbye.' We ended on this note, full of pathos. When he left the room, I turned to Voloshin and said, 'So, Sasha, what have we done? Have we brought the black colonels to power?' Voloshin scratched his head and said, 'I don't think so.'" Testifying in a London court years later, Voloshin could not recall the meeting in detail, saying only that its purpose had been to inform Berezovsky that "the concert is over, the show is over."

Berezovsky says he sat down and immediately wrote a letter to his old protégé, then asked the chief of staff to pass it on. "I wrote about an American journalist who said once that every complicated problem always has one simple solution and that solution is always wrong. And I wrote that Russia is a colossally complex problem and it is his colossal mistake to think that he can use simple methods to solve it." Berezovsky never received a response to this letter. Within days he had left for France, then moved on to Great Britain, joining his former rival Gusinsky in political exile. Soon enough, there was a warrant out for his arrest in Russia and he had surrendered his shares in Channel One.

Three months after the inauguration, two of the country's wealthiest men had been stripped of their influence and effectively kicked out of the country. Less than a year after Putin came to power, all three federal television networks were controlled by the state.

"I'VE ALWAYS TOLD PEOPLE there is no point in going to jail voluntarily," Andrei Sakharov's widow, Yelena Bonner, told a small group of journalists in Moscow in November 2000. Berezovsky, she said, had called her in the summer to ask for advice and she had counseled him to stay out of the country. "Back in dissident times, I always advocated emigration for those under threat," she explained. She had called us in for a press conference announcing Berezovsky's grant to the Sakharov Museum and Human Rights Center in Moscow, which was on the verge of closing.

"What a shitty time we've lived to see," said the museum's director, former dissident Yuri Samodurov, "when we have to stand up in defense of people we don't like at all, like Gusinsky and Berezovsky. We once lived in a totalitarian state that had two main features: totalizing terror and a totalizing lie. I hope that totalizing terror is no longer possible in our country, but we have now entered a new era of a totalizing lie."

Eight

THE DISMANTLING
OF DEMOCRACY

The political system changed so quickly that even political activists and political analysts needed time to get their bearings. In December 2000, I went to a roundtable discussion among political scientists, devoted to analyzing what had happened in the year since Putin was handed power in Russia.

"He has put Russia on ice," said one of them, a man in his fifties with a beautifully chiseled face and tiny wire-rimmed glasses. "That's not necessarily bad. It's a kind of stabilizing effect. But what happens next?"

"It's like the revolution has ended," said another, a former dissident with disheveled salt-and-pepper hair and beard. He meant that the society had reverted to its pre–post-Soviet state. "Old cultural values, old habits are back. The whole country is trying to apply old habits to new reality."

"I don't think anyone really understands anything anymore,"

said a third, a short man with a very big nose and a deep voice. I personally held him to be the smartest man in the room—and he certainly should have been the most knowledgeable, because he worked in the presidential administration.

"But all the changes in the last year have occurred in the area of public consciousness," said another, a liberal political scientist who had come to prominence during perestroika. "The nation has come out of a psychological depression. This is going to be the toughest political era yet, because nationalist ideology is always the strongest."

"But he has to live up to expectations," objected a scholar from a younger generation, a large man with bushy black eyebrows.

The last speaker clearly had not shed the assumptions of the 1990s, when the media or the parliament could call the president to account, as they had many times: Yeltsin had last faced an impeachment attempt in 1999. The older man who had spoken before him, who had once been Mikhail Gorbachev's leading ideological adviser, saw the 1990s for what they had been: a brief period of quasi-democracy, a fleeting vision, a fluke. "They've won, my dears," Alexander Tsipko said to those present. "Russia is a large state floating in an unformed political space. And they try to fill this space with their national anthem, their two-headed eagle, and their tricolored flag. Such are the symbols of Soviet nationalism."

Russia's uncertain identity in the 1990s had manifested, among other things, in its inability to settle on state symbols. Having secured its sovereignty in 1991, the country plunged, almost immediately, into some sort of revolutionary's remorse, which made shedding old symbols and asserting new ones a painful and, as it ultimately turned out, impossible task. The Soviet red flag was immediately replaced with the white, blue, and red flag that had previously served Russia for eight months, between the bourgeois revolution of February 1917 and the Bolshevik revolution in October. The state seal, however, retained its red star, its hammer and sickle, and its stalks of wheat, which had unironically signified plenitude in Soviet times. The parliament debated the seal repeatedly but could not reach any decision except, in mid-1992, for replacing the abbreviation RSFSR (Russian Soviet Federative Socialist Republic) with the words "Russian Federation." At the end of 1993, Yeltsin finally created a state seal by decree: a two-headed eagle would serve as its main image, a symbol Russia shares with Albania, Serbia, and Montenegro, among modern states. It was not until December 2000 that Putin's parliament finally voted to enshrine the two-headed-eagle seal in law.

The national anthem posed an even more implacable challenge. In 1991, the Soviet anthem had been scrapped in favor of "The Patriotic Song," a lively tune by the nineteenth-century composer Mikhail Glinka. But this anthem had no lyrics; moreover, lyrics proved impossible to write: the rhythmic line dictated by the music was so short that any attempt to set words to it—and Russian words tend to be long—lent it a definite air of absurdity. A number of media outlets ran contests to choose the lyrics to go with the Glinka, but the entries, invariably, were suitable only for the entertainment of the editorial staff, and little by little chipped away at the legitimacy of the anthem.

The Soviet national anthem that had been scrapped in favor of the Glinka had a complicated history. The music, written by Alexander Alexandrov, appeared in 1943, with lyrics supplied by a children's poet named Sergei Mikhalkov. The anthem's refrain praised "the Party of Lenin, the Party of Stalin / Leading us to the triumph of Communism." After Stalin died and, in 1956, his successor Nikita Khrushchev denounced "the cult of personality," the refrain could no longer be performed, so the anthem lost its lyrics. The instrumental version would be performed for twenty-one years while the Soviet Union sought the poet and the words to express its post-Stalinist identity. In 1977, when I was in third or fourth grade, the anthem suddenly acquired lyrics, which we schoolchildren had to learn as soon as possible. For this purpose, every school notebook manufactured in the Soviet Union that year bore the new lyrics to the old national anthem on the back cover, where multiplication tables or verb exceptions had once resided. The new lyrics had been written by the same children's poet, who was, by now, sixty-four years old. The refrain now lauded "the Party of Lenin, the force of the people."

In the fall of 2000, a group of Russian Olympic athletes met with Putin and complained that the lack of a singable anthem demoralized them in competitions and made their victories feel hollow. The old Soviet anthem had been so much better this way, they said. So the once recycled Stalinist anthem was again taken out of storage. The children's poet, now eighty-seven, wrote new lyrics to replace the old new lyrics. The refrain now praised "the wisdom of centuries, borne by the people." Putin introduced a bill in parliament and the new old anthem was handily approved.

When the Duma convened in January 2001, the new old anthem was played for the first time—and everyone in the chamber rose, except for two former dissidents, Sergei Kovalev and Yuli Rybakov. "I spent six years in prison listening to this anthem," said Rybakov; the Soviet national anthem had played at the beginning and the end of each day on state radio, which was always on in the camps. "I had been put in prison for fighting the regime that created this anthem, that put people in camps and executed people to the sounds of this anthem."

Rybakov and Kovalev were only two out of 450 members of the Duma, as tiny a minority as dissidents had always been. The Soviet ethos had been restored. The people who held the revolution of 1991 to be theirs were now profoundly marginalized. Nor would the parliament itself, as it had been constituted in the 1990s, exist for much longer.

ON MAY 13. 2000. six days after he was inaugurated, Putin signed his first decree and proposed a set of bills, all of them aimed, as he stated, at "strengthening vertical power." They served as the beginning of a profound restructuring of Russia's federal composition, or, put another way, as the beginning of the dismantling of the country's democratic structures. One of the bills replaced elected members of the upper house of the parliament with appointed ones: two from each of Russia's eighty-nine regions, one appointed by the governor of the region and one by the legislature. Another bill allowed elected governors to be removed from office on mere suspicion of wrongdoing, without a court decision. The decree established seven presidential envoys to seven large territories of the country, each comprising about a dozen regions, each of which had its elected legislature and governor. The envoys, appointed by the president, would supervise the work of elected governors.

The problem Putin was trying to address with these measures was real. In 1998, when Russia defaulted on its foreign debt and plummeted into a profound economic crisis, Moscow had given the regions wide latitude in managing their budgets, collecting taxes, setting tariffs, and creating economic policies. For this and other reasons, the Russian Federation had become as loose as a structure can be while remaining, at least nominally, a single state. Because the problem was real, Russia's liberal politicians—who still believed Putin to be one of them—did not criticize his solution to it, even though it clearly contradicted the spirit and possibly also the letter of the 1993 constitution.

Putin appointed the seven envoys. Only two of them were civilians—and one of these very much appeared to have the biography of an undercover KGB agent. Two were KGB officers from Leningrad, one was a police general, and two more were army generals who had commanded the troops in Chechnya. So Putin appointed generals to watch over popularly elected governors—who could also now be removed by the federal government.

The lone voice against these new laws belonged to Boris Berezovsky, or, rather, to my old acquaintance Alex Goldfarb, the émigré former dissident who just a year earlier had been willing to be charmed by Putin. He authored a brilliant critique of the decree and the bills that was published under Berezovsky's byline in *Kommersant*, the popular daily newspaper Berezovsky owned. "I assert that the most important outcome of the Yeltsin presidency has been the change in mentality of millions of people: those who used to be slaves fully dependent on the will of their boss or the state became free people who depend only on themselves," he wrote. "In a democratic society, laws exist to protect individual freedom. . . . The legislation you have proposed will place severe limitations on the independence and civil freedoms of tens of thousands of top-level Russian politicians, forcing them to take their bearings from a single person and follow his will. But we have been through this!"

No one took notice.

The bills sailed through the parliament. The installation of the envoys drew no protest. What happened next was exactly what Berezovsky's letter had predicted, and it went far beyond the legal measures introduced by Putin. Something shifted, instantly and perceptibly, as though the sounds of the new/old Soviet/Russian national anthem had signaled the dawn of a new era for everyone. Soviet instincts, it seemed, kicked in all over the country, and the Soviet Union was instantly restored in spirit.

You could not quite measure the change. One brilliant Ph.D. student at Moscow University noticed that traditional ways of critiquing election practices, such as tallying up violations (these were on the increase—things like open voting and group voting became routine) or trying to document falsifications (a nearly impossible task) fell short of measuring such a seemingly ephemeral thing as culture. Darya Oreshkina introduced the term "special electoral culture"—one in which elections, while formally free, are orchestrated by local authorities trying to curry favor with the federal center. She identified their statistical symptoms, such as anomalously high voter turnouts and a strikingly high proportion of votes accrued by the leader of the race. She was able to show that over time, the number of precincts where "special electoral culture" decided the outcome grew steadily, and grew fast. In other words, with every election at every level of government, Russians ceded to the authorities more of their power to decide. "Geography disappeared," she said later—meaning, the entire country was turning into an undifferentiated managed space.

IN MARCH 2004, when Putin stood for reelection, he had five opponents. They had overcome extreme obstacles to join the race. A law that went into effect just before the campaigns launched required that a notary certify the presence and signature of every person present at a meeting at which a presidential candidate is nominated. Since the law required that a minimum of five hundred people attend such a meeting, the preliminaries took four to five hours; people had to arrive in the middle of the day to certify their presence so that the meeting could commence in the evening. After the meeting the potential candidate had a few weeks to collect two million signatures. The old law had required half as many signatures and allotted twice as much time to collect them; but more important, the new law specified the look of these signatures down to the comma. Hundreds of thousands of signatures were thrown out by the Central Election Commission because of violations such as the use of "St. Petersburg" instead of "Saint Petersburg" or the failure to write out the words "building" or "apartment" in the address line.

One of Putin's St. Petersburg city hall colleagues told me years later that during his tenure as Sobchak's deputy, Putin had received "a powerful inoculation against the democratic process." He and Sobchak had ultimately fallen victim to the democratic menace in St. Petersburg, and now that Putin was running the country, he was restoring the late-Soviet mechanisms of control: he was building a tyranny of bureaucracy. The Soviet bureaucracy had been so unwieldy, incomprehensible, and forbidding that one could function within it only by engaging in corruption, using either money or personal favors as currency. That made the system infinitely pliant—which is why "special electoral culture" functioned so well.

During the voting itself, international observers and Russian nongovernmental organizations documented a slew of violations, including: the deletion from the rolls of over a million very elderly people and other unlikely voters (when I went to cast my vote, I was able to see that my eighty-four-year-old grandmother's name was in fact missing from the list; my voting precinct was also, coincidentally, located next door to an office of the ruling United Russia party); the delivery of prefilled ballots to a psychiatric ward; precinct staff arriving at an elderly voter's home with a mobile ballot box and leaving hastily when they saw that she was planning to vote for someone other than Putin; and managers and school officials telling staff or students' parents that contracts or financing depended on their vote. In all likelihood, none of these steps was dictated directly by the Kremlin; rather, following renewed Soviet instincts, individuals did what they could for their president.

During the campaign, opposition candidates constantly encountered refusals to print their campaign material, air their commercials, or even rent them space for campaign events. Yana Dubeykovskaya, who managed the campaign of nationalist-leftist economist Sergei

Glazyev, told me that it took days to find a printing plant willing to accept Glazyev's money. When the candidate tried to hold a campaign event in Yekaterinburg, the largest city in the Urals, the police suddenly kicked everyone out of the building, claiming there was a bomb threat. In Nizhny Novgorod, Russia's third-largest city, electricity was turned off when Glazyev was getting ready to speak—and every subsequent campaign event in that city was held outdoors, since no one was willing to rent to the pariah candidate.

Around election time, I interviewed a distant acquaintance, the thirty-one-year-old deputy director of news programming on All-Russia State Television. Eight years earlier, Yevgeniy Revenko had become the youngest reporter working at a national television channel, Gusinsky's independent NTV. He had quickly become known as one of the more enterprising and dogged reporters. The way he worked now seemed to be very different. "A country like Russia needs the sort of television that can effectively deliver the government's message," he explained. "As the state grows stronger, it needs to convey its message directly, with no interpretations." He described his channel's editorial policy as a simple one: "We do show negative stories—we will report a disaster, if it occurs, for example—but we do not go looking for them. Nor do we go looking for positive stories, but we do focus the viewers' attention on them. We never speculate about the reasons for something—say, an official's firing—even if we happen to know the reason. All our information comes from official government statements. In any case, the logic is simple. We are a state television company. Our state is a presidential republic. That means we do not criticize the president." Very occasionally, admitted Revenko over a mug of beer at an Irish pub in the center of Moscow, he felt he had to stifle his creative urge. "But I say to myself, 'This is where I work.'" He grew up in a military family and had some military training himself. That clearly helped.

The late Soviet state had depended on using the many and punishing the few—and the KGB had been in charge of the latter. This system had been more or less restored now. While the vast majority enthusiastically fell in line, those who did not paid the price. Marina Litvinovich, the young woman who had helped create Putin and had urged him to go talk to the families of the *Kursk* crew, was now managing the campaign of his lone liberal opponent in the race, former parliament member Irina Khakamada, who had herself supported Putin four years earlier. During the campaign, Litvinovich got a phone call telling her, "We know where you live and where your child plays outside." She hired a bodyguard for her three-year-old. She was also robbed and beaten. Yana Dubeykovskaya, Glazyev's campaign manager, was also beaten and robbed, and once started driving her car before discovering that the brakes had been cut. A step down on the persecution ladder were apartment burglaries. In the months leading up to the election, opposition journalists and activists of Committee 2008—a group organizing to bring about a more fair election in four years—had their apartments broken into. Often these burglaries occurred concurrently in different areas of Moscow. My own apartment was burglarized in February. The only things taken were a laptop computer, the hard drive from a desktop computer, and a cell phone.

On election night, Khakamada planned a great defeat party. Her campaign rented a spacious Southwestern-themed restaurant and splurged on a spread of salmon, lobster, artichokes, and an open bar. Popular music groups lined up at the microphone, and the country's best-known rock journalist emceed. Nobody came. Waiters seemed to outnumber the guests, and the artichokes lingered. Still, the organizers continued to check all comers against a strict name list. Russian liberals were still struggling to come to terms with just how marginal they had become.

Watching the guests, I was thinking it was understandable that it had taken a while. Four years after putting Putin in office, the few liberals who had switched to the opposition still had personal connections to the many former liberals who remained part of the Russian political establishment. In a vacant dining room off the main hall, Marina Litvinovich perched at one end of a long empty oak table next to Andrei Bystritsky, deputy chairman of the Russian state television and radio conglomerate. Bystritsky, a red-bearded bon vivant in his mid-forties, complained about the wine. "The wine is no worse than our election results," Litvinovich shot back. Bystritsky immediately ordered a hundred-dollar bottle of wine for the table, and then another. It seemed he had come to assuage his guilt. He assured anyone who would listen that he had voted for Khakamada and had even told his two hair-and-makeup people to vote for her. Of course, he had also run the campaign coverage that went out to about forty-five million Russian homes, and told them, over and over again, to vote for Putin. Seventy-one percent of the voters did.

I went to see Bystritsky in his office three days after the election. We had known each other a long time—in the mid-1990s he had been my editor at *Itogi*—so there was no point in pussyfooting around the main question.

"So tell me," I said, "how do you conduct the propaganda of Putin's regime?"

Bystritsky shrugged uncomfortably and busied himself with hospitable preliminaries. He offered me tea, cookies, chocolates, chocolate-covered marshmallows, and finally a CD with the collected speeches, photographs, and video footage of President Putin. The slipcover had five photographs of the president: serious, intense, impassioned, formal smiling, and informal smiling. The serious one had been reproduced widely: on Election Day alone, I came across it on the cover of school notebooks, on preframed portraits for sale at the Moscow Central Post Office (a bargain at $1.50 for a letter-size picture), and on pink, white, and blue balloons for sale in Red Square. The sale of any of these items on voting day was a violation of election law.

"We don't especially do any propaganda," Bystritsky said, settling into a leather armchair. "Look at the election, for example." Russian law left over from the nineties required media outlets to provide all candidates with equal access to viewers and readers. Bystritsky had his numbers ready, and it was funny math: the president, he claimed, had engaged in only one election activity—meeting with his campaign activists—and the twenty-nine-minute meeting was broadcast three times in its entirety during regular newscasts, which had to be extended to accommodate it. On every other day of the campaign, the state television channel also showed Putin during its newscasts—usually as the lead story—but these, Bystritsky explained, were not campaign activities but the stuff of the president's day job. An exhaustive study conducted by the Russian Union of Journalists, on the other hand, concluded that Putin got about seven times as much news coverage on the state channel as did either Khakamada or the Communist Party candidate; other candidates fared even worse. Coverage by the other state channel, the one that had once answered to Berezovsky, was even more skewed, while NTV, which had been taken away from Gusinsky, gave Putin a fourfold advantage over the next-best-covered contender.

This was what Revenko had called "effectively delivering the government's message." Local officials got the message clearly and conducted elections in accordance with it.

SEPTEMBER 1 IN RUSSIA is called Knowledge Day: all elementary, secondary, and high schools all over the country begin the year simultaneously. The first day of school is a rather ceremonial occasion: children, especially first-graders and eleventh-graders (the graduating class), arrive dressed up, bearing flowers, and usually accompanied by their parents. There are speeches, greetings, occasional concerts, collective prayers, and festive processions.

In the summer of 2000—the summer when I had had to briefly leave the country after Gusinsky was arrested—I had adopted a child, a little boy named Vova (eleven months later, I also gave birth to a girl). On September 1, 2004, I took Vova to his first day of classes in first grade. He looked very serious in a blue button-down shirt that kept coming untucked. He gave his new teacher a bouquet of flowers, we listened to the speeches, and the children went inside the school. I got in my car for the long drive to work: Knowledge Day is among the worst traffic days of the year. I turned on the radio and heard the news: a group of armed men had taken several hundred children and their parents hostage at a school in North Ossetia.

Even though I coordinated coverage of the story from Moscow— I was now deputy editor at a new city weekly—in the following three days I did some of the most difficult work of my life. The three-day standoff in the town of Beslan, full of fear, confusion, and several moments of acute hope, culminated with federal troops storming the school building; more than three hundred people died. On the afternoon of September 1, when I came to work, I had said to my colleagues, all of whom were younger and less experienced in covering these sorts of stories: "There will be a storming of the building. There is always a storming." But when it happened, I sat at my desk, hiding my face in my hands, crying. When I finally took my hands away from my face, I found a can of Coke one of my younger colleagues had placed in front of me in an attempt at consolation.

The following weekend, my family and the family of my closest friend huddled together at my dacha. When their eight-year-old daughter briefly stepped out of the front yard, all four of us adults went into a panic. I had the distinct sense that the entire country was similarly traumatized.

It was this shell-shocked nation that Putin addressed, after a fashion, on September 13, 2004. He gathered the cabinet, his own staff, and all eighty-nine governors together, and spoke with them behind

closed doors for two hours. The text of his speech was then distributed to journalists.

"One cannot but weep when talking about what happened in
Beslan," the speech went. "One cannot but weep just thinking about
it. But compassion, tears, and words on the part of the government
are absolutely insufficient. We have to act, we have to increase the
effectiveness of the government in combating the entire complex of
problems facing the country. . . . I am convinced that the unity of the
country is the main condition of success in the fight against terrorism."

From now on, he announced, governors would no longer be
elected; he himself would appoint them and the mayor of Moscow.
Nor would members of the lower house of the parliament be directly
elected, as half of them had been. Now Russian citizens would cast
their votes in favor of political parties, which would then fill their
seats with ranking members. The new procedure for registering political parties made the new procedure for registering presidential
candidates seem quaint in comparison. All political parties now had
to re-register, which meant most would be eliminated. The threshold
for getting a share of the seats in the parliament would be raised from
5 percent of the vote to 7 percent. And, finally, proposed legislation
would now pass through a filter before entering the lower house: the
president would personally appoint a so-called public chamber to
review all bills.

After these changes became law, as they did at the end of 2004,
there remained only one federal-level public official who was directly
elected: the president himself.

IN THE SPRING OF 2005. one of the world's most famous Russians
declared war on Putin. Garry Kasparov, the chess champion, the top-
ranked chess player of all time and also a longtime low-profile political activist, held a press conference to announce he was retiring

from chess to take on the job of restoring Russian democracy. He seemed to have what it might take: fame, money, a relentlessly logical mind combined with oratorical ability that allowed him to make politics make sense to many different kinds of people, and the stamina to campaign nonstop. He spent the summer of 2005 on the stump, and I joined him for a portion of his journey.

In Beslan, the site of the previous year's hostage crisis, Kasparov spent an hour and a half at the cemetery. The New Cemetery, as the locals called it, was a field divided into 330 rectangular plots designed to look identical, though workmen were still laboring every day to cut the granite boxes to frame the graves, cover them with gravel, and place pink granite slabs over them. The plots at the front of the cemetery had been completed, and parents or other relatives had pasted color photographs of the dead children on the stones. Other than that, the only difference among the plots was the size: there were singles, doubles, and triples, and several family graves that included the mother and three or four children, or two sisters and their five children. There were bottles of water, soda, or juice on all the graves: it had become a Beslan tradition to bring open drink bottles for relatives, who had suffered from dehydration before dying. Kasparov paused at every grave, reading the names and the birth and death dates (though every single person buried there was killed on September 3, 2004), and leaned down to place on each grave a red carnation from a box carried by one of his bodyguards. The pace of the visit was like that of a politician moving through a receiving line of voters, except there was no flesh to press.

Then Kasparov went to a house of culture—a sort of all-purpose meeting and entertainment building that exists in every Russian town—where he was scheduled to give a talk. The house of culture was locked up, but about fifty people had gathered on its concrete porch. Many of them were women wearing black dresses and kerchiefs—women in mourning, or, as they had become known all over Russia, the "Mothers of Beslan." They had been the driving force behind an effort to turn the ongoing trial of the single surviving hostage-taker into a full-fledged investigation of what happened at the school. Increasingly, they had come to believe that the responsibility for the deaths of their children lay with federal troops, which concentrated on killing the hostage-takers rather than freeing the hostages—and killed both the captors and the hostages as a result.

"It's lies that killed your children," said Kasparov, addressing the women in black. During the crisis, officials claimed there were 354 hostages in the school. In fact, there were more than a thousand. Former hostages had testified that when their captors, who were watching TV in the teachers' hall, saw the figure 354, they concluded that the government was laying the groundwork for a storming of the building by underestimating the number of potential casualties. It was then, hostages had said, that the hostage-takers stopped giving them water. Other contested official claims included the assertion that the hostage-takers never advanced any demands—while witnesses claimed there was at least one videotape and one letter containing demands that could have led to negotiations. "It's lies that form the foundation of this regime," Kasparov continued. "If the court case here is stifled, if you allow the investigation to wither, then Beslan will happen all over again. I don't want to be in power myself, but I want those who are in power to tell me the truth. I'd force those lowlifes to come here and walk around the entire cemetery." He had tears in his eyes. "I want them to see what their lies led to. Lies!"

Just then there was a dull pop, very much like a gunshot, and the women screamed, "Garry! Garry!" The crowd broke apart, and Kasparov's bodyguards tried awkwardly to shield him while keeping people from trampling one another as they rushed off the porch. A young man standing in front of the building suddenly turned out to be holding a bottle of ketchup, which he shook up violently and then aimed at Kasparov and squeezed. Kasparov was presently covered: his head, his chest, and the right shoulder of his blue sport coat were stained sticky red. The porch was empty now, save for a clear plastic bag with several broken eggs in it that had hit the roof of the porch before landing: that was what had made the popping sound.

An old woman, now standing on the porch with us, tried to clean Kasparov's face with a handkerchief. "Forgive me, forgive me," he whispered over and over again, apologizing for triggering this incident in a town that was already racked with grief. Another woman in black, heavyset, in her forties, said, "Let's go to the school—it's safe there," and Kasparov walked down the street, surrounded by the women, toward the building that had nearly been destroyed in the attack that ended the hostage crisis. For the ten minutes or so that they walked, Kasparov talked about the inevitability of a political crisis, the importance of protest, and the need to put aside political differences in the name of dismantling the regime. The crowd gradually grew as people came out of the houses and apartment blocks along the way to join the walk.

They entered the school through the giant holes in the walls of what used to be the gymnasium. At the end of the siege, this space was filled with children; this was where most of them died. The physical evidence suggested the gymnasium was damaged by tanks firing at point-blank range: there were giant holes in the thick brick wall where steel-grated windows used to be. Inside, the space was charred—by a fire, the Mothers of Beslan believed, started by a flame-thrower used by the Russian troops (the state had acknowledged that flamethrowers were used, but denied that they could have led to a fire).

Kasparov gasped when they entered the gym. "Oh my God, oh my God," he whispered. The women walked to different corners of the ravaged space and began wailing; soon the hall was filled with a muffled, high-pitched sound. Kasparov looked stricken: his eyes red, mouth slightly open, head shaking. It was clear that it would not be possible to talk in here: the room was oversaturated with grief. He asked to be given a tour of the school, and as he walked around with the crowd, now grown to about a hundred people, he talked: "I'm walking through this school, thinking: How do people in Moscow keep walking around, saying something, continuing to lie? Among them, there is someone who gave orders to open fire. If that person gets away with it, we will all be to blame!"

The rest of Kasparov's day was bizarre. He went on to Vladikavkaz, a half-hour's drive away, capital of North Ossetia. He was scheduled to give a talk, but his manager was notified that the curtain in the hall had collapsed onto the stage, so the space was unavailable. About four weeks into his campaign, this was familiar: every venue Kasparov rented anywhere in Russia had something go wrong. Here, not only was the hall unavailable, but in front of the building there was a hastily organized children's event with extremely loud music. Kasparov went anyway and shouted to a crowd of about sixty people, talking about social spending, which constituted about 15 percent of the Russian budget—far less even than in the United States. Several teenagers hovered around the edges of the crowd. One threw a rock at Kasparov and missed. Kasparov kept talking. Then there was a torrent of eggs, two of which hit Kasparov in the head. The teenagers who threw the eggs ran off toward the police vehicles and quickly disappeared: there was no effort to hide that they had been brought there by the police and acted under their protection. When a German journalist who was also hit by an egg tried to chase his assailant, one of the policemen—who later turned out to be the local interior ministry spokesman—grabbed him by the arm and rudely told him to mind his own business. "Their regime is afraid of words!" shouted Kasparov.

Two of his bodyguards, visibly shaken, were whispering to each other. "He was just a kid—I couldn't see it coming," said one. "I was in the wrong position," admitted the other, who tried but failed to shield Kasparov's head. Eggs are not that dangerous, but they served to demonstrate how defenseless Kasparov was, despite his rotating staff of eight bodyguards.

"We've foreseen everything that's foreseeable," Kasparov said to me. "But if I really thought about it, I couldn't go on." One of his bodyguards always watched over food preparation, and Kasparov drank only bottled water he carried with him and ate only food ordered for the entire table.

At a dinner at the close of his trip to North Ossetia—a roughly five-hour affair during which Kasparov played three games of chess, two of them with a local seven-year-old prodigy—Alan Chochiev, an Ossetian activist who had recently served eleven months in prison for distributing antigovernment leaflets, made a toast: "No one has ever tried what you are doing. You are addressing not four hundred thousand people in every city. Not even four hundred at a time, in some large hall. You are talking to fifty or sixty people at a time, in a country with a population of 145 million. It's a crazy task. I want to raise this toast: Here is a man who chose to do the impossible. May it now become possible!"

That was only half the story of Kasparov's impossible task. Kasparov was not just agitating for his point of view; he was also attempting to gather and spread information, turning himself into a one-man substitute for the hijacked news media. He grilled local sympathizers about the situation in their region, then passed this information on. His chess player's memory was invaluable: according to one of his assistants, he had never kept a phone book, because he could not help remembering every phone number he heard. Now he was constantly aggregating and averaging in his mind. He kept a running tally of the percentage of local taxes each region was allowed to keep, the problems opposition activists faced, and details of speech and behavior that he found telling. Now that local and national media existed only to spread the government's message, information had to be gathered in this piecemeal manner.

In Rostov, where Kasparov spoke in front of the public library—he had been scheduled to speak in the library itself, but it had been shut down, under the pretense of a burst pipe—a young man approached his assistant, gave her his business card, and said he wanted to participate as a local organizer. When I asked his name, he said, "That's impossible. I'll get fired immediately." As I later learned from Kasparov's assistant, the man was an instructor at a state college.

Kasparov had flown a chartered plane to the south of Russia, and the plan had been to use it to go from city to city. But after spending most of one day grounded because no airport in the region would give permission to land, the group of thirteen people—Kasparov, his staff, and two journalists—had to switch to cars. When we arrived in Stavropol, it turned out our hotel reservations had been canceled. Standing in the lobby of the hotel, Kasparov's manager called around to every other hotel in the sleepy city; all claimed to be fully booked. This was when the manager of the hotel showed up.

"I am sorry," he said, clearly starstruck. "You must understand the position I am in. But can I take a picture with you?"

"I am sorry," responded Kasparov. "But you must understand the position I am in."

The hotel manager turned beet-red. Now he was as embarrassed as he had been scared.

"The hell with it," he said. "We'll give you rooms."

That evening, only one of several dozen confirmed dinner guests showed up. The local organizer, an entrepreneur, claimed all the invitees had received threatening phone calls warning them against attending the dinner.

In Dagestan, Kasparov was scheduled to award trophies to the

winners of a children's chess tournament. But when our group arrived, the only person waiting for us was a local opposition journalist.
He explained that the head of the Dagestan Chess Federation had
received a phone call from the regional government telling him he
would be fired if Kasparov attended the event, so the drivers—all of
them local policemen, as it turned out—had taken us to the wrong place.

Everywhere Kasparov went, he was followed. There were usually
at least two secret police agents, easily identifiable by their manner,
their dress, and their standard-issue video cameras. Some of these
men videotaped Kasparov, some posed as journalists—they always
asked the same questions and refused to identify themselves—and
some just trailed him. It was impossible to tell whether such extraordinary measures of security, surveillance, and general obstruction
were taken on orders from Moscow or were a local initiative. In any
case, they served to stimulate Kasparov by making him feel that the
regime was scared, and they added weight to his words. At the same
time, they marginalized him: even a world-famous genius begins
to look slightly ridiculous when he is reduced to wearing ketchup-
stained clothes, traveling in a beat-up hired van, and speaking to ad
hoc gatherings in the street time after time.

Kasparov campaigned as doggedly and tirelessly as he had once
played chess: he had played some of the longest matches in the history of the game, and as a perennial outsider in the Soviet sports
establishment, he was no stranger to having the game rigged. But his
political organization failed to grow: with a total television blackout,
his voice, over the years, became more and more marginal. In the end,
his money, his fame, and his mind proved powerless against the regime, even if it was true that the regime was scared of him. Once the
institutions of democracy had been dismantled, it was impossible—it
was too late—to organize to defend them.

Nine

RULE·OF TERROR

On November 23, 2006, a man named Alexander Litvinenko died in a London hospital. He was forty-one years old, he was an FSB officer, and his final days had been broadcast virtually live by the British and some of the Russian media. "Just three weeks ago he was a happy, healthy man with a full head of hair who regularly jogged five miles a day," the *Daily Mail* reported on November 21. Accompanying the piece was a picture of Litvinenko, gaunt and bald, a hospital gown opened on his chest, which was covered with electrodes. "Mr. Litvinenko can barely lift his head, so weak are his neck muscles. He has difficulty speaking and can only talk in short, painful bursts." The day after the article was published, Alexander Litvinenko lapsed into a coma. The following day, trace amounts of the poison that was killing him were finally found in his urine: it was polonium, a very rare and highly radioactive substance. A few hours later, Litvinenko's heart stopped for the second time in two days, and he was dead.

Litvinenko had been a classic whistle-blower. In 1998 he had appeared in a televised press conference with four of his secret police colleagues. They declared they had received illegal assignments from the FSB, including an order to kill Boris Berezovsky. The press conference itself had been organized by Berezovsky, whom Litvinenko had met following an unrelated assassination attempt in 1994, which Litvinenko had investigated. Both men valued being acquainted, and each seemed to place exaggerated hope in the other. Berezovsky believed knowing an honest man in the FSB conferred protection; Litvinenko trusted the influential billionaire to help him change what was wrong with the system. Litvinenko had been in the uniformed services since the age of eighteen. He was one of the youngest lieutenant colonels the Russian secret police had ever had; he was wholly devoted to the system that raised him, but he belonged to that rare breed of people who are incapable of accepting the system's—any system's—imperfections, and who are entirely deaf to the arguments of those who accept things as they are.

Vladimir Putin had been appointed head of the FSB in August 1998, amid allegations of corruption leveled against the previous leadership. "When he was appointed, I asked Sasha who he was," Litvinenko's widow, Marina, told me years later. "He said some people are saying he was never a street officer. That meant they looked down on him—he hadn't come up through the ranks." But Berezovsky arranged for a meeting between his protégé the head of the secret police and his friend the whistle-blower. This was the period when Putin believed his work environment to be so hostile that he held his meetings with Berezovsky in the disused elevator shaft in the FSB headquarters building. Berezovsky wanted the two men to see each other as allies. Litvinenko came bearing charts that he said showed improper connections among FSB departments and the routes that illegal instructions as well as money traveled. He also told Putin about the order to kill Berezovsky, which both the whistle-blower and the oligarch were convinced Putin did not know about. Putin, Litvinenko later told his wife and Berezovsky, was uninterested; the meeting lasted all of ten minutes. He came home dejected and worried about the future—and, as is the way of men like these, resolved to act.

His next step was to hold the press conference on illegal FSB activity. In addition to the order to kill Berezovsky, he claimed to have received instructions to kidnap and beat up prominent businessmen. Putin responded with a televised statement impugning Litvinenko's character, claiming he was delinquent on alimony payments to his first wife (his second wife insisted she had personally made the payments every month and had the stubs to show for it).

Three months later, Litvinenko was arrested on charges of having used excessive force with a suspect three years earlier. The case fell apart, and in November 1999 a military court acquitted him. He was not allowed to leave the courtroom, however: FSB officers entered and re-arrested him on other charges. That case was dismissed without a trial, but a third case was launched immediately. A military judge let him out on his own recognizance, however, pending a new trial; but when Litvinenko learned that the hearings would be held in a small city about a hundred kilometers from Moscow, where few journalists or outside observers were likely to venture, he decided to flee Russia.

In September 2000, he told Marina he would be going to a southern Russian city to visit his elderly parents. He called her almost a month later and directed her to go on vacation. "I said, 'It's not a good time,'" Marina told me. "Tolya, our son, had started his music lessons, why would we go on vacation? He said, 'But you always wanted to go on vacation. You should go now.' And I realized— sometimes he just had this voice that I realized I had to turn my mind off and just do it." She booked a two-week trip to Spain and went there with their six-year-old son. At the end of the two weeks, Litvinenko directed her to get herself to the airport in Málaga at midnight. She arrived, terrified and confused, and was met by an acquaintance who transported her and Tolya to Turkey in a private jet that probably belonged to Berezovsky. Alexander was waiting for her in Antalya, a Turkish resort.

"It was like the movies," she said. "We couldn't believe it." Except no one had scripted their escape. Berezovsky's employee who had accompanied Marina from Málaga had had to leave. After two days of celebrating their reunion at a resort hotel in Antalya, Alexander and Marina began to realize they were fugitives with no place to go. Berezovsky had promised to support them financially, but he had little idea of how to help them logistically, so he called his friend Alex Goldfarb in New York and asked him to fly to Turkey to sort things out. Goldfarb agreed, though his involvement in Litvinenko's escape would cost him his job with George Soros. Goldfarb took Litvinenko to the American embassy in Ankara, where the whistle-blower was interviewed and politely turned down: he had been a secret police agent but not a spy, and the United States had no interest in his information. By going to the embassy, however, Litvinenko had exposed himself to Russian agents who, he knew, kept the embassy under surveillance. Terrified, he needed a solution more urgently than ever.

Goldfarb finally concocted an ingenious plan: the four of them bought tickets with a changeover in London, where the Litvinenkos would surrender to the authorities right in the airport. They did— and wound up in London, their rent and Tolya's school tuition paid by Berezovsky.

After some months at loose ends, Litvinenko began to write. Together with Russian-American historian Yuri Felshtinsky, whom Litvinenko had met when Felshtinsky briefly worked on Berezovsky's media team in Moscow, he wrote a book about the 1999 apartment building explosions. Litvinenko used his professional experience to analyze the evidence that had already been reviewed on Russian television, pointing out numerous inconsistencies in the FSB's official version of the foiled explosion in Ryazan. He and Felshtinsky also reviewed evidence uncovered by reporters for *Novaya Gazeta*, a Moscow weekly specializing in investigative journalism. These journalists had found two conscripts who had sneaked into an air force warehouse in Ryazan in the fall of 1999 in search of sugar to sweeten their tea. They found what they expected: dozens of fifty-kilo sacks marked SUGAR. But the substance they extracted from the sacks made their tea taste so bizarre that they reported the whole incident, including their own breaking, entering, and stealing, to their superior officer. The officer had the substance analyzed and found it to be hexogen, the explosive. Litvinenko and Felshtinsky also found evidence that the air force warehouse was used by the FSB, which, they believed, had stored the explosives there.

Gradually, other evidence began to emerge. An opposition parliamentary deputy, Yuli Rybakov—one of the two men who refused to stand up when the Soviet-Russian anthem was played—gave Litvinenko the transcript of the September 13 Duma session. The speaker had interrupted the session by saying, "We have just received news that a residential building in Volgodonsk was blown up last night." In fact, the building in Volgodonsk would not be blown up for three more days: it seems the FSB plant in the speaker's office—whom Litvinenko was later able to identify—had given the speaker the wrong note at the wrong time, but had known of the planned Volgodonsk explosion in advance.

Another whistle-blower, Mikhail Trepashkin, a former FSB agent who had taken part in Litvinenko's infamous press conference in 1998, joined the investigation. He was able to trace the connections between the FSB and the apartment buildings in Moscow, identifying a businessman whose name was used to rent space in both buildings, the FSB agent who set up the businessman, and even two of the men who had been hired to organize the actual explosions. Most shockingly, Trepashkin had uncovered evidence that the composite portrait of a suspect had been exchanged for a different one. Two men had been arrested, and Trepashkin, who was a lawyer by training, was planning to represent two survivors at the court hearings, using the forum to present his evidence. But just a week before the hearings, Trepashkin was arrested for illegal possession of a firearm; he would spend five years in prison. The court hearings were declared closed to the public; the two suspects received life sentences, but no story ever emerged of who they were and why they had committed their crimes.

ON THE EVENING of October 23, 2002, a couple of friends stopped by for a drink: I had a three-year-old and a one-year-old and was spending most of my evenings at home. The friends, one of whom was a television producer, suggested we turn on the television to watch a recently launched talk show that I had not yet seen. The show had barely begun when a breaking-news announcement interrupted it. A hostage crisis was under way in a Moscow theater. By this time I was editing a small independent political-analysis website, polit.ru. In the next three days I would get a total of about three hours of sleep: my reporters would take turns keeping vigil at the theater and I would be posting their news to our site.

It was a little after nine in the evening when the siege of the theater began. The musical presented that night included a scene in which a real World War II–era airplane appeared onstage. It was then that masked men with machine guns came onstage and around the perimeter of the hall; for a few moments many in the audience thought it was all part of the show. There were about eight hundred people in the hall that night; with the exception of a few dozen young children and foreign citizens the hostage-takers soon released—and some of the actors, many of them also children, who managed to climb out a dressing room window—they would spend the next fifty-eight hours in the hall, growing exhausted, dehydrated, terrified, and ultimately desperate. Though they were ordered to surrender their cell phones to the terrorists, several of them managed to call the leading news radio station at different points during the crisis, so throughout the siege a city frozen in fear and anxiety around the theater heard voices from within it.

Around seven in the morning on the third day of the siege, several cabinet officials entered the meeting hall at a nearby college where relatives of the hostages had spent most of the last three days. "They were very happy and excited," one of the relatives later recalled. "They went up to the microphone. The room froze in silence. They said these sweet words: 'The operation went off without a hitch.' They said all the terrorists had been killed and there were no casualties among the hostages. The room broke into applause, screaming with joy. Everyone was thanking the authorities for saving their loved ones." In this triumphant statement, everything was a lie.

The Moscow theater siege is simultaneously one of the most successfully executed and one of the most absurdly botched hostage-rescue operations in history. Throughout the siege, the terrorists, who gave the impression of being disorganized and disoriented, continued negotiations with just about all comers—and kept gradually releasing some of the hostages. A motley crew of doctors, politicians, and journalists were allowed to go in and out of the building to negotiate better conditions for the hostages. Relatives of the hostages, desperately hoping for a peaceful resolution, gathered for a rally on the second day of the siege and produced a petition that they submitted with more than 250 signatures:

> *Esteemed President:*
>
> *We are the children, relatives, and friends of hostages who are inside the theater. We appeal to your reason and mercy. We know that the building is mined and that the use of force will lead to the theater being blown up. We are certain that no*

concession is too great to grant when at issue are the lives of
seven hundred people. We ask you not to allow people to die.
Continue the negotiations! Accept some of their demands! If our
loved ones die, we will no longer believe that our state is strong
and its government is real. Do not let us be orphaned!

A few hours later, one of our reporters called to say that a hospital right near the theater had been evacuated. The military were beginning to storm the building, I concluded, and were readying space for possible casualties.

At 5:30 on Saturday morning, the third day of the siege, two of the hostages called Echo Moskvy, the city's main news and talk station. "I don't know what's going on," one of them sobbed into the phone. "There is gas. Everyone is sitting in the hall. We ask you, please, we just hope we are not another *Kursk*." Unable to speak further, she passed the phone to her friend, who said, "It seems they are beginning to use force. Please don't abandon us if there is a chance, we beg you." It is heartbreakingly clear that neither the hostages nor their loved ones outside trusted the Russian armed forces to save them. The reference to the *Kursk* made it plain: they did not trust the government to have regard for human life.

In fact, the rescue plan was brilliant: special forces used underground passages to fill the theater with gas that would make everyone inside fall asleep, preventing the terrorists from detonating the explosives planted around the hall—women dressed in black and apparently wearing vests packed with explosives were posted throughout. The sleeping terrorists could then be detained and the hostages freed by troops who would emerge from those same underground passages as well as enter the building through the front doors.

None of it worked out as planned. It took several minutes for the terrorists to fall asleep. Why they did not set off the explosives was unclear, and led to speculation that there were no explosives at all. The hostages, sleep-deprived and severely dehydrated—at least in part because the two different special forces units stationed around the theater could not agree on letting pass a shipment of water and juice the terrorists had consented to accept—fell asleep quickly and required medical help to wake up. Instead of being given immediate medical attention, they were carried out of the building and laid on the steps of the theater, many of them on their backs rather than their sides, as they should have been. Many people choked to death on their own vomit, without ever gaining consciousness, right on the steps of the building. Then the dead and the merely unconscious alike were loaded onto buses, where, again, they were placed sitting up; on the buses, many more people choked to death when their heads flipped backward. Instead of being taken to the hospital next door, the hostages were transported, mostly by bus, to hospitals in central Moscow, where the doctors were helpless to aid them because the military and police authorities refused to tell them what kind of chemical had been used in the theater. Several of the hostages fell into a coma and died in the hospital, some as late as a week after the siege was over. In all, 129 people died.

The government declared victory. Pictures of the terrorists, all of whom were summarily executed in their sleep by Russian troops, were repeatedly shown on television: men and women slumped in theater chairs or over tables, with visible gunshot wounds to their heads. When I wrote a piece on the disregard for human life the government had exhibited by declaring victory in the face of 129 unnecessary deaths, I received a series of death threats myself: the triumph over terrorism was not to be questioned. It was months before some human-rights activists dared point out that Russia had violated a series of international conventions and its own laws by using the gas and applying force when the terrorists were still willing to negotiate. Few Russians ever learned that the terrorists, led by a twenty-five-year-old who had never before been outside Chechnya, had advanced demands that would have been almost laughably easy to fulfill, possibly securing the release of all the hostages. They wanted President Putin publicly to declare that he wanted to end the war in Chechnya and to demonstrate his goodwill by ordering troop withdrawal from any one district of the breakaway republic.

But for all the seeming simplicity of their demands, the terrorists were demanding that Putin act in a way that ran counter to his nature. The boy who could never end a fight—the one who would seem to calm down only to flare up and attack again—now the president who had promised to "rub them out in the outhouse," would certainly rather sacrifice 129 of his own citizens than publicly say that he wanted peace. He did not.

Just two weeks after the theater siege, Putin was in Brussels for a European Union–Russia summit devoted principally to the discussion of the international Islamic terrorist threat. At a press conference after the meetings, a reporter for the French newspaper *Le Monde* asked a question about the use of heavy artillery against civilians in Chechnya. Putin, looking calm and even smiling slightly with the corners of his mouth, said, "If you are ready to become a radical adherent of Islam and you are ready to be circumcised, I invite you to come to Moscow. We are a country of many faiths. We have specialists in this. I will recommend that the operation be performed in such a way that nothing will ever grow there again." The interpreter did not dare translate Putin's response in full, and it did not even make it into the following day's edition of *The New York Times*: the paper demurely translated his last sentence as: "You are welcome and everything and everyone is tolerated in Moscow." But the video of him lashing out at the reporter was still viral on RuTube nine years after Putin made his threat—and demonstrated his utter inability even to pretend to consider a peaceful resolution to the conflict in Chechnya.

ALEXANDER LITVINENKO was now living in a row house in North London, across a narrow street from Ahmed Zakaev, a former actor from
the Chechen capital of Grozny, who had, in the late 1990s, become
the intelligent, charming face of an independent Chechnya. He had
been a key member of the post–cease-fire Chechen government
and Chechnya's representative in the West. In 2000 he was wounded
and left Chechnya for medical treatment, and eventually he sought
political asylum in Great Britain. Now he was living in North London on a stipend he received from his old negotiating partner, Boris
Berezovsky—just like Litvinenko, who had spent much of the second
half of the 1990s in Chechnya, on the side of the Russian troops.
Zakaev's surviving comrades considered him to be the prime minister of Chechnya in exile.

Together, Litvinenko and Zakaev pored over documents and
video footage of the theater siege and made a startling discovery: one
of the terrorists had not been killed; in fact, he seemed to have left the
building shortly before Russian troops stormed it. They identified
the man as Khanpash Terkibaev, a former journalist who, they believed, had long been working for Russian secret police. On March 31,
2003, Zakaev saw Terkibaev in Strasbourg, where both had traveled
for a meeting of the European Parliamentary Assembly as representatives of the Chechen people, Terkibaev sanctioned by Moscow and
Zakaev not. In early April, Litvinenko sought out Sergei Yushenkov,
the liberal colonel with whom Marina Salye had been co-organizing
before she fled Moscow, who was now engaged in a parliamentary
investigation of the theater siege, and gave him all the information he
had collected on Terkibaev. It was two weeks later that Yushenkov was
shot dead in Moscow in broad daylight. Litvinenko was certain this
was a direct result of his theater siege investigation.

But Yushenkov had already given the documents he received from Litvinenko to someone else. Anna Politkovskaya was a journalist in her mid-forties who had spent most of her professional life in relative obscurity, writing excessively researched and confusing pieces on all manner of social ills. During the second war in Chechnya she emerged as a recklessly brave reporter who would spend weeks on end in Chechnya, apparently oblivious of the Russian military's restrictions, documenting allegations of abuse and war crimes. In a couple of years she had become easily the most trusted Russian among Chechens. Gray-haired, bespectacled, the mother of two grown children, she seemed a most unlikely muckraker or war reporter, which probably kept her safe on a number of occasions. During the theater siege, she was allowed to enter the building to attempt to negotiate with the terrorists, and she appears to have been instrumental in getting them to agree to allow water and juice to be delivered.

Politkovskaya found Terkibaev, whom she said she recognized from her time inside the theater, and interviewed him. He turned out to be almost ridiculously vain, and she easily got him to boast of having been inside the theater during the siege, having led the terrorists there, having secured their passage in several vans loaded with arms through checkpoints in Chechnya and police outposts on the approach to Moscow, and of having had in his possession a detailed map of the theater, which both the terrorists and federal troops had lacked. Who was he working for? Moscow, he said.

Politkovskaya drew her conclusions from the interview cautiously. Terkibaev lied a lot, this much was clear. There were also the facts: he had indeed been among the hostage-takers; he was still living; and he moved about freely, including as a member of official delegations abroad. It seemed his claim that he worked for one of the secret services had to be true. And he said one other important thing to Politkovskaya: the reason the terrorists had not set off their explosives, even when they felt the gas filling the hall—an unmistakable

prelude to an attack on the building—was that there *were* no explosives. The women who had been stationed along the theater's rows
of seats, keeping an eye on the hostages and a finger on the button,
were wearing dummy dynamite vests. If this was true—and there was
every reason to think it was—then everyone who died in the siege
died in vain. And, with Khanpash Terkibaev leaving the building before special forces stormed it, the Kremlin probably knew it too.

ON JULY 3, 2003, a second member of the independent committee
investigating the 1999 apartment building bombings died. Yuri
Shchekochikhin, an outspoken liberal politician and a muckraking
journalist—he was deputy editor of *Novaya Gazeta* and, as head of
its investigative team, Politkovskaya's immediate superior—had been
hospitalized two weeks earlier with mysterious symptoms: he had
been complaining of a burning sensation all over his body, and he
had been vomiting. Within a week he was in a coma, skin all over his
body had peeled off, and his hair had fallen out. He died of multiple
organ failure caused by an unknown toxin. Doctors at Moscow's
best-equipped hospital, who diagnosed him with "allergic syndrome,"
had been unable to slow his decline or significantly lessen his pain.

Shchekochikhin had been working on so many investigations
that his friends and colleagues, most if not all of whom believed he
was murdered, were at a loss to suggest which of his suicide missions
actually led to his death. Zakaev was certain that Shchekochikhin was
murdered to prevent him from publishing information he had gathered on the theater siege: namely, evidence that some of the women
terrorists were convicted felons who, on paper, were still serving
sentences in Russian prisons at the time of the siege. In other words,
their release had probably been secured by someone who had extralegal powers—and this, again, pointed to possible secret-police involvement in the organization of this act of terror.

ON SEPTEMBER 1. 2004. as soon as news came of the school siege in Beslan, Politkovskaya, naturally, rushed to the airport to fly to North Ossetia. So did many other journalists, including the other reporter who was well-known in Chechnya, Andrei Babitsky—the man who had been kidnapped by Russian troops at the very beginning of Putin's reign. Babitsky was detained at the airport in Moscow, ostensibly because he was suspected of carrying explosives; none were found and he was released, but he never made it to Beslan. Politkovskaya registered for three consecutive flights, each of which was canceled before it could board, and finally got a seat on a plane to Rostov, the largest city in southern Russia, about four hundred miles from Beslan; she was planning to cover the rest of the way by hired car. Her plan was to act not only as a reporter but also, as much as she could, as a negotiator, as she had two years earlier, during the theater siege. Before leaving Moscow, she had spoken extensively with Zakaev in London, urging him to mobilize any and all Chechen leaders to attempt to talk to the terrorists and negotiate the release of the children. She suggested that rebel leaders should come out of hiding to take on this job, setting no conditions of their own. Zakaev had agreed.

Ever careful—by this time Politkovskaya was the target of constant death threats, and she had seen her editor, Yuri Shchekochikhin, die of poisoning—Politkovskaya brought her own food onto the airplane and asked only for a cup of tea. Ten minutes later, she lost consciousness. By the time the plane landed, she was in a coma. That she was able to come out of it was, in the opinion of doctors who treated her in Rostov, a miracle. Doctors in Moscow, where she was transported two days later, ultimately concluded she had been poisoned with an undisclosed toxin that did severe damage to her kidneys, liver, and endocrine system.

POLITKOVSKAYA, who took months to recover and never fully regained her health, was effectively prevented from covering and investigating the tragedy in Beslan. Other people took up this challenge. These investigators included Marina Litvinovich, Putin's former image-maker. She had quit her job at the Kremlin's pocket political consultancy after the theater siege, not so much because she disagreed with the FSB's handling of it as because she had been kept off the crisis team. She dabbled in opposition politics just as the opposition effectively ceased to exist, went to work for oligarch Mikhail Khodorkovsky, who was promptly arrested, and had wandered into Beslan looking for a way to apply her considerable skills and connections.

"I was scared to go," she told me. "I had never been to the Caucasus." She was too embarrassed to tell me exactly what she had expected, but it seemed she was very much a product of ten years of wartime propaganda, which she herself had helped to create: the last thing she expected to find so close to Chechnya were people like herself. "We went from family to family, from home to home where people had lost children, and everywhere we went, they poured us a 'memorial' shot of vodka. And everyone cried, and I cried, and I cried my eyes out in Beslan. And they just told me their stories and they cried and they asked for help. By that time everyone in Russia seemed to have forgotten about Beslan, so anyone who came, they asked for help. They did not know what kind of help, and at first I did not know, either. I told them banal things, I told them they should organize. It was a strange thing to say to women who had spent their lives making homes—who, if they had a job outside the home, maybe worked at a family store. And gradually I started spending time there, working on a few issues. We created an organization. Then we started collecting eyewitness accounts. And then the trial began."

As with the theater siege, most of the hostage-takers had been summarily executed by Russian troops. By official count, there was a single survivor, and this time he was put on trial. Hearings would go on for two years, and the man's testimony and, more important, eyewitness testimony painted another damning picture of the Russian government's handling of and possible involvement in the hostage crisis. Conducted in tiny Beslan and attended mostly by grief-stricken local residents, the trial would have passed in utter obscurity had Litvinovich not done a simple thing. She made sure every session was audiotaped and the transcript was posted on a website she called The Truth About Beslan.

Using courthouse testimony, Litvinovich succeeded in reconstructing what had happened in the school hour by hour and, on the final day, almost minute by minute. She discovered that there were two rescue efforts working at cross-purposes: a local one directed by North Ossetian governor Alexander Dzasokhov (his official title was president of North Ossetia), and another one directed by the FSB from Moscow. In the early hours of the siege, the hostage-takers had issued a note with their cell phone number and a demand: they named five people, including Dzasokhov, to come in and negotiate with them. Dzasokhov tried to enter the school but was prevented from doing so by troops reporting to the FSB. He did arrange for the former head of neighboring Ingushetia, Ruslan Aushev, to enter the building; Aushev was able to bring out twenty-six hostages, all of them women with infant children. He also brought out a list of demands addressed to Vladimir Putin: they wanted independence for Chechnya, troop withdrawal, and an end to military action. On the second day of the siege, Dzasokhov made contact with Zakaev in London, and Zakaev got the president of the self-proclaimed Chechen republic, Aslan Maskhadov, to agree to come to Beslan and negotiate with the terrorists—an agreement that Politkovskaya had in effect already brokered but that Dzasokhov had had to initiate anew.

There was every indication that the terrorists were willing to negotiate; in most countries, this would have meant the standoff would drag on and on as long as there remained the chance of saving any of the hostages. But as during the theater siege, Moscow did not wait until negotiations were exhausted; in fact, the beginning of military action seems to have been timed specifically to prevent a meeting between the terrorists and Maskhadov, who stood a good chance of brokering a peaceful resolution.

At one in the afternoon on September 3, just minutes after workers from the emergency ministry had come to the building to pick up the bodies of several men killed by the terrorists at the beginning of the siege—this had been negotiated by Aushev—two explosions shook the building. By this time, most of the hostages had been crowded into the school gymnasium for more than two days. They were dehydrated—many of them had begun to drink their own urine—and terrified. They knew the gymnasium was mined—the explosives had been mounted in plain sight—and two of the terrorists were standing guard with their feet on pedals that could set off the explosives.

But the two explosions, coming just seconds apart, originated outside the building. Litvinovich was able to determine that both were the result of Russian troops firing grenade launchers directly at the overcrowded gymnasium. "It was as if something had flown in, a giant ball of fire," one of the former hostages testified. Like most of the adults in the gymnasium, she was a mother who was there with her child. "I looked over," another former hostage said, "and saw that where the door to the schoolyard had been, there was a giant hole in the ceiling, and this hole was burning very, very fast."

"When I came to, there were bodies on top of me," one of the former hostages testified. "Everything was burning," said another. "I was lying on top of dead bodies. There were also dead bodies sitting on the benches." A third testified, "I looked over and saw that my girl was missing her head and her arm and her foot had been crushed completely."

The hostages had spent two days in hell, and now this hell was turning upside down. The terrorists seemed panicked—now they were trying to save the hostages' lives. They herded those who could move on their own into the school cafeteria, which was shielded from immediate fire. They urged those who remained in the gymnasium to stand in the windows and show Russian troops that the room was filled with hostages, that they were firing at women and children. Russian troops continued to use tanks, grenade launchers, and fire launchers, aiming first at the gymnasium and then also at the cafeteria at point-blank range. The terrorists repeatedly attempted to move women and children into rooms that were shielded from the fire. Outside, local police tried unsuccessfully to convince the Russian troops to stop firing. In all, 312 people died, including ten non-FSB officers who died in the fire while attempting to save the hostages.

For the second anniversary of the Beslan tragedy in September 2006, Litvinovich put together a brochure with her findings. Politkovskaya, having been incapacitated, wrote little about Beslan, but her contribution was striking: she secured a police document showing that a man detained four hours before the siege had warned the police of the plan. The warning had been ignored: there was not even heightened security at the school that Day of Knowledge.

HOW WAS ONE TO UNDERSTAND THIS? Some were certain that Beslan had been planned and executed by the secret police start to finish, just as the apartment-block explosions had been. The fact that Putin came out with the initiative of canceling gubernatorial elections just ten days after the tragedy, and that he framed it as a response to terrorism, lends credence to this theory. Zakaev, for one, was certain that the FSB had arranged for a rogue group of Chechens to seize the local governor's office—to provide Putin with an excuse for instituting direct federal control over regional administrations—but something had gone awry and the terrorists ended up at the school.

I believe reality is messier. That the apartment-block explosions were the work of the secret police seems almost beyond doubt—in the absence of an opportunity to examine all of the evidence available and not. The theater siege and Beslan strike me less as well-planned operations than as the results of a series of wrong moves, unholy alliances, and wrecked plans. It appears proven that a number of FSB officers maintained long-running relationships with terrorists or potential terrorists from Chechnya. At least some of these relationships involved the exchange of services for money. It is clear that someone—probably police but likely also secret police—had to aid the terrorists in moving around Russia. Finally, there is every indication that Putin's government worked neither to prevent terrorist attacks nor to resolve crises peacefully when they occurred; moreover, the president consistently and increasingly staked his reputation not only on his own determination to "rub them out" whatever the circumstances but also on the terrorists' perceived ruthlessness.

Did this add up to a series of carefully laid plans to strengthen Putin's position in a country that responded best to the politics of fear? Not necessarily, or not quite. Originally, I think, the organizers of the theater siege and the school siege and their enablers had different motivations: at least some of the Chechen rebels wanted to scare Russians into understanding the nightmare of their war; some of those who helped them execute the attacks on the Russian side were, most likely, motivated purely by profit; others, on both sides, were settling personal scores; still others were indeed engaged in grand political scheming that may or may not have reached to the very top. One thing is certain: Once the hostage-takings occurred, the government task forces acting under Putin's direct supervision did everything to ensure that the crises ended as horrifyingly as possible—to justify continued warfare in Chechnya and further crackdowns on the media and the opposition in Russia and, finally, to quell any possible criticism from the West, which, after 9/11, was obligated to recognize in Putin a fellow fighter against Islamic terrorism. There is a reason that Russian troops in both Moscow and Beslan acted in ways that maximized bloodshed; they actually aimed to multiply the fear and the horror. This is the classic modus operandi of terrorists, and in this sense it can certainly be said that Putin and the terrorists were acting in concert.

ON MARCH 20. 2006. Marina Litvinovich left work just after nine in the evening. She was now working for Garry Kasparov, the chess champion turned politician. They kept their presence in the center of Moscow quiet, working behind an unmarked door, behind which stood two of Kasparov's eight permanent bodyguards. In the evenings, Kasparov and his bodyguards would drive off in his SUV and the rest of his small crew dispersed, driving, walking, or taking the subway by themselves. Litvinovich, who lived nearby, usually walked.

About an hour after she left the office, Litvinovich opened her eyes to discover that she was lying on top of a cellar awning and someone was trying to ascertain if she was all right. She was not: she had apparently been knocked unconscious by a blow or several blows to the head. She had been badly beaten, was bruised all over, and was missing two of her front teeth. Her bag was lying next to her; her notebook computer, her cell phone, and her money were still in it.

She spent three or four hours in the emergency room that night, and she spent another three or four at the police station the following day. The police were unusually solicitous in their manner, but kept insisting she had not been beaten. Had the thirty-one-year-old woman perhaps just passed out in the street and fallen in such an unusual way as to be bruised all over? She objected that she had a large bruise on one of her legs that, the doctors had told her, had probably been caused by a blow with a rubber baton. Had she maybe been hit by a car, then? Litvinovich pointed out that her clothes were so clean that she was wearing the same trousers and coat the following day, so she clearly had not been hit by a car. Moreover, this was one of several signs that she had been attacked by professionals: she must have been held while she was beaten, then laid carefully on the awning on which she found herself.

The attack was a message. The pristine execution and the fact that Litvinovich's valuables were not touched served to underscore this. Another young political consultant, a former colleague of Litvinovich who had made a brilliant career working for the Putin government, spelled out the message in his blog: "Women should not be in this line of work . . . Marina has joined the war, and no one ever said this war would be conducted according to rules." In other words, this is what would happen to those who fought the Kremlin.

ON SATURDAY, OCTOBER 7, 2006, Anna Politkovskaya came home to her apartment building in central Moscow and was shot dead in the elevator.

Who could have done it? Anyone. Politkovskaya could be extremely unpleasant: alongside her extraordinarily empathic personality there seemed to exist another, given to lashing out at the slightest provocation. This was a dangerous trait for a journalist whose sources included any number of well-armed men who were used to violence and not at all used to having women talk back to them. She could be unkind to her sources, as she was to Khanpash Terkibaev, whom she made look vain and stupid after he sincerely tried to impress her. She took sides, a dangerous business in times of clan war. But most of all, she was known as a critic of the Putin regime. Alexander Litvinenko was certain that this was what killed her. "Anna Politkovskaya Was Killed by Putin" was how he titled the obituary he posted that day. "We disagreed occasionally, and we would argue," he wrote of his relationship with Politkovskaya. "But we had complete understanding on one point: we both believed that Putin is a war criminal, that he is guilty of the genocide of the Chechen people, and that he should be tried by an open and independent court. Anya realized that Putin might kill her for her beliefs, and for this she despised him."

The day Politkovskaya died, Putin turned fifty-four. Journalists immediately termed the murder his birthday present. Putin said nothing about Politkovskaya's death. The following day he sent birthday wishes to a figure skater who was turning sixty and a popular actor who was turning seventy, but still uttered not a word about a murder that had shaken the capital and the country. Three days after the murder, he was in Dresden, the city he had once called home, meeting with German chancellor Angela Merkel. When he exited his car in Dresden, he encountered a picket line of about thirty people holding signs that said "Killer" and "Killers Not Welcome Here Anymore." At the press conference following his meeting with Merkel, journalists—and, it seemed, Merkel herself—forced him finally to make a public statement on Politkovskaya's death. Once again Putin showed that, pressed to speak publicly on a matter of emotional significance, he could not comport himself. He seemed to seethe as he spoke:

"That journalist was indeed a harsh critic of the current Russian government," he said. "But I think that journalists know—certainly, experts are aware of this—that her political influence in the country was extremely insignificant. She was known in journalist circles and among human-rights activists and in the West, but her influence on politics in Russia was minimal. The murder of such a person—the cold-blooded murder of a woman, a mother—is in itself an attack on our country. This murder does much more harm to Russia and its current government, and to the current government in Chechnya, than any of her articles."

He was right: Politkovskaya was better known in Western European countries like France and Germany, where her books were translated and promoted widely, than she was in Russia, where she had long since been blacklisted by television (she had once been an articulate talk-show regular), where the newspaper where she worked was perceived as marginal, and where, most important, investigative pieces that would have been bombshells had Russia remained a quasi-functioning democracy were simply ignored. The government never reacted to her interview with Khanpash Terkibaev or her report that the police had ignored Beslan warnings. Not even a low-level police functionary lost his job: nothing happened at all, as though nothing had been said or no one had heard it. And her murder, which put Putin in the position of having to prove his innocence, certainly did more damage to him and to his government than Politkovskaya had in life.

And it was such a terribly crafted statement, and it showed Putin's view of journalists so clearly, that I am inclined to believe he was being sincere.

ON NOVEMBER 1, 2006, just three weeks after the murder of Politkovskaya, Alexander Litvinenko felt ill. Ever mindful that he might be poisoned, he immediately downed four quarts of water, to try to flush whatever it was out of his system. It did not help: within hours, Litvinenko was vomiting violently. He was also in excruciating pain: it felt as though his throat, his esophagus, and his stomach had been burned; eating or drinking was impossible, and when he threw up, he was in agony. After three days of unremitting symptoms, he was hospitalized.

Litvinenko immediately told doctors he might have been poisoned by agents of the Russian government. In response, he got a psychiatric consultation—and decided to keep his theory to himself. Doctors told his wife, Marina, that they were looking for unusual bacteria they believed had caused Litvinenko's severe symptoms. For a while she believed them and patiently waited for her husband to get better. But about ten days into the ordeal, she noticed that Alexander had taken a marked turn for the worse. She also saw that his hospital gown was covered with hair. "I stroked his head," she told me later. "I had a rubber glove on, and his hair stayed on my glove. I said, 'Sasha, what is this?' He said, 'I don't know, my hair seems to be falling out.' And this was when I just stood up right there, where his bed was, and started screaming, 'Have you no shame?' Until then I'd tried to be patient, but this was when I realized I couldn't take it anymore. His attending physician came right away, and I said, 'Do you see what's going on, can you explain to me what's going on?' So they called someone from Oncology and some other specialist and started to consult. And the oncologist said, 'I'm going to take him up to my ward because he looks like someone who has had radiation therapy.' And he took him up to his ward, and still they found nothing."

It was another week before Litvinenko's doctors, the British press corps, and the London police came to believe he had been poisoned. Trace amounts of thallium, a heavy metal historically used in rat poison but long since outlawed in Western countries, had been found in his urine. The discovery gave Litvinenko, his wife, and his friends hope: he would start receiving an antidote and recover. "I thought he might be disabled—I was prepared for that," Marina told me, "but I did not think he would die. I was thinking about treatments we would have to be getting." The discovery also gave the British media a reason to write the story of the "Russian spy," as they insisted on calling him, dying in a London hospital, and Scotland Yard reason to begin interrogating Litvinenko. The former whistle-blower, weak, unable to swallow—during his entire hospital stay he received all his sustenance via an IV line—and overcoming extreme pain to speak, gave about twenty hours of testimony in his final days. But the diagnosis also gave pause to a star toxicologist whom Goldfarb had called in: Litvinenko's symptoms did not really look to him like symptoms of thallium poisoning.

A day or two before he slipped into a coma, Litvinenko dictated a statement that he asked to be released in the event of his death. Alex Goldfarb took it down. It began with three paragraphs expressing gratitude to doctors, Great Britain, and Marina, and continued:

> As I lie here, I sense the distinct presence of the angel of death. It is still possible I'll be able to evade him, but I fear my feet are no longer as fast as they used to be. I think the time has come to say a few words to the man responsible for my current condition.
>
> You may be able to force me to stay quiet, but this silence will come at a price to you. You have now proved that you are exactly the ruthless barbarian your harshest critics made you out to be.
>
> You have demonstrated that you have no respect for human life, liberty, or other values of civilization.
>
> You have shown that you do not deserve to hold your post, and you do not deserve the trust of civilized people.
>
> You may be able to shut one man up, but the noise of protest all over the world will reverberate in your ears,

Mr. Putin, to the end of your life. May God forgive you for
what you have done, not only to me but to my beloved
Russia and her people.

Doctors finally identified the cause of Litvinenko's poisoning a
few hours before he died. It was polonium, a highly radioactive substance that occurs in only minuscule amounts in nature but can be
manufactured. Relatives and loved ones learned the cause from police shortly after Alexander Litvinenko died.

FIVE YEARS AFTER MEETING LITVINENKO and helping him escape, Goldfarb sat down to write a book about the man, coauthored with his
widow, Marina. Less than a year later it would be published in several
languages; its English title was *Death of a Dissident: The Poisoning of
Alexander Litvinenko and the Return of the KGB*. A scientist, a longtime political activist, and a natural skeptic, Goldfarb was able to
reconstruct the story of Litvinenko's murder all the more convincingly because he had never really believed what he called Litvinenko's
and Politkovskaya's conspiracy theories. But his own theory would
have put some of theirs to shame.

At the time of the two murders, Russia's policy in Chechnya
was undergoing a transformation. Without admitting defeat or even
openly negotiating—for Putin would have found either humiliating—
Russia was pulling its troops out of Chechnya and giving free rein
and extraordinary monetary subsidies to a handpicked young Chechen
leader, Ramzan Kadyrov, in exchange for loyalty and the illusion of
peace and victory. For Chechnya's other warlords, big and small, this
meant the end of the road: Kadyrov was ruthless with enemies and
rivals alike. On the basis of extensive circumstantial evidence and
some significant off-the-record interviews, Goldfarb concluded that
one of these warlords had Politkovskaya killed in the hopes of mak-

ing it look like Kadyrov had done it—and discrediting Kadyrov in the eyes of the Russian government. Politkovskaya had been highly and vocally critical of and even insulting to Kadyrov, but Goldfarb believed that the people actually responsible for the murder were Chechens from a rival clan.

Then, Goldfarb suggested, Putin found himself in the position of trying to prove he had not done it—and feeling like he had been framed. Except, thanks in part to his advisers, he did not think he was being framed by Kadyrov: he thought he was being set up by Berezovsky's camp in London. The loudest person by far in that camp was the traitorous FSB agent Litvinenko, who was indeed accusing Putin of the murder. For this, Putin had him killed.

Goldfarb's theory is logically impeccable; everyone in it has motive and means. But I find it too complicated, or, perhaps, too specific. The murder of Alexander Litvinenko is indisputably the work of the Russian government authorized at the very top: polonium-210, which killed him, is manufactured exclusively in Russia. Its production and export are tightly controlled by federal nuclear authorities, and the extraction of the needed dose from the manufacturing chain required top-level intervention in an early stage of the manufacturing process. The authorization for such an intervention had to have come from the president's office. In other words, Vladimir Putin ordered Alexander Litvinenko dead.

Once the poison was identified, British police were easily able to identify their suspects in the murder: polonium, while harmless unless ingested, leaves radioactive traces everyplace it touches. This allowed the police to pinpoint the people who transported polonium to London and the exact place and time at which the poisoning occurred. The two men they identified were Andrei Lugovoy, the former head of security for Berezovsky's business partner, who had gone on to build a lucrative private-security firm in Moscow, and his business partner, Dmitry Kovtun. For reasons the British police will not disclose, they have identified Lugovoy as the murder suspect and Kovtun as a witness. Russia has refused extradition requests for Lugovoy; moreover, he has been made a member of parliament, giving him immunity from prosecution, including extradition requests. Britain, for its part, has treated the case as a purely criminal matter and has not made political demands for Lugovoy's extradition.

No other killing in the long line of murders of journalists and politicians has quite so clear-cut and obvious a story. It is indeed possible that Anna Politkovskaya fell victim to the power struggle in Chechnya. It is possible that Yuri Shchekochikhin was killed by some businessman or politician whose dirty laundry he had aired. It is possible that Sergei Yushenkov was, as the police later claimed, killed by a political rival. It is possible that Anatoly Sobchak died of a heart attack. But all of these possibilities, taken separately, seem unlikely, and taken together seem almost absurd. The simple and evident truth is that Putin's Russia is a country where political rivals and vocal critics are often killed, and at least sometimes the order comes directly from the president's office.

Ten

INSATIABLE GREED

Writing now about Putin's early years as president, I am struck by how quickly and decisively he acted. Even when I was covering the story in real time, it seemed to move at breakneck speed. Putin changed the country fast, the changes were profound, and they took easily. He seemed instantly to reverse Russia's historical evolution. And for an excruciatingly long time, no one seemed to notice.

Or almost no one. After the December 2003 parliamentary election, in which Putin's United Russia took nearly half the seats and the rest were divided among the Communist Party, the absurdist-nationalist and outrageously misnamed Liberal Democratic Party, and a new ultranationalist party called Rodina (Motherland) while all remaining liberals and democrats lost their seats, the Organization for Security and Co-operation in Europe (OSCE) reported: "The . . . elections . . . failed to meet many OSCE and Council of Europe commitments, calling into question Russia's willingness to move towards European standards for democratic elections." *The New York*

Times reported something entirely different, publishing a condescending but approving editorial titled "Russians Inch Toward Democracy." The paper of record did not mention international observers' criticism in its news story the day of the election but published a separate piece on the critics the following day; *The Washington Post* and *The Boston Globe* left the critics out of their coverage altogether. The *Los Angeles Times* went even further: in a mammoth news story, it managed to downplay the OSCE's conclusion in such a way that it sounded like the opposite of itself. The paper quoted an OSCE official saying the balloting "was well-organized and we have not noted any major irregularities." The paper also lauded Putin's now unchallenged control of the Russian parliament as a chance for the president to "push through additional reforms, including cleaning up the entrenched corruption."

Publications outside the United States were more critical. The day before the election, the *National Post* of Canada ran a news item that had the whole story right in the headline: "Racists, killers and criminals run for Duma: Parliamentary elections. Two decades after decadent Yeltsin era, corruption plagues Russia." *The Economist* declared the death of democracy in Russia in an editorial a month before the election, and then followed the election with a special report that called the new parliament "a democrat's nightmare" and stressed the ballooning influence of ultranationalists.

But the world's most influential media, with by far the largest journalist corps in Moscow, were asleep at the wheel. Why? In part, because U.S. politics took precedence. In the fall of 2000, when Putin was nationalizing television, American media were fully focused on the hung Bush–Gore election. I joined the staff of *U.S. News & World Report* then, and I idled through my first few months on the job: the magazine had no room for Russia.

Once the election story was finally over, American media had to deal with the aftermath of the dot-com bubble, beginning a wave of budget cuts and rollbacks that would last more than a decade. Many media outlets cut back on their foreign coverage, including Russia—and sometimes beginning with Russia. It became a self-perpetuating story: having told their audiences and themselves that Russia was safely entering a period of political and economic stability, American media effectively declared the Russian story dead, cut the resources available to cover it, and thereby killed their ability to report the story. ABC, which had had several dozen staffers occupying an entire building in central Moscow, closed its bureau altogether. Other outlets' cuts were not as dramatic but just as drastic: entire bureaus were replaced by part-time freelancers. Only a few papers—*The New York Times*, *The Wall Street Journal*, and the *Los Angeles Times*—maintained complete bureaus with full-time reporters and supporting staff.

In June 2001, George W. Bush met Putin for the first time, famously "looked the man in the eye," and "was able to get a sense of his soul." Exuberant press reports took little notice of the fact that Putin not only was considerably less enthusiastic about his new friend but actually warned the United States that the period of hostility that began with the NATO bombings of Yugoslavia in 1999 was far from over. Then 9/11 happened, and suddenly the Russian war in Chechnya was recast as part of the Western world's struggle with Islamic fundamentalist terrorism—against all available evidence, which included, among other things, Putin's abrogation of an agreement reached under Yeltsin, according to which Russia was to stop selling arms to Iran and selling arms to Arab states to the tune of several billion dollars a year. And by geographic happenstance, major U.S. media started viewing Moscow as not so much the capital of Russia as base camp for reporters traveling to Afghanistan and, later, Iraq. The hunger for war stories was insatiable, and Russia was relegated to the sort of story that reporters did on the run, between truly important assignments. Their dispatches from Russia were articles that could only serve to affirm the existing narrative, shaped by the people who had invented the image of Putin the young, energetic liberal reformer.

That there was not a whole lot to report along this particular story line did not seem to concern most American journalists and editors. They glossed over the nationalization of the media, portrayed the appointment of federal envoys to supervise elected governors as making order out of chaos, completely ignored rollbacks in judicial reform—and increasingly chose to focus on economic topics. Unlike Yeltsin, who seemed always to take two steps forward and one step back on economic reform in a perennial effort to pacify the opposition, Putin filled both his staff's and the cabinet's economic arm with avowed liberals. His premier was the former finance minister, an apparatchik steeped in the Soviet bureaucratic tradition but one sincerely committed to building on the reforms actually instituted in the 1990s—and, conveniently for Putin, focused on this task to the exclusion of any other government business. Even before becoming acting president—while he was still merely the anointed successor—Putin had formed a think tank charged with creating a plan for the economic development of Russia, and appointed a liberal economist who had once worked for Sobchak to run it. After the election, the head of the think tank became minister for economic development, a post created especially for him.

Most notably, Putin appointed Andrei Illarionov to be his economic adviser. It was the president-elect's first appointment, and it was intended as a resonant gesture. Illarionov's views were well-known: a member of the 1980s St. Petersburg economists' club, he had evolved into a full-fledged, articulate libertarian. In the United States, he would have been called ultraconservative (and, fittingly, he eventually took a post at the Cato Institute, a libertarian think tank in Washington, D.C.), but in Russia his views landed him on the politically liberal side of the spectrum. Illarionov did not believe in global warming and did believe in the limitless self-regulating potential of free markets. He was also known for his brilliant analytical mind and his testy temperament, which had kept him on the sidelines of most of the key events of the 1990s. His appointment came as a surprise to everyone, including himself.

ON THE AFTERNOON of February 28, 2000, Illarionov was working in his cluttered office at a tiny think tank he ran in Moscow. Located across Moscow's Staraya Ploshad (Old Square) from the offices of the presidential administration and less than a kilometer from the Kremlin itself, Illarionov's Institute of Economic Analysis was as far from power as it could get, considering that Illarionov was still on a first-name basis with most people who had been making economic policy for years. Illarionov was occasionally called in to give a lecture to the policymakers—as he had, for example, on the eve of the 1998 default, warning of the looming disaster—but his counsel seemed to be perceived as an academic exercise. Frustration had been his status quo for years: he had the respect of his powerful peers but no influence on them.

But at four in the afternoon on February 28, less than a month before the presidential election, his phone rang and he was asked to meet with Putin that evening. The meeting lasted three hours. At some point during the meeting, an assistant entered to inform the president-to-be that federal troops had just taken the city of Shatoy in Chechnya. "Putin was so happy," Illarionov recalled later. "He was gesticulating emotionally, and he was saying, 'We showed them, we did them in.' And since I had nothing to lose, I told them everything I thought about the war in Chechnya. I told him I thought Russian troops were committing a crime under his command. And he kept saying that they were all bandits there and that he would rub them out and that he was here to make sure the Russian Federation stayed intact. The words he said to me in private were exactly the same as what he always said on the topic in public: this was his sincere position. And my sincere position was that it was a crime." The exchange went on for twenty or thirty minutes, growing more heated. The undiplomatic Illarionov knew exactly how these sorts of exchanges always ended: he would never be invited back, and another avenue of potential influence would be closed to him because, as usual, he, with his passionately held views, did not fit in.

And then something remarkable happened. Putin grew quiet for a second, rearranged his facial expression, erasing all passion from it, and said, "This is it. You and I will not be discussing Chechnya." For the next two hours, the two men talked about the economy—rather, Putin allowed Illarionov to lecture him. In parting, Putin suggested they meet again the following day. Illarionov immediately committed two more faux pas: he said no, and he cited the reason for his refusal— he was committed to celebrating the anniversary of his American wife's arrival in Russia, which, because she happened to have moved to Moscow in a leap year, could be celebrated only once every four years. Yet rather than take affront at the refusal, or the reason for it, Putin simply suggested a different date to meet. Illarionov lectured him on economics again, and two weeks after the election, on April 12, 2000, he was appointed the new president's adviser.

Illarionov was very much seduced. For years he had thought that Russian economic reforms were being carried out in a misguided and possibly even harmful manner, but he had been helpless to affect policy. Now he would have unfettered access to the head of state, who seemed genuinely interested in what he had to say—and not at all put off by his communication style. Like most people, when Illarionov encountered traits in others that he himself lacked, he was inclined to interpret them as manifestations of some sort of outstanding ability. Speaking to me eleven years after his appointment, Illarionov insisted that Putin was "an extraordinary person," and cited as primary evidence his ability to control his emotions. Plenty of evidence to the contrary had accumulated by this point, including several instances of Putin losing his temper in public. But as someone constitutionally incapable of keeping his opinions to himself, Illarionov continued to be impressed by Putin's ability simply to "turn off" the talk of Chechnya—and even, it seems, by Putin's flattened affect. At base, Illarionov had a difficult time imagining he might be systematically deceived—which is exactly what allowed him to be deceived for a rather long time.

Illarionov and the other economists in Putin's inner circle sent a strong signal to the U.S. press by their very presence. But most of all, American journalists seemed to miss the essence of the Putin story because some of their most important sources were missing—or willfully ignoring—the story. Big business was happy with Putin. The economy had been growing steadily since hitting a low point in 1998, when the ruble dropped so far that domestic production, inefficient as it was, finally became profitable. By the early 2000s, oil prices began rising, but not yet so much as to render domestic industry irrelevant (this would happen later). This was starting to yield some handsome results for investors who had entered the Russian market when it hit bottom.

A KEY FIGURE among these investors was William Browder, grandson of a former head of the Communist Party USA, and his Russian wife. Browder was a true ideologue: he had come to Russia to build capitalism. He fervently believed that by making money for his investors, he was creating a bright capitalist future for a country it was his legacy to love.

Browder's investment strategy was straightforward and effective. He would buy a small but significant stake in a large company, such as the gas monopoly or an oil giant, conduct an investigation that inevitably exposed corporate malfeasance, and then launch a drive to reform the company. Corruption was pervasive and fairly easy to expose. Most large corporations were conglomerates of companies privatized within the last three to five years, with managers working at cross-purposes, often openly hostile to the new owners. So-called red directors had been stealing from their employers under the Soviets and saw no reason to stop; some of the new owners took a rape-and-pillage approach to their property. Browder's revelations met with various levels of resistance, but more often than not he was able to effect at least some changes. As a result, the value of stocks, which had invariably been purchased at rock-bottom prices, rose exponentially.

The new administration took an active interest in Browder's investigations. More than a few times his people were summoned to the Kremlin, where their PowerPoint presentations never failed to make an impression. Browder was certain he was on a roll. Every time he was able to secure another court or oversight-agency decision that would force another Russian company to pay a bit more attention to the law, a cheer would roll across the ostentatiously named Hermitage Fund offices. "The esprit de corps was like no other office that you've ever had," he told me wistfully years later, "because it's very rare that you could make money and do good at the same time." At its peak, the fund, which had started with $25 million worth of investments, had $4.5 billion invested in the Russian economy, making it the largest foreign investor in the country. Such was the extent of Browder's faith in his own strategy and in the country that even when Russia's richest man was arrested—*especially* when Russia's richest man was arrested—Browder let out one of his cheers: to him it indicated that the new president would stop at nothing to establish law and order.

THE RICHEST MAN in Russia was on tour. Mikhail Khodorkovsky, born in 1963, shared a key character trait with both Illarionov and Browder, one that made all three men extremely different from Putin and vulnerable to him: their behavior was driven by ideas. Khodorkovsky's parents, two Moscow engineers who spent their entire careers working at a measuring-instruments factory, had chosen to keep their own political skepticism from their only son. Theirs was a common dilemma: Speak your mind about the Soviet Union and risk making your child miserable with the constant need for doublethink and doublespeak, or aim to raise a contented conformist. The results of their efforts, however, far exceeded their expectations: they managed to rear a fervent Communist and Soviet patriot, a member of a species that had seemed all but extinct. After getting his degree in chemical engineering, Mikhail Khodorkovsky opted to work at the Komsomol committee. He had no hidden agenda, but in the middle to late 1980s this career choice positioned him well to take advantage of quasi-official and often extralegal opportunities to dabble in business. Before he was out of his mid-twenties, Khodorkovsky had tried his hand at trade, importing personal computers to the Soviet Union, and, more significant, at finance, devising ways to squeeze cash out of the Soviet planned-economy noncash behemoth. He served as an economic adviser to Yeltsin's first government when Russia was still part of the USSR. During the failed August 1991 coup, he was on the barricades in front of the Russian White House, physically helping to defend his government.

By the early 1990s, in other words, the former Komsomol functionary had been completely reformed. He and his friend and business partner, a former software engineer named Leonid Nevzlin, authored a book-length capitalist manifesto titled *Man with a Ruble*. "Lenin

aimed to annihilate the wealthy and wealth itself—and created a regime that outlawed the very possibility of becoming wealthy," they
wrote, exposing the ideology Khodorkovsky had once pledged to uphold. "Those who wanted to make more money were equated with
common criminals. It is time to stop living according to Lenin! Our
guiding light is Profit, acquired in a strictly legal way. Our lord is His
Majesty Money, for it is only He who can lead us to wealth as the norm
in life. It is time to abandon Utopia and give yourself over to Business,
which will make you rich!" By the time the book was published in
1992, Khodorkovsky had his own bank and, like other new entrepreneurs, was buying up privatization vouchers, aiming to take control
of several formerly state-owned companies.

In 1995–1996 the Russian government asked the country's richest men for loans, leveraging controlling shares in Russia's biggest
companies—which, according to the arrangement, they would be
keeping once the government, predictably, defaulted on the loans. As
a result, Khodorkovsky came into possession of Yukos, a newly created
oil conglomerate with reserves among the largest in the world.

His next change of heart came in 1998. The financial crisis that
year put Khodorkovsky's bank out of business. The oil company was
in dire straits: the price of oil on the world's markets was $8 a barrel
but Yukos's outmoded equipment placed the cost of producing one
barrel at $12. The company had no cash to pay its hundreds of thou-
sands of employees. "I would go to our oil rigs," Khodorkovsky wrote
more than ten years later, "and people would not even yell at me.
They were not going on strike: they were understanding. It's just that
they were fainting from hunger. Especially the young people who had
small children and did not have their own vegetable garden. And the
hospitals—before then, we used to buy medication, we would send
people to be treated elsewhere if they needed it, but now we did not
have the money. But the worst thing was these understanding faces.

People were just saying, 'We never expected anything good. We are just grateful you came here to talk to us. We'll be patient.'"

At the age of thirty-seven, one of Russia's richest men discovered the concept of social responsibility. In fact, he probably felt he invented it. It turned out that capitalism alone could make people not only rich and happy but also poor, hungry, miserable, and powerless. So Khodorkovsky resolved to build civil society in Russia. "Until that point," he wrote, "I saw business as a game. It was a game in which you wanted to win but losing was also an option. It was a game in which hundreds of thousands of people came to work in the morning to play with me. And in the evening they would go back to their own lives, which had nothing to do with me." It was a hugely ambitious goal—but, for one of the handful of men who felt they had created a market economy from scratch, not an absurdly ambitious one.

Khodorkovsky formed a foundation and called it Otkrytaya Rossiya, Open Russia. He funded Internet cafés in the provinces, to get people to learn and to talk to one another. He funded training for journalists all over the country, and he sponsored the most talented television journalists to come study in Moscow for a month. He founded a boarding school for disadvantaged children; following the tragedy in Beslan, several dozen survivors became students there. Before long, he was stepping in where Western foundations and governments were pulling out; Russia was considered a stable democracy now, after all. Some said he was funding more than half of all the nongovernmental organizations in Russia; some said he was funding 80 percent of them. In 2003, Yukos pledged to give $100 million over ten years to the Russian State University for the Humanities, the best liberal arts school in the country—the first time a private company in Russia had contributed a significant amount of money to an educational institution.

Khodorkovsky also became preoccupied with the idea of transforming his company into a properly managed, transparently governed corporation. He hired McKinsey & Company, the global management consulting giant, to reform the management structure, and Price-waterhouseCoopers, another world giant, to create the accounting structure from scratch. "Before Pricewaterhouse came along, all the Yukos accountants knew how to do was stomp their feet and steal a bit at a time," Khodorkovsky's former tax lawyer told me. "They had to be taught everything." His partners grumbled—Khodorkovsky's efforts seemed to be misplaced—but he was determined to turn Yukos into the first Russian multinational corporation. To this end, he hired a Washington, D.C.–based public relations firm. "We would set up five interviews in New York, and we would spend the day going from interview to interview," the consultant who worked with him remembered. "Not many CEOs would spend this kind of time. We got a *Fortune* cover story. He was a poster boy for what people hoped would happen in Russia." The capitalization of Yukos grew exponentially, owing only in part to the growing price of oil, in part to newly modernized drilling and refining systems, which drastically reduced the cost of production, and in part to the new transparency. Khodorkovsky was the richest man in Russia, clearly on his way to becoming the richest man in the world.

On July 2, 2003, Platon Lebedev, the chairman of the board of Yukos's parent company, Group Menatep, was arrested. Several weeks later, Yukos's head of security, a former KGB officer, was behind bars. Khodorkovsky himself was told by those in the know and those who could simply follow the obvious logic of events that he, too, would be arrested soon. Someone even wrote up a prescription for Khodor-kovsky of things to do to avoid arrest; the document, commissioned by one of his public-relations people, was never seen by Khodor-kovsky because another of his publicity men ripped it up in outrage. In any case, it was obvious what Khodorkovsky should do: leave the country. His partner and coauthor with him of *Man with a Ruble*,

Leonid Nevzlin, did just that: he moved to Israel. Khodorkovsky went to the United States briefly but returned—and went on tour.

There was a talk Khodorkovsky had been giving for a bit over a year at this point. I had heard it once when he addressed a group of young writers, assembled at his request. The point of the speech was that Russia should join the modern world: stop running its companies like medieval fiefdoms at best and prisons at worst; transform its economy into one based on the export of knowledge and expertise rather than oil and gas; value its smart, educated people—like us writers—and pay them well. Khodorkovsky was not a great public speaker: he tended to be stiff, and his voice was soft and incongruously high for a man of his height, his looks, and his wealth. But he had the force of conviction and the weight of his reputation on his side; people generally wanted to know what he wanted to say to them.

So instead of leaving the country or genuflecting before Putin—for this was precisely the advice the ripped-up paper had contained—Khodorkovsky decided to create his own lecture circuit. He hired Marina Litvinovich, Putin's former image-maker, to coach him on public speaking. She told him he had a way of belaboring an idea even after the audience had come over to his side, and this caused him to lose his tempo. Khodorkovsky, a few assistants, and eight bodyguards commenced several months of living out of a chartered jet. He went around the country speaking to students, workers, even military recruits on one occasion (though that engagement seems to have been an organizers' error). Litvinovich sat in the front row with a letter-size piece of paper with the word "Tempo" written on it; whenever Russia's richest man perseverated, she held up the sign for him to see.

Over the weekend of October 18, 2003, the Khodorkovsky team was in Saratov, a city on the Volga River. It snowed and, unusual for that time of year, the snow stayed on the ground. For some reason no one quite understood or at least no one articulated, the entire group went outside and wandered in the vast white expanse. They then returned to their hotel, Khodorkovsky abruptly bade everyone good night and disappeared, and the rest of the group got quickly and morbidly drunk. The next morning Khodorkovsky told Litvinovich to return to Moscow: she had not seen her three-year-old son in weeks, and Khodorkovsky could manage the next destination without her.

The phone calls came in the dark predawn hours of October 25: Khodorkovsky had been arrested at the Novosibirsk airport at eight in the morning, five in Moscow. *So that's why he sent me home*, thought Litvinovich. Anton Drel, Khodorkovsky's personal lawyer, got a cryptic message through a third party: "Mr. Khodorkovsky requested that you be informed that he has been arrested. He said you would know what to do." *Typical Khodorkovsky*, thought Drel, who had no idea what to do. In the late morning, he received another phone call: "This is Mikhail Khodorkovsky. Would it be convenient for you to come to the prosecutor general's office now?" he asked with trademark formality; he had already been transported to Moscow. Several hours later, Khodorkovsky was indicted on six charges, including fraud and tax evasion.

EIGHTEEN MONTHS LATER. Khodorkovsky would be found guilty not on six but on seven counts and sentenced to nine years in a prison colony. Long before that sentence was up, he would be indicted on a new set of charges and then sentenced again, this time to fourteen years behind bars. Lebedev, the former chairman of his board, would stand trial alongside Khodorkovsky both times. Other Yukos affiliates, including the former head of security, lawyers, and a variety of managers not only at Yukos but at several subsidiaries, would face other charges and similarly harsh sentences; dozens of others would flee the country. Eventually, even Amnesty International, openly reluctant at first to take on the case of a billionaire, would declare Khodorkovsky and Lebedev prisoners of conscience. No one—not even his jailers, it seemed—would doubt, after a certain point, that he was unfairly imprisoned, but even eight years after his arrest no one would be quite certain what exactly Khodorkovsky had done that had cost him his freedom and his fortune.

Khodorkovsky himself and many of his staff believed that he was being punished for speaking out about corruption. In February 2003, Putin had gathered Russia's wealthiest businessmen for a rare discussion that was open to the media. Khodorkovsky arrived with a Power-Point presentation that consisted of eight simple slides containing facts that all of those present certainly knew and just as certainly tried to pretend they did not know. Slide six was titled "Corruption Costs the Russian Economy over $30 Billion a Year" and cited four different studies that had arrived at more or less the same figure. Slide eight was titled "The Shaping of a New Generation" and contained a chart comparing three different institutions of higher learning: one that graduated oil-industry managers, one that trained tax inspectors, and one that prepared civil servants. Competition to get into the last college reached almost eleven persons per spot, aspiring tax inspectors had to beat out as many as four competitors, while future oil-industry managers had to fight fewer than two other people—even though official starting salaries in the oil industry were two to three times those in the government sector. These, Khodorkovsky indicated, were just the official figures; high school students were making their career plans counting on income from corruption.

When he was speaking, Khodorkovsky also mentioned the recent merger of the state-owned oil giant Rosneft with a smaller, privately held oil company. "Everyone thinks the deal had, shall we say, a second layer," said Khodorkovsky, alluding to the glaringly high price Rosneft had paid. "The president of Rosneft is here—perhaps he'd like to comment." The president of Rosneft did not care to comment, and this looked very much like an embarrassing and public admission of guilt.

The person who responded to Khodorkovsky was Putin himself. He got the same smirk on his face with which, at the press
conference a few months earlier, he had suggested that the French
journalist be castrated—the facial expression that indicated he was
having difficulty containing his anger. "Some companies, including
Yukos, have extraordinary reserves. The question is: How did the
company get them?" he asked, shifting in his chair to raise his right
shoulder in a gesture that made him seem bigger and smiling a thuggish smile that made it plain this was a threat, not a question. "And
your company had its own issues with taxes. To give the Yukos leadership its due, it found a way to settle everything and take care of all
its problems with the state. But maybe this is the reason there is such
competition to get into the tax academy?" In other words, Putin accused Khodorkovsky of having bribed tax inspectors and threatened
a takeover of his company.

Then there was the school of thought that the reason for Khodorkovsky's trouble was politics: he meddled too much. He made donations to political parties, including the Communists. Immediately
following Lebedev's arrest in July, Khodorkovsky asked Prime Minister Kasyanov, with whom he had a distant but genial relationship, to
find out what had happened. "It took three or four attempts," Kasyanov told me. "Putin kept saying that the prosecutor's office knew what
it was doing. But finally he told me that Yukos had been financing
political parties, not just the [small liberal parties], which Putin had
given him permission to finance, but also the Communists, which he
did not allow him to fund." Eight years later, Nevzlin—the Yukos
partner who left the country—maintained that the company's donations to the Communist Party had "of course" been cleared by the
Kremlin. Some people in Khodorkovsky's circle took to calling the
party-financing situation "the double-cross cross," believing Khodorkovsky had been set up by someone close enough to Putin to tell

Khodorkovsky—falsely—that his funding the Communists had been cleared. All these discussions were taking place in the lead-up to the December 2003 parliamentary election—the one after which *The New York Times* reported that Russia was "inching toward democracy."

A third group of observers had the simplest of all explanations for Khodorkovsky's fate. "He did not go to prison for tax evasion or stealing oil, for God's sake," Illarionov said to me seven and a half years after the arrest. "He went to prison because he was—and remains—an independent human being. Because he refused to bend. Because he remained a free man. This state punishes people for being independent."

But in October 2003, when news of the arrest broke, its darkly absurd nature was far from obvious to everyone. William Browder, for one, applauded the arrest. In an op-ed piece published in the English-language daily *The Moscow Times* and distributed to investors, he wrote, "We should . . . fully support [Putin] in his task of taking back control of the country from the oligarchs."

ON NOVEMBER 13, 2005, Browder was returning to Moscow from London. He had been living in Russia for nine years, and though he spoke no Russian, he felt as much at home in Moscow as anyone could. His money guaranteed a level of comfort familiar to the very wealthy in oil-producing countries: he traveled on a luxurious separate track from the moment he landed in Moscow, where he would be whisked through airport formalities and picked up by his driver, a former police officer who retained his badge, which made him king on the lawless roads of Moscow. But this time Browder found himself stuck in the airport's VIP lounge: his passport was apparently held up at the border. A couple of hours later, he landed in the detention area of the airport, a blank room with cold plastic chairs and several other detainees, each a prisoner of his own uncertain fate. Fifteen hours after arriving, Browder was put on a flight back to London: his Russian visa had been revoked.

Surely this was a massive misunderstanding. Browder called the cabinet ministers and the Kremlin staffers who had liked his Power-Point presentations so much. They were vague, evasive, noncommittal. After several phone calls, it began to sink in that his visa issues would not be resolved anytime soon. For all his faith in Putin's best intentions, one thing Browder knew for certain was that no business should be left unattended in Russia. He began moving his operation to London. The analysts moved; the fund divested itself of $4.5 billion worth of stock in Russian companies, without anyone's seeming to notice. By the end of the summer of 2006, the Hermitage Fund's Russian companies were empty shells with a small office in Moscow occasionally visited by the company's secretary.

She was there, along with a staff member visiting from London, when twenty-five tax police officers descended on the office and turned it upside down. Soon the same number of officers, led by the same colonel who had run the first raid, appeared at the offices of the Hermitage Fund's law firm, apparently looking for stamps, seals, and certificates for three holding companies through which the Hermitage Fund had managed its investments. When a lawyer objected that they lacked the appropriate search warrants, he was taken to a conference room and beaten there.

Four months later, Browder was notified of multimillion-dollar judgments against his companies issued by a court in St. Petersburg. Put on notice by his visa annulment, frightened by the tax police raids, he was now downright terrified by a sequence of events for which there could no be reasonable explanation. Why would the tax police need registration papers, seals, and stamps for empty shell companies? How could there be judgments against these companies if their representatives had not even known of any lawsuits or court hearings? Browder asked his Moscow lawyers to investigate.

It was not a lawyer but a young accountant who, after more than a year of sleuthing, finally reconstructed an absurd, barely believable, but nonetheless logical sequence of events. The three empty shell companies, Sergei Magnitsky discovered, had been re-registered in the names of other people, all of them convicted felons. Then the companies had been sued by other companies, which produced contracts supposedly showing that the stolen companies owed them money. Three different courts in three different Russian cities held speedy hearings and issued judgments against Browder's former companies totaling a billion dollars, which just happened to be exactly the amount of profit the three companies had reported in the previous tax year. Then the companies' new owners filed claims with the tax authority, requesting a refund of all the taxes they had paid: they appeared to qualify for it because, on paper, the companies no longer had a profit. The refunds, totaling $230 million, were processed in a single day in December 2007; they were transferred to the companies' new owners and disappeared from the Russian banking system.

It appeared Magnitsky had uncovered an embezzlement scheme that involved the tax authority as well as the courts in at least three cities: had the judges not been in on the deal, they would hardly have rubber-stamped judgments with such ease and speed. Nor would the tax authority have processed the refund so fast—or at all, considering that Browder's lawyers had already filed six different complaints alleging the theft of his companies—had the entire scheme not been orchestrated at or near the top of the agency.

Browder, ever the ideologue, saw an opening. By now he believed that his own banishment from Russia had come from the very top: even if he still did not know the exact reason, he could believe that someone whose toes he had stepped on could have conspired to convince the president or someone very close to him that Browder was an undesirable. But now Browder had a chance to save Russia all over again. "There is no way the president of the country could allow $230 million of the country's money to be stolen," he reasoned. "I mean, the tax crime is so cynical. If you made a move about it, people would say it's just too far-fetched. We expected SWAT teams and helicopters to swoop down from the sky and get all the bad guys."

Magnitsky wrote fifteen different complaints aimed at exposing the embezzlement and starting an investigation. But instead of SWAT teams swooping down from the sky, criminal probes came raining down on lawyers Browder had engaged. Seven attorneys at four different law firms received notice that they were being investigated on various criminal charges. At this point Browder knew enough to offer all of his lawyers refuge in Great Britain. "You know, I was trained as a financial analyst," he told me a couple of years later, in part by way of explaining how difficult the process had been for him, in part by way of justifying why it took him so long to realize the full gravity of the situation. "I wasn't a soldier. I wasn't trained that people would be putting their lives at risk. And I went to every single one of our lawyers and I said, 'I am truly sorry that this has happened. It was not my intention to have put you in physical harm and it is not my intention to leave you in physical harm and I want you to leave Russia at my expense, and come to London at my expense, and stay in London at my expense.' It wasn't an easy conversation to have with any of these guys. They were all in their forties, at the top of their careers, some of them didn't speak a word of English. And I was asking them to give up their lives, their professions, their whole community, to go into exile at a moment's notice to protect themselves from danger."

Six of the seven lawyers accepted Browder's offer and moved to London. The one who refused was Sergei Magnitsky, the accountant, at thirty-six the youngest of the group—which was how Browder explained his refusal to himself: "Sergei was from a generation who thought that Russia was changing. There was a new Russia, maybe an imperfect Russia, but a getting-better Russia. The basic fundamental principles of law and justice existed—that was his premise. He said, 'This is not 1937. I've done nothing wrong and I know the law. There's no legal means that they could come and arrest me.'"

On November 24, 2008, Sergei Magnitsky was arrested in connection with the very embezzlement scheme he had tried to expose. Like his client three years earlier, he was certain at first that it was a misunderstanding that would soon be cleared up with the help of his lawyers. At his first court hearing, he argued he should be released, among other reasons, because his young son was ill with the flu; he was clearly certain his ordeal would be over in a matter of days. Not only was he not released, however, but the conditions in which he was held deteriorated steadily as he was shuttled back and forth between two Moscow jails. He was not allowed to see his wife or mother. His became ill and was consistently denied the medical care he required. On November 16, 2009, Sergei Magnitsky died in prison at the age of thirty-seven.

After his death, the prison released to his family his notebooks, in which Magnitsky had meticulously copied every complaint, appeal, and request he wrote: once he realized that his arrest was no misunderstanding, he had waged a fierce one-sided battle, writing 450 documents in his 358 days in jail. He created an encyclopedia of the abuse he had suffered. He described the overcrowded cells in which he was reduced to eating and writing while sitting on his cot. In one of the cells, the glass in the windowpanes was missing and temperatures inside hovered around freezing. In another, the toilet— or, rather, the hole in the floor that served as the toilet—overflowed, flooding the room with sewage. He described being systematically denied hot meals and, often, any food at all for days on end. Most egregiously, he was denied medical attention even as his chronic abdominal pain grew so severe he could not sleep, even as he wrote letters documenting his symptoms and spelling out his legal rights regarding health care. He died of peritonitis.

Browder and his investment fund staff were finally fated to become soldiers. They launched a highly visible, vocal, and effective campaign they called Justice for Sergei Magnitsky. They collected copious evidence against the people who had been connected to the jailing and torture of their colleague and against those involved in the embezzlement scheme he had uncovered. Within a few months, bills that would require visa bans and freeze any local assets of these officials were pending in the U.S. Congress, the European Parliament, and parliaments of European Union member states.

BY THIS TIME, the dominant Russia story had finally changed in the U.S. media. It had taken most of Putin's second term in office to transform the narrative: "emerging democracy" slowly gave way to "authoritarian tendencies," which gradually yielded to a picture of what had become for all intents a criminal tyranny. Back in 2003, when Khodorkovsky attempted to talk to Putin about corruption, the global organization Transparency International ranked Russia as more corrupt than 64 percent of the world's countries: in its annual rating it looked slightly more corrupt than Mozambique and marginally less corrupt than Algeria. In its 2010 report, the organization showed Russia as more corrupt than 86 percent of the world: it now fit in between Papua New Guinea and Tajikistan.

Russia finally lost its bona fides in the eyes of international business and media. Browder was spending his time criticizing the Russian regime not only in the world's parliaments but also at forums such as the annual big-business gathering in Davos, Switzerland. Andrei Illarionov had resigned his post. "Everyone had their own turning point," he explained to me. "Mine was Beslan. That was when I realized it was a modus operandi. There was the real possibility of saving lives, and he [Putin] opted instead for the killing of innocent people, the killing of the hostages. I mean, I was at work, and I could watch and listen, and I could see it all clearly close up. I could see that if the standoff continued for at least a few more hours, lives would be saved, all of them or most of them. There would be no attack and the children and their parents and their teachers would be saved. And if this was the case, then there could be only one explanation for storming the school building when they did. It all became clear to me that day, September 3, 2004."

Illarionov resigned his position as sherpa—Putin's personal representative—to the Group of Eight; winning Russia's full membership in the G8 had been one of Illarionov's main accomplishments. "Being an adviser is one thing," he explained. "Being an adviser is being an adviser: it's an important post, but it's not the same thing as personally representing someone. And I told my employer that under the circumstances I could no longer function as his personal representative."

Six months later, Illarionov resigned his job as the president's adviser as well. "It had just become ridiculous. No one was heeding my advice on the economy or on anything else. The train of the Russian state was moving full speed ahead on a completely different set of rails." He proceeded to write a series of scathing articles defining this "different set of rails." Russia, he wrote, had become the opposite of a liberal economy: an unfree, warmongering state ruled by a corporate group. Like Browder, Illarionov became a tireless and vocal roaming critic of the Putin regime.

Mikhail Kasyanov, the prime minister, had also left. His turning point came when Khodorkovsky was arrested. "There had been signs before," he told me. "There was the television takeover and the handling of the theater hostage crisis—these were all signs—but I did not think this was a plan. I thought these were mistakes that could be corrected. And I kept thinking this way right up until the point when Lebedev and Khodorkovsky were arrested. This was when I realized these were not accidental mistakes—this was policy, this was his general understanding of life."

Kasyanov had conscientiously observed Putin's request that he stay "off his turf"— meaning out of politics—so conscientiously, in fact, that he had willfully blinded himself to the political life of the country. So, in the summer of 2003, when Putin told him that the prosecution of Lebedev and Khodorkovsky was their punishment for donating funds to the Communist Party, Kasyanov was shocked. "I could not believe something that was legal required special permission from the Kremlin." The conflict between Putin and his premier quickly became public: Kasyanov openly criticized the arrests, calling them an unwarranted and extreme measure. It was clear Putin would not keep this outspoken premier around for his second term, but the president's patience seemed to run out early: in February 2004, a month before the election, he fired his cabinet.

After firing Kasyanov, Putin planned to keep him on in a less public position. He made him three job offers, each more insistent than the last: there was the option of heading the security council or running a new state-affiliated bank venture, an offer Putin made twice. When Kasyanov finally said no, his former employer's tone turned from seductive to menacing. "I was already at the door when he said, 'Mikhail Mikhailovich, if you ever have a problem with the tax police, you may ask for help, but make sure you come to me personally." Kasyanov interpreted Putin's parting words as both a threat and an offer to keep a door open. Tax trouble duly began: Kasyanov's consulting company, which he formed right after losing his job, was audited. Kasyanov chose not to seek help, which meant not only that the tax audit dragged on for two years (the two sides finally managed to settle on an extremely minor violation, improperly entering in the books a box of writing paper), but also that Kasyanov became persona non grata in Russian politics. In the years following his firing, he tried to run for office and register a political party—reportedly even managing to collect the absurdly high number of signatures required—but his papers were consistently turned away by the registration authorities. With no access to television or large newspapers, Kasyanov went from mainstream to marginal as fast as any politician ever had.

THE KHODORKOVSKY CASE came to trial in mid-2004 and dragged on for ten months, despite the fact that nearly all motions by the defense were denied, drastically cutting the number of witnesses and cross-examinations at Moscow's Basmanny Court. As the verdict neared, Igor Shuvalov, a lawyer and a newly prominent assistant to Putin, said, "The Yukos case was a show trial intended as an example for other companies using various schemes for minimizing their tax burden. If it hadn't been Yukos, it would have been another company." Even the Moscow press corps, used to writing about some of the most cynical politicians on the planet, were shocked by the open use of Stalin-era language to mean more or less exactly what Stalin had meant: that the courts existed to do the bidding of the head of state and dole out punishment as he saw fit to those he saw fit to punish.

In fact, only two of the seven charges against Khodorkovsky concerned alleged tax evasion, and what happened in the Moscow court was more show than trial. The defense called few of its witnesses— not only because the court turned down so many of its motions but also because the prosecution's case seemed so flimsy it hardly warranted a full-force defense, especially since testifying for the defense seemed to incur considerable risk. Ten Yukos affiliates, including two lawyers—both of them women—had already been arrested, and nine more evaded arrest by fleeing the country; soon these numbers would seem quite small, as dozens of people would be in prison and hundreds on the run.

Finding itself in the middle of a Kafkaesque trial, the defense adopted a pointedly understated style. In his final arguments, Genrikh Padva, Khodorkovsky's lead attorney and possibly the country's most famous defense lawyer, sounded more like a schoolteacher than the passionate participant in a judicial contest. Over the course of three days of hearings, Padva read his arguments, methodically listing all of the prosecution's errors, aiming to show that the prosecutors failed to supply any documents even proving that the defendants were in any way involved with some of the companies listed in the charges, much less actually guilty of the crimes. "And I won't even mention the fact that the charges are filed in accordance with laws that went into effect years after these supposed deeds took place," was a typical Padva aside. His tone conveyed that he entertained no illusions about his ability to convince the judges of anything, but in the interests of history and future appeals to international judicial bodies, he needed to get all his arguments on record. The judges, three overweight women around forty, each sporting a shiny helmet of combed-back hair, sat still, their lips pursed in identical demonstrations of displeasure. Their demeanor seemed meant to say: The decision has long been made, and your insistence on procedure and proper discussion is an offensive waste of everyone's time.

Khodorkovsky and Lebedev were each sentenced to nine years in a prison colony; three months later, an appeals court cut a year off the sentences. The men were shipped off to different colonies, each as faraway and difficult to get to as a colony could be. To visit their client, Khodorkovsky's lawyers had to travel nine hours by plane and another fifteen hours by train. Russian law mandated placing convicts in prisons within easy travel distance of their homes—so the law had to be changed, retroactively, to accommodate the Khodorkovsky case.

For six months following his arrest, Khodorkovsky tried to run his company from jail. Finally realizing this was untenable, he signed his shares over to Nevzlin, the partner who had moved to Israel. But the company, bombarded with tax liens and lawsuits, its assets inside Russia long since seized by the state, was cracking. Within a year of Khodorkovsky's arrest, Russia's largest and most successful oil company, which had once paid 5 percent of all the taxes collected by the federal government, was facing bankruptcy proceedings. Its most attractive asset, a company called Yuganskneftegaz, owner of some of Europe's largest oil reserves, was up for auction. The state gas monopoly, now run by Putin's former deputy in St. Petersburg, looked poised to win the auction. To prevent the deal, Yukos's lawyers filed for bankruptcy in a Texas court and then sought a staying order on the sale of the company there; Gazprom, the Russian company, certainly was not going to listen to an American court on this matter, but it so happened it planned to buy Yuganskneftegaz with funds borrowed from American and West European banks. The financing was pulled and it looked, briefly, like the takeover might be temporarily averted—when a newly registered company called Baikalfinansgrup appeared out of nowhere to register for the auction. Journalists immediately descended on its registration address in Tver, a godforsaken town about three hours outside Moscow; it turned out to be a small building that was used as a legal address by 150 companies, none of which appeared to have any physical assets.

Nor did Baikalfinansgrup have financial assets. According to its registration documents, filed two weeks before the auction, its capitalization was ten thousand rubles, or roughly $300. But somehow the state-owned oil company Rosneft—the one whose president had declined to respond to Khodorkovsky's questions about perceived corruption a year earlier—lent the unheard-of company more than $9 billion to buy Yuganskneftegaz; this was less than half the company's estimated worth at the time. The auction, held on December 19, 2004, lasted all of two minutes.

Speaking in Germany two days after the auction, Putin bristled at the suggestion that Yukos assets had been bought by an unknown entity. "I know the stockholders of the company, and they are individuals," he said. "They are individuals who have been working in the energy sector for a long time." Another two days later, Rosneft, the state oil company, bought Baikalfinansgrup, taking control of the Yukos assets—but also ensuring that it could never be sued for having purchased it in the course of a rigged auction.

It had been just over a year since Khodorkovsky's arrest, and it was now clear Russia had passed two milestones. With the country's former richest man behind bars indefinitely, no one, not even the rich and powerful, could afford free agency. And with the assets of the country's largest private company hijacked in broad daylight, Putin had claimed his place as the godfather of a mafia clan ruling the country. Like all mafia bosses, he barely distinguished between his personal property, the property of his clan, and the property of those beholden to his clan. Like all mafia bosses, he amassed wealth by outright robberies, as with Yukos, by collecting so-called dues and by placing his cronies wherever there was money or assets to be siphoned off. By the end of 2007, at least one Russian political expert—someone believed to have access to the Kremlin—estimated Putin's personal net worth at $40 billion.

THE $40 BILLION FIGURE can be neither confirmed nor disproved, but there was one story I was able to report in detail. It shed light not only on the scale of Putin's personal fortune but also on the mechanics of amassing it. It took my good reportorial luck and one very brave man to tell it.

In the early 1990s, Sergei Kolesnikov had been one of hundreds of Soviet scientists turned Russian entrepreneurs. A Ph.D. in biophysics, he started out manufacturing medical equipment and then began importing it. During the Sobchak administration, he formed a joint venture with the city and created a successful business outfitting St. Petersburg's clinics and hospitals. After Sobchak was voted out of office, he bought out the city's share and took the company private, staying in the same line of business.

As soon as Putin was elected president, Kolesnikov was contacted by an old business associate from his St. Petersburg days. He outlined a scheme: some of Russia's wealthiest men would donate significant sums of money earmarked toward purchasing medical equipment for Russian facilities. Kolesnikov would use his expertise to procure the equipment at significant volume discounts. The difference between the list price of equipment, which would be reported to the donor, and actual money spent had to be no less than 35 percent; if Kolesnikov obtained an even greater discount, he could keep the difference as profit. The 35 percent had to be deposited in a bank account set up in Western Europe and would later be used to invest in the Russian economy.

Kolesnikov had no qualms about agreeing to the scheme. Like Browder, he thought he was living well while doing good for Russia: the much-needed medical equipment was an unquestionable good; on top of that, his new partners would be investing large amounts of money into the Russian economy. Sure, they were skimming off the top—more than a third of the money donated—but they were investing it in Russia, not lining their own pockets. And also, "we knew this was not money made by backbreaking labor. You can't come by that kind of money honestly."

The first donor was Roman Abramovich, a secretive Russian oligarch, and future owner of the Chelsea Football Club. He donated $203 million, of which about $140 million bought equipment for the Military Medical Academy in St. Petersburg (run by Putin's friend the minister of health, who had once helped ferry Sobchak out of the prosecutor's office and out of Russia) and over $60 million stayed in a European bank account. His donation was followed by a number of smaller ones. By 2005, about $200 million had accumulated in this bank account. Kolesnikov and his two partners—one had started out with him in St. Petersburg and the other had brought him into this new line of business—formed a new company called Rosinvest, a wholly owned subsidiary of a Swiss company, which did business through a third company, also Swiss, ownership of which was fixed in bearer shares. In other words, whoever was in physical possession of the papers was the legal owner. Each of the three men got 2 percent of the shares; the remaining 94 percent was handed over to Putin himself.

The newly formed company had sixteen different investment projects, mostly in industrial production; they were well chosen, naturally afforded a variety of tax and legal benefits, and brought a handsome profit—94 percent of which belonged to Putin. All along, there was also what Kolesnikov thought of as a small personal project of Putin's, a house on the Black Sea budgeted at $16 million. "But things kept getting added," Kolesnikov told me. "An elevator to the beach, a marina, a separate high-voltage line, a separate gas pipeline, three new motorways that led directly to the palace, and three helicopter pads. The building itself was changing, too: an amphitheater was added, then a winter theater. And then it all had to be decorated too: furniture, artwork, silverware. It's all very expensive!" Kolesnikov traveled to the Black Sea coast twice a year to monitor the project; last time he was there, in the spring of 2009, what had been a house had become twenty buildings, and the total budget had long since passed the billion-dollar mark.

Something else had happened a few months earlier. In the aftermath of the world financial crisis, Kolesnikov's partner informed him that Rosinvest would no longer be making investments: its only purpose now was the completion of the Black Sea palace. Kolesnikov, who had not exactly been a stickler for legalities but had been very proud of his work and sincerely convinced that he was creating wealth for his country, was deeply offended. He fled Russia, taking the company's documentation with him, and paid a Washington law firm a considerable sum of money to review the papers and verify his story. And then he went public with the story of what became known as Putin's Palace. But the story, while it attracted a fair amount of attention when I wrote about it in Russia, drew little reaction from the government: first Putin's press secretary dismissed it as rubbish and then, when copies of some building contracts were published by *Nevaya Gazeta*, the Kremlin confirmed that the Black Sea project existed.

IT WOULD BE fair to assume that the palace scheme was just one of many similar schemes for squeezing wealth out of Russia. The question is: What is the nature, the motivating principle, behind these schemes? In other words, the question is, once again: Who is Mr. Putin?

There is the story of Putin the bureaucrat who did not take bribes—a key narrative that explains Boris Berezovsky's attraction to him, which, in turn, was key to making Putin president. Berezovsky's right-hand man, Yuli Dubov, who had long since become one of the London exiles, told me one of the most striking of the upstanding-Putin stories. Once, in the early 1990s, Dubov was having trouble with some of the documentation for the car service station Berezovsky was opening in St. Petersburg. He needed Putin to make a phone call to facilitate the process, and to this end he scheduled lunch with him. Dubov arrived at city hall early, as, uncharacteristically, did Putin. As they both waited for their appointed time to be able to leave for lunch, Dubov broached the subject of the phone call. Putin immediately took care of the matter, but then refused to go to lunch: "Either you have me help you with your business, or you take me to lunch," Dubov remembered him saying. This was clearly not just a bureaucrat who did not take bribes: this was a bureaucrat whose entire identity rested on his incorruptibility.

And then there was the Putin on whose guard $100 million worth of contracts evaporated, as Marina Salye documented. The remarkable part of this story is not the occurrence of theft—it is abundantly clear that some theft occurred absolutely everywhere in Russia in those days and in similar situations, which was the reason Salye's revelations never gained momentum—but that *all* the funds appear to have been stolen. I suspect that if Putin had shaved off only 5, 10, 20, even 30 percent, he would not have created an enemy for life, as he did with Salye—just as Kolesnikov would not have waged his campaign had the palace stayed merely a very expensive side project.

But it is as if Putin could not resist taking it all. And I think this is literally true. On several occasions, at least one of them embarrassingly public, Putin has acted like a person afflicted with kleptomania. In June 2005, while hosting a group of American businessmen in St. Petersburg, Putin pocketed the 124-diamond Super Bowl ring of New England Patriots owner Robert Kraft. He had asked to see it, tried it on, allegedly said, "I could kill someone with this," then stuck it in his pocket and left the room abruptly. After a flurry of articles in the U.S. press, Kraft announced a few days later that the ring had been a gift—preventing an uncomfortable situation from spiraling out of control.

In September 2005, Putin was a special guest at New York's Solomon R. Guggenheim Museum. At one point his hosts brought out a conversation piece that another Russian guest must have given the museum: a glass replica of a Kalashnikov automatic weapon filled with vodka. This gaudy souvenir costs about $300 in Moscow. Putin nodded to one of his bodyguards, who took the glass Kalashnikov and carried it out of the room, leaving the hosts speechless.

Putin's extraordinary relationship to material wealth was evident when he was a college student, if not earlier. When he accepted the car his parents won in a lottery, though the prize could have been used to greatly improve the family's living conditions, or when he spent almost all the money he made over the summer to buy himself an outrageously expensive coat—and bought a cake for his mother—he was acting in ways highly unusual and borderline unacceptable for a young man of his generation and social group. Ostentatious displays of wealth could easily have derailed his plans for a KGB career, and he knew this. The story told by the former West German radical—of Putin demanding gifts while in Dresden—completes the picture. For a man who had staked most of his social capital on conforming to the norm, this was particularly remarkable behavior: it seems he really could not help himself.

The correct term is probably not the popularly known *kleptomania*, which refers to a pathological desire to possess things for which one has little use, but the more exotic *pleonexia*, the insatiable desire to have what rightfully belongs to others. If Putin suffers this irrepressible urge, this helps explain his apparent split personality: he compensates for his compulsion by creating the identity of an honest and incorruptible civil servant.

Andrei Illarionov discovered this less than a month after becoming Putin's economic adviser: just days after his inauguration, Putin signed a decree consolidating 70 percent of the country's alcohol manufacturers in a single company and appointing a close St. Petersburg associate to run it. At the time, oil prices had not yet taken off and alcohol was arguably the country's most lucrative business. As Illarionov found out, no one on the new president's economic team had been consulted about or even informed of the decision. Over the next few months, Illarionov would grow accustomed to this: Putin continued to talk a good economic line to the public and the media, and continued to appear to listen to his sterling team of liberal advisers, while consistently broadsiding them with decisions that consolidated all of the country's resources in the hands of his cronies.

Is this what happened with Khodorkovsky? Did Putin have him arrested because he wanted to take possession of his company rather than for reasons of political and personal competition? Not exactly. He put Khodorkovsky behind bars for the same reason that he abolished elections or had Litvinenko killed: in his continuing attempt to turn the country into a supersize model of the KGB, there can be no room for dissidents or even for independent actors. But then, independent actors are inconvenient in part because they refuse to accept the rules of the mafia. And once Khodorkovsky was behind bars, the opportunity to rob him presented itself. In seizing this opportunity, Putin, as usual, failed to distinguish between himself and the state he ruled. Greed may not be his main instinct, but it is the one he can never resist.

Eleven

BACK TO THE USSR

O n October 2, 2011, Boris Berezovsky was jumping around his office excitedly. I was in London to cover a trial he had initiated in an attempt to recover some of his assets more than ten years after he became an exile, and he had asked me to come to his office the Sunday before hearings started, to reveal to me what he was thinking about the Russian political situation.

"You understand?" he began. "The Russian regime has no ideology, no party, no politics—it is nothing but the power of a single man." He was painting a picture of a Wizard of Oz figure, clearly feeling no need to acknowledge that he had invented the man. "All someone has to do is discredit him—him personally." Berezovsky even had a plan, or a couple of plans—but here I was sworn to secrecy.

I went away amused at the man who would not give up being kingmaker, yet I had to admit Berezovsky's analysis was correct. The whole edifice of the Russian regime—which, in the eyes of the world, had long since graduated from showing "authoritarian tendencies" to full-fledged authoritarianism bordering on tyranny—rested on this one man, the one Berezovsky thought he had chosen for the country a dozen years earlier. This meant the current Russian regime was essentially vulnerable: the person or persons to topple it would not have to overcome the force of an ingrained ideology—they would merely have to show that the tyrant had feet of clay. It also meant the tipping point in Russia was as unpredictable as in any tyranny—it could come about in months, years, or decades, triggered perhaps by a small event, most likely the regime's own mistake that would suddenly make its vulnerability evident.

I had seen something like this happen in Yugoslavia eleven years earlier: Slobodan Milošević, who had held on to power using terror on the one hand and exploiting nationalist fervor on the other, called an early election, mistakenly certain that he would win—and lost, and understood that he was losing too late to quash the rising wave of protest. And in 2011, we had seen Arab dictators drop like dominoes, toppled by crowds made suddenly fearless by the power of the word and the example of others. The problem with Russia, however, was that the huge country was as atomized as it had ever been. Putin's policies had effectively destroyed public space. The Internet had developed in Russia over the last ten years, as it had in other countries, but it took on the peculiar shape of a series of information bubbles. American researchers who "mapped" the world's blogospheres found that unlike the American blogosphere—or, for that matter, the Iranian one—which formed a series of interlocking circles, the Russian blogosphere consisted of discrete circles, each unconnected to any other. It was an anti-utopia of the information age: an infinite number of echo chambers. Nor was this true just of the Internet. The Kremlin was watching its own TV; big business was reading its own newspapers; the intelligentsia was reading its own blogs. None of these groups was aware of the others' realities, and this made mass protest of any sort seem unlikely.

IN THE 2000 ELECTION, Putin got almost 53 percent of the vote, while his ten opponents each garnered between 1 and 29 percent. When he ran for reelection in 2004, he had 71 percent—a typical authoritarian-regime result—and his five opponents received between 0.75 and 14 percent apiece. As Putin's second term was drawing to a close in 2007, the politicized classes in Russia wondered what would happen. Would Putin change the constitution to allow himself more than two con-secutive terms? Would he go the Yeltsin route and direct the country to vote for a handpicked successor? For a time, Putin seemed to be favoring Defense Minister Sergei Ivanov, a former KGB colleague. But in December of that year, Putin held a televised meeting with the leaders of four puppet parties, who together declared they wanted to nominate First Deputy Prime Minister Dmitry Medvedev for presi-dent. Medvedev just happened to be present for this well-scripted watershed event. In the election that followed, in March 2008, he garnered more than 70 percent of the vote, while his three opponents each received between zero and 17 percent. Once inaugurated, Med-vedev appointed Putin his prime minister.

Forty-two-year-old Medvedev made Putin look charismatic. At just over five feet (his exact height was a carefully guarded secret, but rumors abounded, as did pictures of Medvedev sitting on a pil-low or standing on a step stool to reach a microphone), he also made Putin look tall. He was a lawyer by education, he had worked in city hall in St. Petersburg, and he had never held a job leading a team or running anything, much less a country. He mimicked Putin's robotic way of enunciating his words, except where Putin made every syl-lable sound menacing, Medvedev sounded like a voice synthesizer. And unlike Putin, Medvedev did not make vulgar jokes. That—and perhaps a desperate need to vest someone with hope—was enough to endear Medvedev to Russia's intellectuals.

For the first time since Putin destroyed the media and shut down Russian politics, the man in the Kremlin addressed the thinking public of Russia. Medvedev talked of what his speechwriters thought to call "The Four I's": *institutions, infrastructure, investment,* and *innovation.* Flashing an iPhone and, once it had been introduced, an iPad, Medvedev seemed to be trying to imbue his own dense vocabulary with a modern, Western spirit. The intelligentsia ate it up. When Medvedev called on human-rights activists, liberal political analysts, and assorted thinking others to join a newly formed presidential council, they all came, willingly sacrificing their time to write white papers that evidently were never read. When journalists at opposition media dared criticize not only Putin but also Medvedev, editors pulled their stories. When Medvedev told a group of activist historians he would finally approve a long-stalled plan for a national museum honoring the memory of victims of Stalinist terror, the historians dropped everything to draw up plans, draft documents, and do the work federal bureaucrats should have been doing, all to enable Medvedev to sign the decree—which he never did. What he did was keep giving speeches, promising to fight corruption and modernize the country, while nothing changed. Mikhail Khodorkovsky stood trial for the second time. Sergei Magnitsky died in prison. And Vladimir Putin not only built his palace on the Black Sea but continued to run the country.

Medvedev's role was almost exclusively ceremonial, but in their addresses to the public, the two leaders divided and conquered the country. Medvedev, with his refined diction, his talk of innovation, and his promises to fight corruption, played to the once vocal minority of activists and intellectuals, and succeeded in pacifying them. For the majority, Putin produced ever more of his memorable vulgarisms. After two deadly explosions on the Moscow subway in March 2010, he reprised his 1999 "Rub them out in the outhouse" pledge regarding terrorists: "We know they are now lying low," he said. "But it is up to law enforcement to scrape them up off the bottom of the gutter." In July 2009, responding to President Barack Obama's observation that the prime minister had "one foot in the old ways of doing business and one foot in the new," Putin said, "We don't spread our legs." In July 2008, when the majority owner of a metals and coal factory failed to attend a meeting at which Putin planned to dress him down, Putin said, "I understand that an illness is an illness, but I would recommend that Igor Vladimirovich [Zyuzin] get better as soon as possible. Or I'll just have to send a doctor to see him and take care of the problem altogether." In August 2010, Putin told a newspaper reporter that opposition activists who engaged in unsanctioned demonstrations (by this time, most opposition demonstrations were unsanctioned) should expect "to be hit over the head with a stick." These thuggish one-liners were his way of still campaigning for popularity, as were a stream of topless photographs of him vacationing in the northern region of Tyva and, later, coverage of his diving in the Black Sea and emerging with two sixth-century vases planted there in advance by archaeologists. This was a dictator's campaign, one that tolerated neither opposition nor scrutiny, but allowed for careful orchestration.

Putin was campaigning to remain the undisputed leader of the country—a surprisingly easy goal to accomplish in the presence of a sitting president—and, as a natural consequence of his obvious ongoing leadership, to become president again once Medvedev's term ran out in 2012. Indeed, within six months of becoming president, Medvedev introduced—and the parliament passed—a measure changing the constitution to increase the presidential term to six years. The plan, ostensibly, was for Medvedev to sit out his four years doing nothing but talking pretty, and then to cede the throne to Putin, this time for two consecutive six-year terms. But transparent as that plan was, hope persisted that Medvedev was sincere in his intentions or that, after being called president for a few years, he might develop actual presidential ambitions—or simply that the system Putin had created might crack, as all closed systems eventually do.

The system's greatest vulnerability stemmed from Putin's and his inner circle's pleonexia, the insatiable desire to have what rightfully belonged to others, that was exerting ever greater pressure on the regime from inside. Every year, Russia slid lower on the Corruption Perceptions Index of the watchdog group Transparency International, reaching 154th out of 178 by 2011 (for the year 2010). By 2011, human-rights activists estimated that fully 15 percent of the Russian prison population was made up of entrepreneurs who had been thrown behind bars by well-connected competitors who used the court system to take over other people's businesses. By mid-2010, a thirty-four-year-old attorney named Alexey Navalny was drawing tens of thousands of daily hits on his blog, where, by combing government websites to find evidence of excess hidden in plain sight, he monitored the many outrages of an unaccountable bureaucracy. Here was the Voronezh region holding a tender to purchase five gold wristwatches at a cost of $15,000. Here was the city of Krasnodar in southern Russia offering to pay about $400 million for technical documentation on a planned railroad crossing. Here were two beds and two bedside tables plated with 24-karat gold, which the Ministry of the Interior was purchasing. Navalny dubbed the people in charge of Russia "The Party of Crooks and Thieves"—a name that caught on immediately. In the fall of 2010, the magazine I was editing published a long and detailed interview with Navalny, and in the lead I wrote, "An actual politician has suddenly been discovered in Russia." Other magazines followed, putting the handsome blond Navalny on the cover, the attention culminating in a *New Yorker* profile in April 2011.

On February 2, 2011, Navalny announced that he was taking his one-man anticorruption campaign public, and called for contributions to his newly formed organization. Within three hours he had his first $5,000, in donations ranging from five kopecks (less than a cent) to the equivalent of $500. Within twenty-four hours, he had his first million rubles (roughly $30,000)—an all-time speed record for online donations to any cause in Russia. This was as clear a sign as there could be that Russians were fed up with being had—and were willing to pay for change. But it was also clear that a lone fighter like Navalny could not bring about change. As chess champion Garry Kasparov had already learned, having money, being popular, and being right did not enable an outsider to put a dent in the system. Only someone who was already on the inside could crack the monolith.

THAT MAN APPEARED to come on the scene in May 2011. Surprising everyone, including himself, Mikhail Prokhorov, now the second-richest man in Russia, announced that he was entering politics. Forty-six-year-old Prokhorov's life story resembled that of other Russian superrich: he had entered business as a college senior, made his first money in the late 1980s by buying and selling anything he could get his hands on, amassed a fortune in the 1990s by privatizing wisely, and by shrewdly investing and reshaping what he had privatized. Unlike Gusinsky, Berezovsky, and Khodorkovsky, he had kept a distance from the Kremlin for most of his career, preferring to remain a hands-on manager and leave politics to his business partner.

Entering politics now was not exactly his own idea—although he would protest that it was. He had been solicited on behalf of the president and the prime minister to take the reins of a foundering right-liberal political party. It was a familiar pattern by this point: every election year, the Kremlin would anoint one rightist party and one leftist party that would be allowed on the ballot, to take part, alongside Putin's United Russia, in what amounted to a mock election. Real political parties with actual leaders and agendas, meanwhile, would be denied registration on the basis of the convoluted laws and regulations adopted in the early 2000s. So Prokhorov had been chosen to serve as the figurehead of a dormant rightist party that would be briefly resuscitated in time for the December 2011 parliamentary election: he would be expected to play a scripted role, perhaps make a few careless rich-guy statements that would help drum up support for regular-guy Putin, and then retire to the sidelines when so instructed.

But I thought that this time the Kremlin puppeteers might have grown overconfident and made a fateful mistake. I knew Prokhorov a little: for the last three years I had been editing a magazine in which he was the principal investor. He seemed constitutionally incapable of being a figurehead. Moreover, he was actively looking for an arena in which he could apply himself fully. He had accomplished all he had set out to do in business in Russia, he was profoundly depressed about the state of the country, and he had been considering the disheartening option of selling off his assets and moving to New York, where he had bought the NBA team that would become the Brooklyn Nets. Now the alternative had presented itself: instead of leaving the country, he could fix it. He would get down to work, master this new undertaking just as he had set out to master metallurgy and the intricacies of management on the factory-floor level when he came into possession of the metals giant Norilsk Nickel, which he prided himself on having reformed from the bottom up, securing the workers' support for the many changes he had instituted. Prokhorov was brilliant; at six-foot-eight he was, literally, a giant, and I believed he just might topple the system.

Over the next few months, I watched Prokhorov undergo a remarkable transformation. He received expert coaching: he got out of baggy navy Brioni suits and into tailored beige and gray ones. He unlearned his Aspergian way of answering questions in complete, grammatically correct paragraphs, sounding completely certain, and learned to leaven his speech with qualifiers and misplaced modifiers.

Most important, he gathered dozens of experts in politics, economics, and media to help him develop nuanced positions on Russian politics and started to form a power base. He blanketed the country's largest cities with billboards featuring his face and slogans such as "Plan for your future." He had the money not only to buy all the advertising space in the land but also to replace his ads immediately after local authorities in more than a few places, taken aback by his audacity, took them down.

Whoever came up with the idea of using Prokhorov as a stand-in for the opposition obviously had not expected him to take the job so seriously. Vladislav Surkov, an assistant to Putin who had over the years built a reputation as the Kremlin's chief puppet master—effectively taking the place vacated by Berezovsky—began calling Prokhorov in for almost daily talks. Prokhorov, unaccustomed to reporting to anyone, nonetheless submitted to a ritual he found odd and distinctly humiliating: giving Surkov a complete accounting of his political activities. Surkov in turn made suggestions, on at least one occasion advising Prokhorov to drop someone from the party's rolls. Prokhorov ignored the suggestions and pressed on with what he thought was right—until September 14, 2011, when he found himself locked out of his own party's scheduled congress. Many of the activists Prokhorov had recruited over the previous three months were not allowed to take part in the congress either, and an entirely different group of people elected an entirely different leadership. Whoever had given Prokhorov the party had now decided to take it away.

Watching one of the richest and tallest men in Russia feeling utterly lost, confused, and betrayed was painful. Prokhorov called a press conference to announce that the lockout was illegal. He convened an alternative congress the following day and spoke there. He promised to see to it that Surkov would lose his job. He promised to fight. He promised to come back in ten days and lay out his detailed plans for a political battle.

Of course, Surkov—if it was indeed Surkov—was not the only one to have miscalculated badly. Prokhorov, living in the information bubble shaped by his experience in business, at a safe distance from the Kremlin, had overreached catastrophically. In the days after the congresses, he received enough messages about what would happen to him and his business to force him to give up on the idea of being a politician. Prokhorov never did come out with his battle plan; he all but disappeared from the public eye.

It seemed that whoever had chosen Prokhorov to oppose Putin had made a classic mistake of overconfidence—but had caught it in plenty of time.

ON SEPTEMBER 24, 2011, United Russia held its own party congress. Dmitry Medvedev addressed the throngs.

"I believe it would be right to support the candidacy of Vladimir Vladimirovich Putin for president," he declared. The hall erupted in a standing ovation. When it finally quieted, Medvedev unselfconsciously told the crowd that he and Putin had made the arrangement back when Medvedev first became president. And now, when Putin returned to the post of president, Medvedev would be his prime minister.

Within hours, the Russian blogosphere filled with pictures of Putin doctored to look older and conspicuously like Leonid Brezhnev, the Soviet leader who died after eighteen years in office, virtually immobile and completely incoherent. Putin, the bloggers reminded one another, would be seventy-one by the time his second six-year term was over.

And with this, the transformation of Russia back into the USSR was, for all Putin's intents and purposes, complete.

EPILOGUE:
A WEEK IN DECEMBER

Saturday, December 3, 2011

I am driving my family to see a vapid American comedy at an expensive shopping mall in central Moscow. Snow is late this year, and the city feels like it has been plunged into a permanent wet darkness. Excessive lighting on the Garden Ring, the eight-lane road that circles the city center, does little to change that feeling. But I am struck by a giant illuminated structure. One might call it a poster or a billboard, but neither description would do justice to the scale of the thing. It sits atop a two-story building from the eighteenth century, and it appears taller than the building. It is backlit and also illuminated brightly around the edges, some sort of King Kong digital photo frame. Inside the frame, Putin and Medvedev, one wearing a red tie and the other a blue, look resolutely past each other, over a giant caption: UNITED RUSSIA. TOGETHER WE WILL WIN.

Tomorrow is the parliamentary election. That makes today, by

law, a "day of silence," meaning any and all campaigning is banned—
outdoor advertising included. I pull over at an intersection, take a
picture of the monstrosity with my cell phone, and upload it to Facebook. Within an hour, the picture collects seventeen comments—no
world record, but more reaction than I expected on a Saturday night.
Even more surprising, those commenting are not my usual gang of
politically engaged friends. "Pigs!" writes a marketing manager. "You'd
think we've seen worse, but it still makes you want to throw up,
doesn't it?" writes a former political reporter who gave up journalism
fourteen years ago.

I have not voted in a parliamentary election for more than a
dozen years, because Putin's laws rendered elections meaningless:
political parties could no longer get on the ballot without the Kremlin's approval, members of parliament were no longer elected directly, and the results were rigged by election officials anyway.

But a couple of months ago, when a group of well-known liberal
writers, artists, and political activists called on people to go to the
polls and write an obscenity on the ballot, I criticized the idea online
as a losing tactic. The government had made a mockery of elections,
but, I argued, you cannot outmock a cynic. What we really needed
was a meaningful alternative to the mockery—like, perhaps, a reason
to vote. In the back-and-forth that followed in various publications,
a few people chimed in with actual reasons to go to the polls: first, to
make sure the Party of Crooks and Thieves did not vote in your name;
second, to vote for one of the quasi-opposition parties on the ballot,
so that Putin's United Russia did not win a constitutional majority in
parliament. Amazingly, these geeky exhortations went viral.

Having written her dissertation on elections, my girlfriend is a
principled always-voter. She woke up the other day and asked me,
"Did I dream it, or did you say you were going to vote?"

"Yes, I am going to vote."

"Why?" she asked.

"I can't quite explain it," I said. "But I feel something is afoot."

I said this because over the last few days I have had several discussions with my friends, who are also going to vote: we have been trying to decide which so-called party to pick. And thousands of people, including a number of my friends, have registered and trained as volunteer election observers either on their own or as part of an effort called Citizen Observer, organized by a prominent political scientist, Dmitry Oreshkin (who also happens to be my girlfriend's father). They will be spending tomorrow at the polls trying to forestall attempts at falsification. And people are discussing the picture of Putin and Medvedev on my Facebook page as if, all at once, they really cared.

Sunday, December 4

I go to the polls a half-hour before they close, as the geeks told me to, so that I can catch the election thieves red-handed if they have already used my name to vote. But no, neither I nor my ninety-one-year-old grandmother, registered at the same address, has voted. Nor do I observe any other violations. I cast my vote uneventfully, photograph it, post it to Facebook as a potential aid in exposing vote-count violations (another geek idea), and go to a former colleague's fortieth-birthday party.

It is a mixed crowd: book-publishing people, journalists, designers, and at least one wealthy manufacturer—my friend is one of those people who seem to know everyone. And everyone is talking about the election. Thirty-somethings come in declaring, "I voted for the first time in my life!" After a while it gets predictable that anyone who reached legal majority after Putin came to power will utter this phrase within minutes of walking through the door. A couple of guests who worked as volunteer election observers regale us with tales of violations: young people who were paid to hide prepared ballots under their clothing and slip them in along with their own; election officials who removed observers once the counting began. (Tomorrow we will find out that many officials simply forged their final tallies, with no regard for the actual ballots.)

None of this is news to me or Darya.

What is new is the fact that we are talking about all this at a party, late into the night. And that we all voted. And something else, too: the election observers tell us that their fellow observers included a schoolteacher, a businessman's wife who arrived in a Range Rover, and other people who are . . . not like us. Something has shifted, and not only for us media junkies glued to our Facebook pages.

"What do you think it will take for people to take to the streets?" Vladimir, a smart young reporter from the leading business daily's presidential pool, asks those gathered in the kitchen.

"I'm not sure," I say, "but I feel like something is in the air."

Monday, December 5

Driving the kids to school, I listen to reports of partial returns on the radio. United Russia supposedly has just under 50 percent of the vote. I know this is not an accurate figure, but it is considerably lower than the similarly falsified results of the previous parliamentary election, when United Russia supposedly got 66 percent. Perhaps this time the true numbers are so low that some local election officials felt they could take the lie only so far. As I will also find out later today, some precincts resisted altogether the pressure to cook their numbers. Citizen Observer's five hundred election observers, posted at 170 precincts in Moscow, saw no major violations of voting procedures at thirty-six of them. When the results from just those precincts were tallied, United Russia came in second, with just over

23 percent of the vote, trailing the Communist Party. Assuming this selection of precincts was representative, it would appear that the official count more than doubled the real one. Citizen Observer also reports that 49 percent of eligible voters took part—far more than in any other recent Russian election.

A protest is planned for tonight, and I plan to go. I do not want to: protests in Moscow are dreary or dangerous, or both. The way it works now, anyone planning to stage any kind of public rally or demonstration has to notify the authorities ten to fifteen days in advance; the city can then deny permission or grant it, for a specific location and a specific number of participants. If permission is denied but the demonstration goes on anyway, participants are likely to be arrested, and roughed up in the process. If permission is granted, the police set up cordons marking off space for the expected number of participants, and metal detectors at the perimeter. Protesters have to undergo a sometimes unpleasant search procedure and then hold their rally behind the police cordon, quite literally talking to themselves. I dislike the legal gatherings even more than the illegal ones, but once every few months, I feel I must go. This is one of those times.

My friend Ana instant-messages me with a quote from today's *New York Times* article on the Russian election. Ana, whom I met in Kosovo, spent several years in Moscow as a foreign correspondent, and now lives in The Hague. "'Democracy is in action,' Mr. Medvedev said, standing with Mr. Putin at United Russia's campaign headquarters, where both appeared a bit shaken." She adds: "If it wasn't sooo sad, it would be quite funny."

"Yeah," I respond. "Something is afoot, but it isn't going anywhere."

And I go to the protest. It is still unseasonably warm for Moscow, which means it is cold and miserable: temperature around freezing, and pouring rain. Who is going to brave this kind of weather to fight the hopeless fight for democracy?

Everyone.

At least, everyone I know. I approach the park where the protest is slated to take place with two friends, Andrei and Masha, and as we walk, people attach to our small clump. One of Andrei's younger brothers, and then another. Two of my former reporters—the ones who took turns calling in from the scene of the theater-siege disaster nine years ago. One of them, Anton, is now a radical art activist, and has spent a fair amount of time in jail for prank protests. The other, Grisha, recently quit his editorial job in a dispute over preelection censorship: he had been instructed to exclude critical articles from his digests of foreign media coverage of Russia. As we draw closer, we cannot even make out the metal detectors through the crowd. Then word spreads: The cordoned-off area has filled up, the police will not be letting any more people through. This means there are at least five hundred people in the park—and that, by contemporary Moscow standards, is huge.

We walk in the street along the park, looking in over a low fence. There are not hundreds but thousands of people in the park. We find ourselves in an informal phalanx about ten across. Parked all along the street are buses that brought the police here, and waiting prisoner-transport vehicles. "We are blocking traffic," Andrei says. "They'll detain us." The police look on indifferently as about a dozen of us climb over the fence to join the demonstrators. The rain keeps coming. My hair is soaked, and my feet feel like they are about to fall off. I am happy to be standing there freezing and endlessly saying hello to friends appearing from every direction.

There comes my friend the photographer, with whom I traveled the war zones in the 1990s. There, arriving separately, is his son, a college sophomore born a year after the Soviet Union collapsed. And now Tatyana, who was my editor more than fifteen years ago. "I've lost it, you know," she tells me. "Remember how we used to count the number of people at a demonstration in the nineties, by mentally breaking the crowd into quadrants? I can't do it anymore." Neither can I: I cannot remember the technique, nor can I distinguish anything in the thick crowd, in the rain, in the dark. But I am certain there are more than five thousand people here—estimates will range up to ten thousand—and that makes this the largest protest in Russia since the early 1990s.

As the rally breaks up, I invite the group to my apartment, which is just down the block. The women accept the invitation, but the men say they are going to join a march to the Central Election Committee building. The march is clearly illegal, and I fear they will be arrested. Indeed, there will be about three hundred arrests, and there will be violence. But there will be something else, too: in about an hour, when I am cooking a late supper and people are sipping cognac in my apartment, still trying to warm up, Grisha will tweet that Andrei has just pulled his two younger brothers out of a prisoner-transport vehicle by their coat collars. In another hour, six young men—Grisha, Andrei, Andrei's two brothers, and two men I have not met—will be at my apartment, disheveled and self-satisfied in a romantic, revolutionary way, embellishing the story of the prisoners' rescue as they tell and retell it.

I think, *I have seen this before.* This is the moment the fear lifts. Someone enters a prisoner-transport vehicle to rescue his brothers, and the police in riot gear move aside and let him. It is a tiny moment of great change.

The young men eat and decamp to the police precincts where their less fortunate friends are being held.

Tuesday, December 6

Driving the kids to school, I choose the route that takes me past a police precinct where some of last night's detainees were taken. I see a small crowd just outside: about a hundred people spent the wet, freezing night here, demanding—unsuccessfully—that lawyers be allowed into the building.

Another, illegal protest is called for tonight. All day I debate whether to go, and finally decide against it. I have taken part in illegal protests before, and have always managed to slip away (once sliding between a riot cop's legs). But my girlfriend is seven months pregnant, and it seems a particularly bad idea to risk fifteen days' administrative arrest, which is what many of the detainees will get.

I go about my business with a strange feeling. I go to the gym and then to a café, to meet with the general director of the publishing house where I am going to start working next week. The café is not far from the square where tonight's protest will take place, and because of this my phone's reception keeps fading in and out: word has it, cellular service is being jammed. Driving home, I pass armored vehicles and police buses, which now seem to be parked in every square in the center of town. According to radio news reports, tens of thousands of police have been pulled into Moscow from other cities.

I do not register where I learn this—from a friend, from Facebook, or from the radio—but another legally sanctioned protest is scheduled for Saturday. That makes the troops and the jamming feel more exciting than ominous: Monday's protest was not a fluke. Perhaps this is not necessarily going nowhere after all.

I worry, though, that the brewing revolution has no unifying symbol, no clear slogan. At 2:43 a.m. an advertising executive named Arsen Revazov writes a Facebook post:

The Snow Revolution, or A Clean Slate

When and if several million people put white ribbons on
their arms or tie them to their cars, to their handbags or their
lapels, etc., it will become impossible to forge or falsify

anything at all. Because it will all be out in the open and everyone will know.

It will snow. The entire city will turn white. Citizens don white ribbons. First they are ten percent of the population, then thirty, then fifty, then seventy-five. Once it's more than thirty, no one is afraid anymore. And suddenly everyone—or almost everyone—loves and respects everyone else because of this. . . .

We have to keep this up through March. Then God will decide. I am convinced that if several million people don white ribbons (or even paper napkins) in our city, everything will change for the better fast and without violence.

Within hours, nearly a thousand people "like" the post and more than seven hundred repost it. Moreover, it turns out that a separate white-ribbon effort began a couple of hours earlier. The revolution now has a symbol.

Another three hundred people have been detained at the illegal protest. A friend starts a Facebook group to coordinate aid efforts for the detainees. I join, as do several hundred others. By tomorrow, there will be regular food deliveries, courtesy of the café where I had my business meeting today, and sleeping bags and blankets will be bought or donated for all the detainees, who are otherwise reduced to sitting on hard benches or standing. The group is called HELP-Revolution, and at three in the morning I am bursting with pride to have been made an administrator.

Wednesday, December 7

Before I went to bed last night, the number of people who clicked "I'm going" on the coming Saturday demonstration's Facebook page was nearing three thousand. This morning, it is over five thousand. Eighty-year-old ex-president Mikhail Gorbachev has called for a revote. In a post for the *International Herald Tribune* opinion blog, where I am a regular contributor, I describe Monday's protest and try to put into words what is by now the unmistakable sense that Russia has passed a turning point.

> The problem with the Soviet regime—and the one created by Vladimir Putin in its image—is that they are closed systems whose destruction is unpredictable. There is no obvious cause-and-effect relationship between street protests and the ultimate fall of the regime because there are no mechanisms that make the government accountable to the people.
>
> Even the most obvious recent parallel, Ukraine's 2004 Orange Revolution, fails as a model: There the stand-off between street protesters and the government that had stolen an election was resolved by the Supreme Court, which ordered a recount and a re-vote. But Russia has no justice system independent of the executive branch. And worse, neither a recount nor a re-vote would work, since election laws have long since been rigged to allow only Kremlin-sanction parties on the ballot.
>
> So the people who are protesting the stolen election are, in effect, demanding the dismantling of the entire system. And that, for lack of better parallels, brings us back to the fall of the USSR.
>
> That process took five years and proceeded in a two-steps-forward-one-step-back manner. Protests were allowed, then banned, then allowed again. Dissidents were freed, then their apartments were ransacked by the police. Censorship was lifted in fits and starts. At the height of the protest

movement, hundreds of thousands flooded the streets, defying
not only the police but tanks, and yet it was impossible to tell
whether their actions had direct consequences—because, just
as now, the people had no mechanisms for holding the
government accountable.

But one thing is clear in retrospect: Once the process
was underway, the regime was doomed. The more hot air
it pumped into the bubble in which it lived, the more
vulnerable it also became to growing pressure from the
outside. That is exactly what is happening now. It may take
months or it may take a few years, but the Putin bubble
will burst.

What will happen next? The Kremlin seems to be flailing. Yesterday tens of thousands of young people bused in from out of
town were herded into the center of Moscow for a United Russia
victory rally. They were issued bright vests and blue drums, which
they discarded unceremoniously after the event. Pictures of the
drums, dented, stained, and soaked, piled on the sidewalk, flooded
the blogs. They seemed to symbolize the regime perfectly: a lot
of noise and pomp, then an inglorious abandonment in the dark
freezing rain. What are the government's other options? Most of
the people detained on Monday and Tuesday are still in police holding cells, and they have already overtaxed the facilities' and the
courts' capacity: mass arrests at Saturday's protest are simply not
an option. Violence is possible but feels doubtful, because Putin, I
suspect, has not yet realized how desperate his situation is. More
likely, he will attempt to mollify the protesters by throwing them
a bone. Vladislav Surkov, the Kremlin's chief puppeteer, has already
suggested that a new party be formed to accommodate "irritated
urban communities." Putin and his inner circle seem unaware that

the whole country is irritated with them, so they probably think that allowing a handpicked ersatz opposition candidate on the ballot in the March presidential election will let off enough steam. The protests will have to continue until those in power realize that they are a tiny and despised minority—and then they will act like a cornered animal. What is in their limited repertoire—a terrorist attack that will allow Putin to declare a state of emergency? Such a move will not save his regime, but might delay its demise by a year or two.

In the evening, I go to a meeting of Rus' Sidyashchaya (Russia Behind Bars), an organization formed a couple of months ago by Olga Romanova, a former business writer who became a full-time prisoners' rights activist after her entrepreneur husband was arrested and sentenced to eight years' imprisonment for fraud. After bribery failed to set him free, Romanova launched her own investigation, turning up evidence that her husband was sentenced on the basis of forged documents—provided, she believes, by his former business partner, who also, until last year, was a senator. Romanova made it to the Supreme Court, which overturned the verdict—and after Moscow City Court ignored that decision, she made it to the Supreme Court again, and again got the verdict overturned. She then flew to a distant prison colony to collect her husband, who had been behind bars for more than three years already. The video of their reunion instantly went viral.

Rus' Sidyashchaya meets at a café in the center of town, the sort where thoughtful young men and women choose among eighteen varieties of excellent tea before proceeding to a few varieties of mediocre wine. But these Wednesday-night gatherings are mostly of women who look like they work as accountants or middle managers. Except they are working full-time to get their "business prisoner" husbands out of jail. I sit at a table with Svetlana Bakhmina, a former mid-level Yukos lawyer who served four and a half years in prison, and a shy young bespectacled woman who tells me her husband has been sentenced for alleged fraud.

"And here is Irek Murtazin!" shouts Romanova, who is forty-five and heavyset, with dyed red hair.

A slight man in his late forties enters. He is a former television executive from Tatarstan who was fired in October 2002, over his coverage of the theater siege. He became a popular blogger, and in 2009 was arrested for allegedly libeling the president of Tatarstan. He was sentenced to twenty-one months in prison for libel and, the court ruled, for "inciting enmity against a specific social group," defined as government officials.

"I have good news and bad news," says Murtazin. "The bad news is, a Tatarstan judge who hit and killed a young man while driving drunk last summer has just been acquitted."

The room issues a collective sigh: this bad news is hardly news at all, so common are accidents involving state officials—and their acquittals.

"The good news," says Murtazin, "is that nearly half the justices of the peace who were getting cases of those detained in the protests Monday and Tuesday called in sick today. That's eighty judges with the flu."

Now, this is news. And it turns out that because detention facilities are overflowing, some of the detainees are being released and casually instructed to show up for court at a later date. Corruption fighter Alexey Navalny, however, appeared before a judge today and was sentenced to fifteen days for his role in leading the illegal march on Monday.

One of the women at the meeting is handing out white ribbons to everyone. In less than twenty-four hours, the revolution's symbol has become official.

When I get home, the number of people who have clicked "I'm going" on the Facebook page for Saturday's protest has passed ten thousand.

Thursday, December 8

More than twenty thousand Facebook users now plan to attend the protest on Saturday.

I talk with someone who is in daily contact with members of the presidential administration and the federal government. "They are hysterical," he says. "No one knows what to do, they make decisions based on the mood in which they wake up in the morning. Yesterday, Medvedev wanted to turn off [the independent cable television channel] Dozhd. We were barely able to stop him." In a few days, I will learn that cable providers did get calls directing them to stop providing access to Dozhd, but decided to resist the request, citing contractual obligations. No one was more surprised than the owner and director of Dozhd. President Medvedev, meanwhile, has un-followed Dozhd on his Twitter account.

City workers have hastily started repairs of some kind in Revolution Square, where Saturday's protest is slated to take place—a classic tactic of last resort to keep demonstrators away.

Friday, December 9

I am anxious. Driving the kids to school, I listen to the radio and worry—even as the newscaster reports that more than twenty-five thousand people plan to come on Saturday. It is like that moment early in a passionate love affair when all the same words are being said as yesterday, but somehow the heat seems to have been turned down a notch. I drop the kids off, go home, and go back to sleep.

But when I wake up a couple of hours later, the revolution is still on, and passions are just as high as they need to be. The issue of concern now is that, while Saturday's protest is technically legal, the organizers' original application—filed ten days ago—specified three hundred participants. In the past, those in the overflow have been detained. Yet it will be impossible to detain an overflow of thousands, or tens of thousands—and that may translate into police violence.

Two organizers—a career politician and a magazine editor—go to Moscow city hall to try to negotiate. In the middle of the afternoon, the editor, Sergei Parkhomenko, posts the result of their negotiations on his Facebook page: the city has offered a new location for tomorrow's protest, granted the organizers license to have as many as thirty thousand participants, and extended the duration of the protest from two to four hours. Soon the city also agrees to provide all those who mistakenly go to Revolution Square with unimpeded passage to the new location, a half-hour's walk away. The only bad news is that instead of the fabulously named Revolution Square, the protest will take place at Bolotnaya (Swampy) Square. A friend, prominent poet and political commentator Lev Rubinshtein, immediately terms this "a linguistic challenge."

The country's best-loved best-selling author, Grigory Chkhartishvili, who pens historical detective novels under the name Boris Akunin, writes in his blog:

I Could Not Sit Still

Why does everything in this country have to be like this?
Even civil society has to wake up when it's most inconvenient
for the writer.
    I went away to the French countryside for some time
in peace, to write my next novel. But now I can't concentrate.

I guess I'm going home. That's 500 kilometers behind the wheel—and then wish me luck getting on a flight.

I hope I do make it and get to see the historic occasion with my own eyes and not via YouTube.

But the reason I am writing this post is that I have been asked to warn all those who don't yet have this information:

THE PROTEST WILL TAKE PLACE IN BOLOTNAYA SQUARE (not in Revolution Square).

At parent-teacher conferences in the evening, I notice many of the other children's parents are wearing white ribbons.

When I put my daughter to bed, she asks if she can go to the protest with me tomorrow.

"No, I'm sorry, I don't think it's a good idea to take kids yet."

"But this is a legal protest, right?" She knows that otherwise I could be detained.

I assure her that it is and that nothing bad is likely to happen to me. "I'll probably be going to a lot of protests these coming months," I say, "and I probably won't be able to take you with me. But I'll take you to the last one, when we have a celebration."

"You mean, when there is no more Putin?" She catches her breath, as if the thought were too much to contemplate. She is ten; she was born after Putin came to power, and she has heard conversations about him her entire life. When my kids were little, they made Putin into a sort of household villain, the bogeyman who would come get you if you did not mind your table manners. I put a stop to that, and as they have grown I have tried to give them a reasonably nuanced picture of politics, but I think I may have neglected to say that no one rules forever.

Saturday, December 10

Driving in from our dacha, where the children and Darya will be while I am at the protest, I listen to the radio and fret. So what if thirty-five thousand people have stated on Facebook that they are going to the protest? I have heard of people getting seven hundred Facebook RSVPs for a party—and not a single actual guest. It is the weekend, after all: people will be feeling lazy, they will want to sleep in or stay at their dachas, and they will figure someone else will go to the protest.

As I get closer to Bolotnaya Square, I see people flowing to it from every direction: in groups, in couples, alone; young, old, middle-aged. People wearing white ribbons, white scarves, white hats, even white trousers, carrying white balloons and white carnations. It still has not snowed, so the white they wear and carry has to compensate.

I meet up with a group of friends, including Andrei and two of his brothers. At the metal detectors, the police are calm and polite. Inside, we wander the square, scanning for familiar faces. At Monday's protest, I knew everyone was there because I could see them all; today I know they are all here because I cannot see them for the crowd. Even texting becomes impossible, as the volume exceeds the capacity of Moscow's cellular networks.

We gawk at homemade banners people have brought. One features a graph of the official results reported by the Central Election Committee, overlaid with a bell curve that tells a different story: it shows what normal distribution of support for United Russia would look like. "We Don't Trust You, We Trust Gauss," says the poster, referring to Carl Friedrich Gauss, the mathematician who gave the world the bell curve.

"I Did Not Vote for These Assholes," proclaims another banner, carried by a young man with a reddish beard, "I Voted for the Other Assholes. I Demand a Recount."

"There are so many people here!" a very young man shouts into his cell phone. "And they are all normal! I've heard like a million jokes, and they were all funny!"

If you have spent years feeling as if your views were shared by only a few of your closest friends, being surrounded by tens of thousands of like-minded people really does feel like hearing a million funny jokes at once.

Somewhere in the distance, there is a stage. I cannot see it, and I can hardly hear any of the speakers. One of my friends remembers a trick from the early 1990s, when people would bring portable radios to rallies and use them to listen to the speakers: she turns on the radio on her cell phone (cellular service may be overtaxed, but this public square features free wireless) and gives us the highlights of speeches. We look around, and occasionally join in chants: "New Elections!" "Freedom!" "Russia Without Putin!"

The speakers include Boris Akunin (he made it from the south of France in time), a well-loved, long-blacklisted television anchor, and assorted activists. Darya's father speaks about election fraud. None of those who pass for opposition politicians—"the other assholes"—are here. They have not yet gotten the message that power has shifted away from the Kremlin. Navalny is still in jail, so a journalist reads his address to the protesters. And Mikhail Prokhorov, the billionaire who suspended his political career two months ago, is still silent. On Monday he will announce that he is running for president, but by then it will be too late to win cred with the revolutionary crowd: he will immediately be branded a Putin plant.

I am wearing thermal underwear, two jackets, and moon boots; there is no way to dress for standing still in a Russian winter. After a couple of hours my friends and I decide to leave. Other people are still arriving. Walking away from the protest, I stop on a pedestrian bridge to look back at the crowd. There are a lot more than thirty-five thousand people; later estimates will range as high as a hundred fifty thousand.

We take a large table at a restaurant that, like all the eateries in the neighborhood, is filled with protesters ordering mulled wine in an attempt to warm up. Friends and strangers are shouting the latest news across tables. Andrei is the first to read a couple of lines from a radio station's website: "The protest is drawing to a close. A police representative has mounted the stage. He says, 'Today we acted like the police force of a democratic country. Thank you.' There is applause." At our table there is a momentary silence. "This is great," all of us start saying then, looking at one another incredulously. "This is great." How long has it been since any of us was able to say, unequivocally, "This is great" about something happening in our city?

I leave my friends at the restaurant to return to my family at the dacha. I drive over the Big Stone Bridge—the largest bridge over the Moscow River—just as the police leave Bolotnaya Square. There are hundreds upon hundreds of them, moving along the sidewalk four and five across, the length of the bridge. For the first time that I can remember, I do not get a knot in my stomach while I look at police in riot gear. I am stuck behind an orange truck with a snowplow. It still has not snowed, so I am not sure what the truck is doing out in the street, but I notice a white balloon tied to the corner of the plow.

Protests were held today in ninety-nine cities in Russia and in front of Russian consulates and embassies in more than forty cities around the world.

In the evening, Putin's press secretary, Dmitry Peskov, tells journalists that the government has no comment on the protest and promises to let them know if a comment is formulated.

A few minutes later, NTV, the television channel taken away from Vladimir Gusinsky ten years ago and eviscerated, airs an excellent report on the protest. I watch it online—it's been years since I had a working television in the house—and I recognize something I have observed in other countries when I covered their revolutions. There comes a day when you turn on the television and the very same goons who were spouting propaganda at you yesterday, sitting in the very same studios against the very same backdrops, start speaking a human language. In this case, though, this moment gives my head an extra spin, because I can still remember these journalists before they became goons, when they last spoke human about a dozen years ago.

As I approach our dacha, it starts to snow. By morning, the countryside will be covered in white.

AFTERWORD

On March 1, 2012, this book was published in the United States, Great Britain, and many other countries outside Russia (a Russian publisher confessed to being too scared to touch it). Three days later, Putin declared victory in the first round of the presidential election, with 63 percent of the vote. Holding a virtual monopoly on the ballot, the media, and the polls themselves, he could have claimed any figure—he could even have opted for less than half the votes and chosen to stage a runoff, to try to disarm his critics with a show of democracy—but he opted for a landslide, and a slap in the face to the Movement for Fair Elections, which had kept up the pressure with large-scale protests through the winter.

I felt an odd sort of satisfaction when the election results were announced: as disheartening as they were for the protest movement and as hopeless a future as they promised for my country, they were also an integral part of the story I had been writing. Putin and the regime he had built were as inflexible and unsubtle as ever. Some political scientists and editorial writers had suggested that Putin would institute soft reforms in response to the protest movement, perhaps allowing change to occur gradually from within the system. The Putin I had studied—the main character I had described in this book—would never allow this, not just because he abhorred any manifestation of what he perceived as weakness but also because he had been too deeply traumatized by perestroika, which had begun with Gorbachev's soft reforms and ended with the collapse of the Soviet Union.

Watching the Russian presidential election from my book-tour perch in the United States, I felt displaced and helpless. Friends comforted me with assurances that telling the West about Russia was a better use of my time than placing my body in a Moscow street protest. And I felt I had done this job well by predicting, accurately, that Putin would be unyielding in the face of resistance—and that meant a crackdown was inevitable. Things would get a lot worse before they got better.

But there was a strain in the story I had been telling that made me slightly uncomfortable. I had been saying that working as a journalist in Russia had become virtually impossible: my colleagues had been killed, maimed, and threatened; the government worked in mysterious ways, behind closed doors, turning the job of describing Russian politics into guesswork at best; reporting had become dangerous and pointless at the same time. Yet my own professional life seemed to belie this story: I managed to stay employed in Russia, rising, by the time of my book tour, to editor in chief of a publishing house that put out a line of books and two monthly magazines, one of which I also edited. The catch was, it was a popular-science publishing house and the books were travel guides and popular-science titles. I loved this work—much of my journalism over the years and two of my books had been popular-science, and my colleagues and I believed that by educating our readers we made our country better.

Yet the growing gap between my political writing and my day job sometimes made me feel like a fake, or at least a split personality. During my book tour, I would go on talk shows to speak about Putin's regime and the protest movement, and then go back to my hotel to edit a story on vertical climbing in the animal kingdom. Somewhere along the line, without noticing it, I had done what the Soviet intelligentsia of my parents' generation had done: retreated into areas of research that were obscure enough to escape the regime's attention. At the same time, I could hardly complain: I did work I loved, got to hire people I liked and respected (several of them also former political journalists), and was paid well for it.

BY THE TIME I returned to Moscow from my book tour, the crackdown had begun. A legal, peaceful march on May 6, the eve of Putin's inauguration, ended in clashes with riot police when they decided to prevent people from joining the rally at the end of the route; 650 people were arrested and dozens injured, including several policemen. Darya and I, with our infant, were separated from my ten-year-old daughter and she ended up in the thick of the violence; she was safe in the end but terrified and traumatized. In June, the Duma began rubber-stamping bills that came flooding from the Kremlin. One bill greatly expanded the government's ability to ban protests—and to punish protesters. Authorities could now declare unlimited areas off-limits to protesters in perpetuity; protesters were no longer allowed to attend demonstrations wearing face masks (including surgical ones) or anything that could be used to cover the face; individual organizers could be fined 300,000 rubles (just under $10,000) for any violations—including exceeding the maximum number of participants vetted by the authorities. The government also reserved the right to determine for itself who the organizers were, rather than continuing to hold responsible the people who had petitioned local authorities for a demonstration permit. The arrests began soon after: more than a dozen people, apparently picked at random from among the protesters, were thrown in jail and charged with inciting public disorder on May 6; they would be sentenced to upwards of four years in prison. In July the Duma passed laws effectively banning Russian nongovernmental organizations from accepting foreign funding. In August a Moscow court sentenced three young women who called themselves Pussy Riot to two years behind bars for a forty-second anti-Putin performance inside a Moscow cathedral. In September the Duma passed amendments to laws on high treason and espionage, essentially making it possible to convict anyone of either crime—with sentences up to life in prison. On October 1, the U.S. Agency for International Development, which had been funding some civic organizations in Russia, including ones that provided essential help to small independent newspapers, was summarily kicked out of the country. The space for any sort of independent activity was rapidly shrinking.

I went to Australia for the Sydney Writers' Festival to promote this book and wrote a story for my magazine—on the Sydney Harbour Bridge. With friends and acquaintances dealing with arrests and apartment searches, I felt increasingly schizophrenic in my popular-science haven—especially because I had begun attending endless meetings with representatives of an organization called the Russian Geographic Society. The organization was a nonprofit with a twist: it was more than one hundred and fifty years old and had been all but forgotten through much of its history—until some powerful people took an interest in it. Now its president was the minister of emergencies, Sergei Shoygu, and its chairman of the board was Vladimir Putin. This meant the nongovernmental organization could have anything it wanted—like a four-story building a stone's throw from the Kremlin, which was being renovated to house the Society's headquarters. At some point RGS decided it wanted to have its own magazine—and *Vokrug Sveta*, the magazine I edited, seemed like a fitting candidate: It was also one hundred and fifty years old, the oldest continuously published magazine in the country—and its name meant "around the world," which seemed fitting for a geographic society's magazine.

When an organization patronized by the most powerful men in Russia develops an interest in a business, it usually ends with a takeover. Sergei Vasilyev, the owner of *Vokrug Sveta*, knew this well: he had been coerced into selling his large advertising business, where he was now a hired manager. He negotiated with the RGS for a few months and then placed the words "Magazine of the Russian Geographic Society" on the cover. While Vasilyev retained nominal ownership of the magazine—and full financial responsibility for it—we now had an obligation to print at least one RGS-related story in every issue.

I had my own concerns about RGS. One was that Vasilyev would be forced to get rid of me: he and I had discussed the political risks he was taking by hiring me and I had promised to leave if my name or my politics became an issue. But no one demanded my resignation. In fact, suddenly I seemed able to pass through walls: as a representative of RGS-affiliated *Vokrug Sveta* I was invited to state television and radio, where I had been blacklisted for years. I never went, but one of our editors used a live state-radio broadcast to speak up for Pussy Riot—and no one said a word to me. Did anyone even know? I put out feelers and soon found out that Putin's press secretary, Dmitry Peskov, who was working on the RGS/*Vokrug Sveta* project most closely, had not known I was the magazine's editor at the time the partnership was announced—by Putin himself. Peskov found out from a mutual acquaintance of ours several weeks later.

What would he do now? I wondered. Would he go to Putin and tell him they had an issue with the magazine the president himself had praised so highly? How would he define the issue? Did Putin even know I existed—let alone that I had written this book, which had received extensive press in the West? I had begun to suspect strongly that he did not. For him to know, someone would have had to tell him—to have been the bearer of bad news. And now the news was doubly bad: Peskov would have had to tell Putin both that he had not done his homework on *Vokrug Sveta* and that I had written this book. I had a feeling he had not and would not. And from my accidental new perch I was getting a view that confirmed my earlier suspicion: that Putin had fulfilled his dream of re-creating the late-Soviet-period KGB, an organization that collected and produced mountains of useless paper but missed Mathias Rust, the nineteen-year-old West German amateur pilot who landed his plane in Red Square in May 1987, having illegally crossed into Soviet airspace from Finland.

MY OTHER CONCERN regarding RGS was professional. To produce the monthly stories, our journalists would go along on RGS expeditions, which were many, exotic, and lavishly funded. On one hand, these expeditions afforded us opportunities to go places few journalists can get to—like the New Siberian Islands, for example. On the other hand, RGS representatives were usually hard-pressed to explain the actual purpose of their expeditions, making me suspect that RGS functioned like any Russian bureaucracy, spending money just because it could.

And I had another concern—or, rather, a fear. Putin himself had been taking an increasing interest in RGS activities and in nature-preservation efforts in general. He had, for example, personally placed a satellite-transmitter collar on a wild Siberian tiger in 2008—but four years later environmentalist bloggers reported that the tiger had been taken from the Khabarovsk Zoo so that Putin could be photographed performing his feat. As *Vokrug Sveta* reporters started going on RGS expeditions, they brought back other, similar tales. There was the time, in 2010, when Putin placed a satellite collar on a polar bear—locals told our reporter two years later that the bear had been captured several days in advance and heavily sedated in anticipation of Putin's visit. And they said there was a time when Putin wanted to be photographed in a Far Eastern national park—but his security service plotted a route through a part of the park that had been clear-cut. Inventive park rangers procured tree trunks and tied them to stumps for the photo op.

But this was all hearsay. Our reporters had not seen any of this and, as a popular-science magazine, we were under no obligation to investigate these allegations. If anything was clear, it was that Putin's nature-preservation efforts had little to do with science of any sort. As an editor, I hated taking this position: in all my years as a political reporter and editor, I had never shied away from investigations, including high-risk ones. I had not expected to face gut-wrenching ethical choices at a popular-science magazine. I had brought several young editors on board with me when I came to *Vokrug Sveta*, and as the summer of 2012 wore on, we spent longer hours in the garden of our publishing house having that conversation, endlessly familiar from the Soviet era, about whether the compromises we were making or might make were justifiable. We talked about the sense that a slow rot had set in, and we turned and looked back on our building with nostalgia, as though we had already lost the magazine.

On the morning of September 1, a Saturday, I got a call from my publisher: Peskov had called requesting a *Vokrug Sveta* writer-photographer team to accompany Putin on a hang-glider flight geared to reintroduce West Siberian cranes into the wild. My heart sank. I was sure the journalist would witness something along the lines of tigers borrowed from the zoo or trees tied to stumps. I would feel we had an obligation to write about it, and then there would be

trouble: at the least, I would get fired, and at the most, the magazine's takeover would turn hostile.

I said no, and I was fired on the spot.

THE FOLLOWING MONDAY I went to the publishing house, signed the
requisite papers, made an announcement to the staff, and, in the late
afternoon, tweeted that I was leaving my job. I used a hashtag that
had been part of a brief fad the previous year: people would write
tiny poems where the first line rhymed with the hashtagged "and you
can thank Putin for that"; the allusion was to a Stalin-era tradition,
when the dictator was often thanked, in verse, for everything ranging
from a happy childhood to a sunny day. I wrote "I am leaving *Vokrug
Sveta* #youcanthankPutinforthat"; it rhymed. I got a flurry of media
calls, gave a few quotes, and went home to celebrate my firing with
two of my closest friends.

Early the following morning I flew to Prague for a job interview.
I was in a taxi, tired, hungover, and slightly disoriented, when my
phone rang. A male voice asked me to hold. I listened to silence for
two minutes, fuming. A different male voice came on: "Don't hang
up. I will connect you." I blew up: "I didn't ask to be connected with
anyone! Why do I have to hold? Who are you connecting me to? Do
you want to introduce yourself?"

"Putin, Vladimir Vladimirovich," said the president's voice on
the other end of the line.

"I heard you were fired," he continued, while I scrambled to
formulate some sort of message for him while also saying something that indicated I realized this might be a prank. "And that I
unwittingly served as the reason for it. But you should know that
my nature-preservation efforts have nothing to do with politics.
Unfortunately, for a person in my position it is difficult to separate
the two."

This turn of phrase was vintage Putin: asking for sympathy while subtly denigrating the office of president—something I'd always felt a genuinely elected leader would not do. "So if you have no objections, I propose we meet and talk about this," he said.

"I have no objections. But how do I know this is not a prank?" Putin promised I would get a call arranging the meeting and he would show up for it, thereby demonstrating the phone call had not been a prank. Right around this point in the conversation my cab passed Franz Kafka's grave.

I spent the following week worrying that the meeting would be cancelled. I had, after all, spent years studying this man, poring over everything he ever said, rewinding and playing his smirks and grimaces dozens of times over—and I had never physically been in the same space with him. Secretly, I felt I had made him up.

At the same time, how could the meeting possibly happen? I knew I had been blacklisted: I had not even been able to get accredited for a Kremlin press conference in the last dozen years. The RGS relationship had changed much of that, but I still felt that happened in a parallel reality: I did not believe I could pass through the Kremlin walls before someone remembered who I was and why I was blacklisted in the first place. Would Peskov not find it necessary to tell his boss about my book? And whether or not he did, how could he possibly spin the meeting? If I was right about the state of decay of the presidential administration, Peskov would not warn Putin and would not even think about the media reaction to our meeting until after it had happened.

A week after the phone call, I was waiting for Putin in the Kremlin. The day before, I had received no fewer than eight calls from different people in the administration and in the press office: first they were openly competing for the right to be making arrangements for my visit and then they could not figure out which gate I should be using to enter the Kremlin and kept calling back to change the arrangement. The press-office employee who met me at the gate asked whether I had been to the president's working office before and was crushed to hear I had not: she did not know the way. We walked the Kremlin grounds asking policemen for directions. So far my theory seemed to be correct.

I waited in the cafeteria a few doors down the hall from the president's office. It had as much gold leaf as the Cathedral of Christ the Savior, and it smelled of borscht: it looked like an early-post-Soviet restaurant, somebody's unimaginative idea of what wealth looks like. It was also heavily subsidized: a double espresso was fifteen rubles (about fifty cents), or a tenth of its Moscow street price. I knew I would have to wait a long time: wait times of four hours were average, and six or more hours was not unheard of. I had brought a book to read. I had wanted to bring my own book as a gift to Putin, but my friends and family begged me not to; a midnight text-message plea from a colleague finally convinced me not to do it. I was reading Peter Matthiessen's brilliant book about cranes, *The Birds of Heaven*. In the introduction Matthiessen quotes a Long Island neighbor asking him, "Who cares about cranes?" He explains: "Like many people on many continents, I care profoundly about cranes and tigers, not only as magnificent and stirring creatures but as heralds and symbols of all that is being lost."

I had planned to use the wait time to find the words to say to Putin: I assumed I might have time for a single statement. My issue with Putin's apparent interest in cranes and tigers—and also in polar bears and snow leopards—was that he appeared interested in them as symbols of his own power: he chose the largest predators and the largest flying birds to dominate on camera, to show he was not only president but also king of the jungle. Notwithstanding his professed interest in projects aimed at saving Siberian cranes, tigers, and snow leopards, Russia under his rule had made disregard for the environ-

ment a matter of state policy. Among other things, Putin had personally sanctioned restarting the paper mill that has been polluting the
Baikal, the world's oldest and deepest fresh-water lake: the president
toured it in a mini-submarine and said it seemed clean enough to
him. But would accusing him of hypocrisy even register?

The wait was two hours—very short by Putin standards, as his
press secretary would later point out. A senior press-office employee
walked me to his office.

"What is the format of the meeting?" I asked.

"What do you mean?" she asked, apparently surprised. "Are you
asking if it's public or private?"

"Yes," I said. "Is it on the record or off, how long is it planned to
last, what is the agenda?"

"I have no idea," she answered with a smile.

Chalk up one more for my no-one-is-driving-the-bus theory.
Plus, I was now free to write about the meeting.

Sergei Vasilyev, my former publisher, had also been invited—
and had apparently waited in the press office. The press secretary
now walked him to the door.

Putin was sitting at his desk when we walked in—a classic
Russian-bureaucrat gesture of power, which forces the visitor, who
might have expected to be met at the door, to approach the desk
instead. The office had not changed much from the Kremlin of the
1990s, which, in turn, had been a spiffed-up version of the Soviet-era
Kremlin: polished-wood 1960s bureaucrat furniture, a large desk and
a conference table. The Soviet-era buttonless plastic phones—the
Kremlin's equivalent of direct dial—sat on both the desk and the
table. In perfect accordance with this power protocol, Putin waited
for us to reach the middle of the room before he rose to greet us. He
shook our hands and showed us to the conference table: he would
sit at the head of it and Vasilyev and I to either side of him. Vasilyev

was red-faced and sweating and I found it painful to look at him. Putin looked bloated in a way that hinted at too much plastic surgery, so looking at him was difficult, too.

"Before we start," he said, "I want to see if this conversation makes sense. Did you like your job? Or do you maybe have other plans and the status of a persecuted journalist will help your career along?"

He clearly had not been briefed. He had no idea who I was—aside from having been fired as editor of a popular-science magazine he now considered his own. He did not know about the book, or my role in the protest movement, or the many articles about him and his administration that I had written in the Russian press. And, it seems, he had not asked for any information in advance of our meeting—further evidence that he had grown as isolated and solipsistic as only a dictator can. He had taken an interest in me only because he now considered the magazine his own, he liked it just the way it was, and he did not like someone firing the editor in chief without consulting him. I had come to meet my nemesis, but he was merely calling a meeting with a member of his vast staff.

"I liked my job very much," I told him honestly. "And I do not find my career to be in need of a boost."

"Good," he smiled. "Then we can talk. I like kitties and puppies and little animals." He said he felt his public efforts on behalf of endangered species helped draw attention to important problems. "And I came up with the Siberian cranes project myself."

This was news to me. The project to restore the Siberian crane population dates back to the late 1970s. I asked him to clarify what he meant by claiming authorship of the idea. Putin explained that he had heard of the program several years ago and learned that it had lost funding—so it had been his idea to finance the project again.

"So," said Putin, addressing me, "I am sure you will tell us your reasons for refusing to send a reporter, but you were wrong. And you," he said, addressing my former boss, "were also wrong to open fire like that. Sure, there should be discipline at a magazine, just as there should be in the army."

Now was apparently my chance to deliver my message. "Vladimir Vladimirovich, I agree with everything you said about the importance of drawing attention to these issues, and about the potential the head of state has of influencing nature-preservation programs," I said. "But, unfortunately, the way things work in this country is that as soon as you get involved, your person becomes more important than the cause. You are probably aware that when you put a satellite collar on that Siberian tiger, the tiger had actually been borrowed from the Khabarovsk Zoo. And when you put a collar on the polar bear, that bear had been captured days ahead of time and kept under heavy sedation until you arrived—"

"Of course, there are excesses!" Putin interrupted me rather cheerily. "And I have taken people to task for that. But it is so much more important that I draw attention to the issues! Sure, the leopard had been sedated," he said (I had said nothing about a leopard). "But what's important is that I was the one who came up with the whole leopards project! And the tigers. After I did that, twenty different countries that have tigers also started working on the problem. Sure, there are excesses," he repeated. "Like that time I dove for the amphorae."

I could not believe he was the one drawing the analogy to the amphorae fiasco—the time, about a year earlier, when Putin had posed for the cameras emerging from the bottom of the Black Sea bearing two ancient amphorae, which, as it quickly turned out, had been planted there for him to find. "So then everyone started writing that the amphorae had been planted. Of course they were planted! I wasn't diving to be able to blow my gills wide," he said, by which, I think, he meant some sort of sea-creature equivalent of self-aggrandizement. "I was diving to draw attention to the history of that place. And then everyone started writing that I'd come up with planted amphorae like a dickhead. But some people actually started reading up on history."

The word he used—*mudak*—was one of those words Russians consider entirely unsuitable for mixed company. Like the "gills" crack, it was a vintage Putin vulgarism but also a faux pas unworthy of a man who once fancied himself a trained KGB recruiter. His speech was pitched all wrong for me and for the occasion.

Putin turned to Vasilyev again and demanded to know if he was willing to offer me my job back. The publisher said yes.

"But one more thing," I said, when Putin turned back to me. "You said a magazine should be run like an army. It should not."

"Depends on the army." Putin winked. Another miss.

"No, it does not. A magazine should not be like any army." I was about to cite Russia's law on mass media, which explicitly prohibits publishers from interfering in editorial policy, but Putin suddenly wiped his thin smile off his face and stood up.

"I've got enough experience with this," he said coldly. "We'll discuss this issue another time."

The meeting was over.

WHAT HAD I learned? That the person I had described in this book—shallow, self-involved, not terribly perceptive, and apparently very poorly informed—was indeed the person running Russia, to the extent Russia was being run.

Rather than feeling satisfied, I left upset. I really had loved my job. I felt heartbroken for Vasilyev, who had been humiliated for trying too hard, but who had, with the exception of the cranes episode, been an ideal publisher: smart, encouraging, yet generally hands-off. I rode my bicycle to a nearby cafe, where a small group of friends and colleagues were waiting to debrief me. I downed a glass of Jameson and recounted the conversation blow-by-blow; Andrei recorded it.

"What should I do?" I asked at the end.

"Are you out of your mind?" asked my friend Vera, human sciences editor at *Vokrug Sveta*.

That was enough to bring me to my senses. The editors in chief of many Russian publications were appointed by the Kremlin, and I did not want to work at any such publication—especially as the editor in chief. I went home and wrote Vasilyev a letter saying that if he still wanted me back after regime change, I would be willing to return as the cleaning lady. But not until then.

"I hope we get a chance to work together soon," he responded.

POSTSCRIPT:
APRIL 2014

If Vladimir Putin were the kind of man who could be inspired, then one might suspect that in the spring of 2012 he had been blessed with inspiration. But he is not, and he was not, and what seems to have happened in the spring of 2012 was a stroke of luck that could only be called dumb—dumb and huge. Putin took a primitive political step that set in motion a chain of events that, in barely a year and a half, would transform him from the quintessential post-ideological politician into a man with a mission, an aspiring general in a new worldwide culture war.

In the spring of 2012, Putin decided to pick on the gays. In the lead-up to the March 2012 election, faced with mass protests, Putin briefly panicked and reshuffled his staff, firing his chief ideologue, Vladislav Surkov, and replacing him with one Vyacheslav Volodin. Surkov was a snob, an intellectual, an aesthete—worse, a poet and a novelist—who had been partial to complicated schemes and endless intrigue: he liked to create movements, such as the pro-Putin youth organization Nashi, flirt with the opposition, such as it was, dabble in setting editorial policies for television stations, and insert himself personally into conflicts between media personalities or politicians. When the protests broke out in December 2011, the angry consensus around the Kremlin was that Surkov, with his propensity for intrigue, was to blame: he had allowed things to become too complicated—he had allowed simply too much.

Volodin was the exact opposite, incapable of any subtlety of thought or language. His political decisions were straightforward. When Putin supposedly ran for reelection (against a ballot stacked with four nonentities), it was most likely Volodin who decided to decree a definitive victory with 63 percent of the vote; Surkov's style would have been to hew closer to the facts and to good taste by claiming just over 50 percent. And faced with the protest movement, the new Kremlin crew reached for the bluntest instrument it could find: it called the protesters queer.

The queers themselves did not know this was happening. The protesters, including those among them who were, like me, gay, were not in the habit of watching state-controlled television. We lived in a happy little bubble where people ate and drank well, dressed even better, worked in well-designed centrally located offices doing something at least vaguely creative, vacationed with discernment, and rarely, if ever, encountered homophobia while we did any of these things. Meanwhile, in April 2012, a prominent news anchor, Dmitry Kiselev, who was also a highly placed executive in the state broadcast monopoly, was railing: "It is not enough to ban propaganda of homosexuality! We must ban blood and sperm donations by them, and if they should die in car accidents, we must burn their hearts or bury them underground, for they are unsuitable for the aiding of anyone's life." The biggest TV channel's most prominent commentator, Maxim Shevchenko, recorded a series of opinion pieces in which he explained that gays and lesbians *were* the Antichrist. As the campaign gathered steam, the patriarch of the Russian Orthodox Church weighed in, saying that the international trend toward legalizing same-sex marriage was a sign of the coming apocalypse. And by the fall of 2013, when the antigay campaign had become a mainstay of Russian politics, an hour-and-a-half-long investigative report on the topic aired in prime time. It explained that homosexuals were plotting to overthrow the Russian government and destroy the Russian family. It also claimed that the meteor that had fallen on the city of Chelyabinsk earlier that year had been God's wrath against the sodomites. It was classic war rhetoric: gays were portrayed as simultaneously extremely dangerous—and less than human.

By 2013, the antigay campaign had burst my information bubble. The media in the United States and Western Europe also noticed the campaign, which looked particularly bizarre in the summer of 2013 against the backdrop of the Supreme Court's decision in *United States v. Windsor* to uphold the right to same-sex marriage. While many people in the United States celebrated the decision as the ultimate victory of the gay rights movement, Russia was careening into the Middle Ages, a shift that suddenly warranted many newsprint inches. The Western media's consensus was that the Putin regime's antigay campaign was a distraction, meant to divert attention from thinking of the country's ominously slowing economy.

It was not. The Kremlin's antigay campaign was as blunt and sincere an expression of Putin's worldview as any the world had seen. When Putin learned of the protests, he had known immediately that he was dealing with the enemy, the enemy not just of his regime but of Russia itself, for he had long since forgotten there was a distinction. If they were the enemy, then they were not really Russians. They were the Other. And there is no one who represents the Other better than gay people.

Putin struck propaganda gold. He and Volodin and whoever else may have helped hatch the antigay campaign believed that gays were the one minority they could beat up on with impunity—that is, without incurring any diplomatic costs. This did not turn out to be true: the world reacted slowly, but it reacted strongly. But by this point, the campaign was working too well to be turned around. There was a kernel of truth at the heart of the antigay propaganda: there had been no gay people in Russia before the Soviet Union collapsed. There had been men who loved men, and women who loved women, but gay identity and its politics really were a post-Soviet Western import. And this really did make gays the quintessential foreign agent. Beating up on gays could unite the nation.

But there was more. For the first time, while looking back wistfully toward the USSR, as Putin had always done, he also—quite by accident—found himself looking into the future. The lonely nostalgic idea of hiding behind the Iron Curtain was replaced with the radical vision of opening a new chasm, starting a war against the West.

To start this new war, Russia would be forming a new alliance rather than simply re-creating the old Soviet one. It could be joined not only by many members of the old Soviet bloc but by African nations, Muslim countries, and some Latin American ones. There might even be splintering in the West and allies to be found there. Countries in the former Soviet Union started taking up antigay legislation that copied the "homosexual propaganda" law passed in Russia: Kazakhstan, Kyrgyzstan, Armenia, Georgia, Moldova—which was yanked back by the threat of being denied membership in the EU—and Lithuania, which was already a member and therefore not afraid. Countries like Uganda and Nigeria, passing ever more inventively brutal antigay legislation, now nodded toward Russia: if even a Western nation like Russia could not stomach the gay agenda, surely they were on the right path. And countries like Ecuador and Malaysia joined Russia's new informal "traditional values" bloc in the United

Nations, which succeeded in pushing three different antigay resolutions through that organization's misleadingly named Human Rights Council.

In this burgeoning international alliance, a rich source of rhetoric opened up for the Kremlin, imported by far-right evangelicals who were feeling increasingly marginalized in the United States. In Russia, Paul Cameron, a former psychologist expelled by the American Psychological Association, addressed members of the Duma, feeding them bogus statistics of the sort that had gotten him censured by professional associations in the United States—like claiming that a majority of gay people favor sex with children. The World Congress of Families, an international antigay organization, secured a plan to hold its annual conference in Moscow—in the Kremlin's Congress Hall and the giant Cathedral of Christ the Savior, both. Here in Moscow, "traditional values" was once again an applause line, and the junk science Cameron and others imported, by the likes of the discredited American sociologist Mark Regnerus, formed the basis of long treatises typed up by the new generation of Russian bureaucrats. These, in turn, were used to support legislation not only banning "homosexual propaganda" but also "protecting children from harmful information," which meant, first and foremost, any mention of homosexuality, but also any mention of death, violence, suicide, domestic abuse, unhappiness, and, really, life itself.

Most important, this "traditional values" rhetoric, some of it newly imported and some of it newly rediscovered in the writings of early-twentieth-century Russian Slavophile thinkers, gave rise to a Kremlin ideology—something that had not really existed in nearly a quarter century. In his December 2013 state-of-the-federation address before parliament, Putin outlined this ideology. It was a first: for fourteen years, as both president and prime minister, Putin had stuck to the pragmatic in his speeches, putting himself forward as a problem solver but never a leader. Now he said, "We will strive to be leaders." He meant himself—and Russia, which now had a new relationship to the world.

Claiming leadership, said Putin, "is absolutely objective and understandable for a state like Russia, with its great history and culture, with many centuries of experience not of so-called tolerance, genderless and childless, but of the real organic life of different peoples existing together within the framework of a single state." In relaying his speech into English, the Kremlin's translators chose to write "neutered and barren" rather than "genderless and childless"— a more poetic rendition that pulled a subtle veil over the statement's homophobia. What Putin was really saying, though, is that Russia's new role in the world was to protect itself and others from sliding into the Western trap of immorality, decadence, and, of course, homosexuality.

"Today many nations are revising their moral values and ethical norms, eroding ethnic traditions and differences between peoples and cultures," he continued. "Society is now required not only to recognize everyone's right to the freedom of consciousness, political views and privacy, but also to accept without question the equality of good and evil, strange as it seems, concepts that are opposite in meaning." For centuries Russians had been told that homosexuality was wrong, foreigners were bad, and the empire was right; then, with the collapse of the Soviet Union, they had been asked to change their minds about all of these things. No more! It was time to resist this scourge of tolerance and diversity creeping in from the West, said Putin. "We know that there are more and more people in the world who support our position on defending traditional values," he asserted. Russia's role was to "prevent movement backward and downward, into chaotic darkness and a return to a primitive state."

It was a perfect mixture of Slavophile anti-Western fear-mongering and Western antiliberal fear-mongering, a sweet potion for a country that had always drawn strength and unity from fear-mongering. Russia and the Soviet Union had always been a fortress under siege, a country that derived its national identity from the sense of impending assault and catastrophe. The United States and its allies had been the enemy since the middle of the twentieth century, but for a quarter century, there had been a gaping hole where national identity used to be. In the mid-1990s Yeltsin had even formed a special commission to fill it, to formulate the "national idea," but none materialized. Now a suitable new nemesis had finally been named. "Neutered and barren tolerance" was the enemy.

I was the enemy.

Darya and I packed up our family and left the country. In the end, it was not a big decision: there was nothing to decide. In June 2013 the Duma passed a ban on "homosexual propaganda" and another on adoptions by same-sex couples—a law that could be used to annul our oldest son's adoption—and announced its intention to create a mechanism for removing biological children from same-sex families as well (we had two of those). In some of the discussions, the politicians mentioned me and my family by name. The self-proclaimed leader of a "Russian Orthodox activist movement"—a gang of thugs who specialized in beating up LGBT protesters in plain view of the police and television cameras—volunteered to adopt my children. The only thing we had to discuss was when we would leave the country. We set our deadline for the end of the 2013–2014 school year (we had already paid tuition), and a few weeks later we moved it up to December 2013, a month shy of the twentieth anniversary of my residence in Moscow as an adult.

In the final weeks, our Moscow apartment—the one I was renovating at the beginning of this book, a small architectural treasure that had long been my claim to safety and home—had turned into an ongoing yard sale. And during those same weeks, protesters stood in the main square in Kyiv, demanding the resignation of President

Viktor Yanukovych, who had reneged on a pledge to form a closer alliance with the European Union. The Duma finally decided to pass a resolution on the matter—and before it did, the head of the foreign relations committee, Alexey Pushkov, a well-traveled former career diplomat turned Mikhail Gorbachev's speechwriter, turned foreign-affairs columnist, and finally turned politician, warned that if Ukraine went west, that would lead to "a broadening of the sphere of gay culture, which has become the European Union's official policy." Over the next couple of months the image of the Western threat menacing Ukraine broadened to include not only the gays but also the Americans, for whom the gays were always a stand-in anyway.

We were living in New York City when Russia annexed Crimea in March 2014. From everything I could tell, the invasion was wildly popular. Putin's approval ratings shot up above 70 percent. Even many of the long-marginalized opposition politicians praised what they called his victory. My friends in Moscow felt smaller and more isolated than ever. It had been a long and unusually cold winter in New York, but the day after Putin announced the annexation was, finally, warm enough to put on a light coat. I reached into the pocket and pulled out some bills. They were Ukrainian: the last time I had worn it, a few months earlier, several of my close-friend colleagues and I had done one of our periodic runs to Kyiv to conduct a reporting workshop. Here was something that would never happen again, for so many reasons at once, but really because one man had unleashed a war against my kind—the gays—and my other kind—the journalists—and against Ukraine as well.

In his speech to parliament announcing the annexation of Crimea, Putin warned not only of external threats but also of an internal one: "some kind of a fifth column and national-traitors of various sorts." The "national" in traitors was meant to call to mind the National Socialists, harking back to the time of the Soviet Union's greatest fears and biggest military triumph, when it beat back Nazi Germany: the "national traitors," the enemy within, were on the side of an external enemy as evil and dangerous as Hitler. A few weeks later, a giant poster briefly went up on a storefront in central Moscow, with portraits of five prominent performers and political activists who had criticized the invasion of Ukraine. THE FIFTH COLUMN. ALIENS AMONG US, read the caption.

Meanwhile, the Ministry of Culture was rapidly drafting the country's new Policy on Culture, so essential in a time of war. The resulting document contained twelve sections, with an epigraph from a speech by Putin and extensive quotes from Putin in all but one of the sections. "In his recent speeches V. V. Putin has pointed out significant distinctions between cultural trends that dominate in the West and values that are traditional for Russia," read the document, and proceeded to quote him. "The policy should list the values that characterize Russian culture," the document continued, and proceeded to quote Putin five times in a row, for an exhaustive list of Russian values. These appeared to be: protecting the rights of the majority; resisting the push for tolerance; protecting "traditional values"; standing up for conservatism; ensuring that any culture that was promoted was national in nature. In sum, the document said, the country's new credo is "Russia is not Europe." The document, published in its entirety in the daily *Izvestia*, just as every important document of the Soviet era used to be, summed up the two most important things about the state of Russia in spring 2014: it was now a country that defined itself in opposition to the West; and every nuance of its new identity was dictated directly and personally by its supreme leader.

At the end of March 2014 President Barack Obama met with other NATO leaders in Brussels to discuss Russia and Ukraine and then gave one of his clear, cogent speeches. "This is not another Cold War that we're entering into," he said. "After all, unlike the Soviet Union, Russia leads no bloc of nations, no global ideology."

He was tragically wrong. He had missed Putin's transformation from a bureaucrat who had accidentally been entrusted with a huge country into a megalomaniacal dictator who believed he was on a civilizational mission—and who was apparently supported in this view by the people of his huge country. This transformation had been drastic and sudden—the collective mind of American foreign policy, deliberative and collaborative as it is, had just learned to think of Putin as an authoritarian ruler, but this view was already outdated. Much more important now was that he had upset the entire post-WWII world order and felt justified and inspired in his aggression.

For once, it was the American president who was looking backward, describing the state of the world—and of Putin in it—as it had been a couple of years or even a couple of months earlier, before Putin had discovered and put forth his ideology. It was the Russian president who was looking forward, to unleashing an all-out culture war against the West and its values. He will score many victories in this war, and cause many more casualties, before the full gravity and danger of Putin's transformation becomes clear to Western politicians. But the ultimate casualty will be Russia itself, a country in which the 1990s flirtation with progress and democracy will be remembered as an anomaly, if it is remembered at all, and which is once again staking its future on fighting the Western world and isolating itself from it.

Acknowledgments

I am grateful to Cullen Murphy, who first suggested I write a piece about Vladimir Putin for *Vanity Fair*, and to my agent, Elyse Cheney, who noticed that the resulting piece wanted to become a book. My editor, Rebecca Saletan, made that book immeasurably better than it would have been without her. Many other people helped along the way, and I hope someday soon I will be able to thank them in print without fearing that such recognition might be harmful. You know who you are, and I hope you know how grateful I am. Two people cannot avoid mention, however: my friend and colleague Ilya Kolmanovsky, whose research and insights were crucial in the early stages of this project; and my partner, Darya Oreshkina, who has made me happier and more productive than I have ever been.

Notes

PROLOGUE

Page 3   **a draft law on *lustratsiya*:** The full text of the law is available at http://www
.shpik.info/statya1.html. Accessed July 14, 2010.

Page 3   **she learned that the KGB:** Marina Katys, "Polozhitelny itog: Interview s depu-
tatom Gosudarstvennoy Dumy, sopredsedatelem federalnoy partii Demokrati-
cheskaya Rossiya Galinoy Starovoitovoy," *Professional*, July 1, 1998. http://www
.starovoitova.ru/rus/main.php?i=5&s=29. Accessed July 14, 2010.

Page 3   **1991 post–failed-coup decree:** Constitutional Court decision citing the decree
and overturning its most important provisions. http://www.panorama.ru/ks/d9209
.shtml. Accessed July 14, 2010.

Page 4   **a decree forbidding protests:** In fact, the ban on protests was a one-two punch:
the cabinet issued a ban, and Gorbachev followed with a decree creating a special
police body to enforce the ban. Both were deemed unconstitutional by the Russian
government, whose authority Gorbachev, in turn, did not recognize. http://iv.garant
.ru/SESSION/PILOT/main.htm. Accessed July 15, 2010.

Page 6   **she immersed herself in an investigation:** Andrei Tsyganov, "Seleznev dobilsya
izvineniya za statyu Starovoitovoi," *Kommersant*, May 14, 1999. http://www
.kommersant.ru/doc-rss.aspx?DocsID=218273. Accessed July 15, 2010.

ONE. THE ACCIDENTAL PRESIDENT

Page 14   **experienced overall improvement:** Andrei Shleifer and Daniel Treisman, "A Normal Country: Russia After Communism," *Journal of Economic Perspectives*, vol. 19,
no. 1 (Winter 2005), pp. 151–74. http://www.economics.harvard.edu/faculty/
shleifer/files/normal_jep.pdf. Accessed April 30, 2011.

Page 15   **importing used European cars:** David Hoffman, *The Oligarchs: Wealth and
Power in the New Russia* (New York: PublicAffairs, 2002).

Page 15   **"He was the first bureaucrat":** Author interview with Boris Berezovsky, June
2008.

Page 17   **swindled Russia's largest carmaker:** Hoffman.

Page 17   **acquired part of a large oil company:** Whether Berezovsky was an actual owner
of 25 percent of Sibneft and 49 percent of ORT, the Channel One company, is in
fact unclear: as this book goes to press, a London court is trying to determine just
this. What is uncontested is that he was the sole manager of the television company
and drew significant income from the oil company.

Page 18   **"someone who is capable of doing it":** Natalia Gevorkyan, Natalya Timakova, and Andrei Kolesnikov, *Ot pervogo litsa: Razgovory s Vladimirom Putinym.* http://archive.kremlin.ru/articles/bookchapter1.shtml. Accessed Feb. 7, 2011.

Page 20 **"Chubais believed":** Tatyana Yumasheva (Dyachenko)'s blog, entry dated Feb. 6, 2010. http://t-yumasheva.livejournal.com/13320.html#cutid1. Accessed April 23, 2011.

TWO. THE ELECTION WAR

Page 24 **one hundred people died:** Number of victims cited according to the Moscow City Court's sentence in the case of A. O. Dekushev and Y. I. Krymshahalov. http://terror1999.narod.ru/sud/delokd/prigovor.html. Accessed May 5, 2011.

Page 26 **the decree was also illegal:** Speech by Duma member Sergei Yushenkov, Kennan Institute, Washington, D.C., April 24, 2002. http://terror99.ru/commission/kennan.htm. Accessed May 5, 2011.

Page 26 **"We will hunt them down":** Putin's Sept. 24, 1999, TV appearance. http://www.youtube.com/watch?v=A_PdYRZSW-I. Accessed May 5, 2011.

Page 27 **resemblance to Mussolini:** Unpublished memo leaked to me by Berezovsky's team in November 1999.

Page 27 **"Everyone was so tired of Yeltsin":** Author interview with Marina Litvinovich, July 1, 2008.

Page 30 **"My friends . . . My dears":** Boris Yeltsin's address, Dec. 31, 1999. Text: http://stra.teg.ru/library/national/16/0. Accessed May 6, 2011. Video: http://www.youtube.com/watch?v=yvSpiFvPUP4&feature=related. Accessed May 6, 2011.

Page 31 **"Russia's new century":** Vladimir Putin's address, Dec. 31, 1999. Text: http://stra.teg.ru/library/national/16/2/print. Accessed May 6, 2011. Video: http://www.youtube.com/watch?v=i4LLxY4RPwk. Accessed May 6, 2011.

Page 32 **"Berezovsky would keep calling me":** Author interview with Natalya Gevorkyan, June 2008.

Page 33 **"He was working directly for the enemy":** Pavel Gutiontov, "Zauryadnoye delo." http://www.ruj.ru/authors/gut/100303_4.htm. Accessed May 8, 2011.

Page 34 **"This is February 6, 2000":** Transcript of a Feb. 9, 2000, NTV newscast. http://www.library.cjes.ru/online/?a=con&b_id=426&c_id=4539. Accessed May 7, 2011.

Page 35 **attempt to break free:** Andrei Babitsky, *Na voine*, transcripts of Russian-language recordings of a book manuscript prepared for a French publisher. http://somnenie.narod.ru/ab/ab6.html. Accessed May 7, 2011.

Page 35 **face charges of forgery:** Transcript of Andrei Babitsky's press conference on March 1, 2000. http://archive.svoboda.org/archive/hr/2000/ll.030100-3.asp. Accessed May 8, 2011.

Page 35 **probably been no exchange:** Oleg Panfilov, *Istoriya Andreia Babitskogo*, chapter 3. http://www.library.cjes.ru/online/?a=con&b_id=426&c_id=4539. Accessed May 8, 2011.

Page 35 **"the information he transmitted":** Panfilov, *Istoriya Andreia Babitskogo.*

Page 35 **funded by an act of Congress:** Broadcasting Board of Governors FAQ. http://www.bbg.gov/about/faq/#q6. Accessed May 8, 2011.

Page 35 **issued a statement condemning:** Congressional Research Service report, "Chechnya Conflict: Recent Developments," updated May 3, 2000. http://www.fas.org/man/crs/RL30389.pdf. Accessed May 8, 2011.

Page 36 **"The Babitsky story":** Author interview with Natalya Gevorkyan, June 2008.

Page 37 **returned to the car and left:** For the chronology of events in Ryazan, I have relied primarily on Alexander Litvinenko and Yuri Felshtinsky, *FSB vzryvayet Rossiyu*, 2nd ed. (New York: Liberty Publishing, 2004), pp. 65–108, which combines many press reports with original reporting, and on *Ryazanski sahar: Nezavisimoye rassledovaniye s Nikolayem Nikolayevym*, the NTV television program that aired on March 24, 2000. http://video.yandex.ru/users/provorot1/view/54/. Accessed May 8, 2011.

Page 38   in at least one of the Moscow explosions: "13 sentyabrya v Rossii—den' traura
po pogibshim ot vzryvov," an unsigned news story on Gazeta.ru, Sept. 10, 1999.
http://gazeta.lenta.ru/daynews/10-09-1999/10mourn.htm. Accessed May 8, 2011.

Page 38   "The more alert we are": ITAR-TASS, as cited by Litvinenko and Felshtinsky,
FSB vzryvayet Rossiyu.

Page 39   "First, there was no explosion": *Ryazanski sahar.*

THREE. THE AUTOBIOGRAPHY OF A THUG

Page 43   the Siege of Leningrad: Michael Jones, *Leningrad: State of Siege* (New York: Basic
Books, 2008).

Page 44   "Imagine a soldier": Ales' Adamovich and Daniil Granin, *Blokadnaya kniga.*
http://lib.rus.ec/b/212340/read. Accessed Feb. 7, 2011.

Page 44   *Burzhuikas:* Harrison Salisbury, *The 900 Days: The Siege of Leningrad* (New York:
Da Capo Press, 2003), pp. vii–viii.

Page 44   a wood-burning stove in every room: Oleg Blotsky, *Vladimir Putin: Istoriya zhizni*
(Moscow: Mezhdunarodniye Otnosheniya), p. 24.

Page 44   His parents . . . had survived the siege: Gevorkyan et al.

Page 45   twice as many women: Yuri Polyakov, Valentina Zhitomirskaya, and Natalya
Aralovets, " 'Demograficheskoye ekho' voyny," published in the online journal
Skepsis. http://scepsis.ru/library/id_1260.html. Accessed Feb. 7, 2011.

Page 45   given him up for adoption: Irina Bobrova, "Kto pridumal Putinu gruzinskiye
korni?" *Moskovski komsomolets*, June 13, 2006. http://www.compromat.ru/
page_18786.htm. Accessed Feb. 7, 2011.

Page 45   inclined to believe the story: Author interview with Natalia Gevorkyan,
June 2008.

Page 46   the Putins' apartment: Childhood friend Viktor Borisenko, quoted in Blotsky,
Vladimir Putin: Istoriya zhizni, pp. 72, 89.

Page 47   a striking assertion: Gevorkyan et al.

Page 47   the Putins emerge as practically rich: Yevgeniy Putin, quoted in Blotsky, p. 46.

Page 48   "Some courtyard this was": Viktor Borisenko, quoted in Blotsky, pp. 68–69.

Page 48   "If anyone ever insulted him": Viktor Borisenko, quoted in Blotsky, p. 68.

Page 49   "The labor [shop] teacher": Viktor Borisenko, quoted in Blotsky, p. 67.

Page 49   "Why did you not get inducted": Gevorkyan et al.

Page 50   as a sixth-grader: Teacher Vera Gurevich, quoted ibid.

Page 50   "We were playing": Grigory Geilikman, quoted in Blotsky, p. 160.

Page 50   "We were in eighth grade": Nikolai Alekhov, quoted in Blotsky, p. 161.

Page 50   "He once invited me": Sergei Roldugin, quoted in Gevorkyan et al.

Page 51   "Someone picked on him": Ibid.

Page 52   hand-to-hand combat: Blotsky, p. 259.

Page 52   theme song from the miniseries: "S vyslannymi iz SshA razvedchikami vstre-
tilsya Vladimir Putin," July 25, 2010. http://lenta.ru/news/2010/07/25/spies/.
Accessed Feb. 25, 2011.

Page 52   "When I was in ninth grade": Blotsky, p. 199.

Page 53   subversive troops: Y. Popov, "Diversanty Stalina." http://militera.lib.ru/h/popov_
au2/01.html. Accessed Feb. 25, 2011.

Page 53   one of only four survivors: Gevorkyan et al.

Page 53   "some intelligence officer for sure": Ibid.

Page 54   "A man came out": Blotsky, pp. 199–200.

Page 54   "He surprised everyone": Gevorkyan et al.

Page 55   Putin graduated from secondary school: Blotsky, p. 155.

Page 55   number of cars: http://www.ref.by/refs/1/31164/1.html. Mikhail Blinkin,
"Avtomobil' v gorode: Osobennosti natsionalnogo puti," http://www.intelros.ru/
pdf/arc/02_2010/42-45%20Blinkin.pdf. Accessed Oct. 27, 2011.

Page 55   gave the car to their son: Gevorkyan et al.

Page 56   Putin made a thousand rubles: Ibid.
Page 56   an overcoat for himself: Gevorkyan et al.; Blotsky, pp. 226–27.
Page 56   "All through my university years": Gevorkyan et al.
Page 57   "not particularly outgoing": Blotsky, p. 287.
Page 57   "He says, 'Let's go'": Ibid., pp. 287–88.
Page 57   "Once I tried": Sergei Roldugin, quoted in Gevorkyan et al.
Page 58   "That's how it happened": Gevorkyan et al.
Page 58   a tiny minority: Sergei Zakharov, "Brachnost' v Rossii: Istoriya i sovremennost'," *Demoskop Weekly*, Oct. 16–29, 2006, pp. 261–62. http://www.demoscope.ru/weekly/2006/0261/tema02.php. Accessed Feb. 27, 2011.
Page 58   "One evening": Gevorkyan et al.
Page 59   such was his cover: Ibid.
Page 59   "I was most amazed": Ibid.
Page 60   "Only the Central Committee": Vadim Bakatin, *Izbavleniye ot KGB* (Moscow: Novosti, 1992), pp. 45–46.
Page 61   Article 190': Bakatin, pp. 32–33.
Page 61   constant surveillance and harassment: Filipp Bobkov, *KGB i vlast* (Moscow: Veteran MP, 1995).
Page 61   thoroughly familiar with the way it was organized: Gevorkyan et al.
Page 61   A perfectly laudatory memoir: Vladimir Usol'tsev, *Sosluzhivets* (Moscow: Eksmo, 2004), p. 186.
Page 61   "It was an entirely unremarkable school": Ibid.
Page 61   Counterintelligence officers in Moscow: Bobkov.
Page 61   assigned to the intelligence unit: Gevorkyan et al.
Page 62   did his job well: Ibid.
Page 63   a little Stasi world: Ludmila Putina, quoted ibid.
Page 63   Putin drank beer: Gevorkyan et al.
Page 64   Putin was assigned: Author interview with Sergei Bezrukov (former KGB agent in Berlin), Düsseldorf, August 17, 2011.
Page 64   Putin and his two colleagues: Usol'tsev, pp. 70–74; author interview with Sergei Bezrukov, Düsseldorf, August 17, 2011.
Page 64   small monthly hard-currency payments: Usol'tsev, p. 36.
Page 65   they made a lot more money: Ibid., p. 30.
Page 65   so unreachable for someone like Putin: Author interview with Sergei Bezrukov, Düsseldorf, August 17, 2011.
Page 65   a former RAF member: Author interview with the man, Bavaria, August 18, 2011; he asked that his name not be printed.
Page 65   every other officer . . . had his own office: Usol'tsev, p. 62.
Page 66   Former agents estimate: Usol'tsev, p. 105; author interview with Sergei Bezrukov, Düsseldorf, August 17, 2011.
Page 66   Putin's biggest success: Author interview with Sergei Bezrukov, Düsseldorf, August 17, 2011.
Page 66   The KGB leadership: Bobkov.
Page 66   a public statement condemning secret-police crimes: O. N. Ansberg and A. D. Margolis, eds., *Obshchestvennaya zhizn' Leningrada v gody perestroiki, 1985–1991: Sbornik materialov* (St. Petersburg: Serebryany Vek, 2009), p. 192.
Page 68   demonstrations in East Germany continued: Elizabeth A. Ten Dyke, *Dresden and the Paradoxes of Memory in History* (New York: Routledge, 2001).
Page 69   shoving papers into a wood-burning stove: Gevorkyan et al.
Page 70   "I was scared to go into stores": Ludmila Putina, quoted ibid.
Page 70   "They cannot do this": Sergei Roldugin, quoted in Gevorkyan et al.

FOUR. ONCE A SPY

Page 74   "The people of our generation": *Obshchestvennaya zhizn'*, p. 502.

Page 75   "stop misinforming people": Sergei Vasilyev, memoirs published in the *Obvodny Times*, vol. 4, no. 22 (April 2007), p. 8, quoted in *Obshchestvennaya zhizn'*, p. 447.

Page 75   "It seems, after the dust": Alexander Vinnikov, *Tsena svobody*, quoted in *Obshchestvennaya zhizn'*, p. 449.

Page 76   "We all found one another": Yelena Zelinskaya, "Vremya ne zhdet," *Merkuriy*, vol. 3 (1987), quoted in *Obshchestvennaya zhizn'*, pp. 41–42.

Page 76   a living page: Vasilyev, quoted in *Obshchestvennaya zhizn'*, p. 447.

Page 76   a group of young Leningrad economists: *Obshchestvennaya zhizn'*, pp. 47, 76.

Page 77   Leningrad saw its first political rally: Ibid., pp. 51, 52, 54, 74.

Page 77   "The rules were, anyone could speak for five minutes": Ibid., p. 632.

Page 78   start eating their lemons: Ibid., p. 633.

Page 79   a rally in memory of victims of political repression: Ibid., p. 112.

Page 79   the People's Front: The first meeting of the People's Front, held in Leningrad in August 1988, was attended by representatives of twenty organizations from different Russian cities and twelve more from other Soviet republics. http://www.agitclub.ru/front/frontdoc/zanarfront1.htm. Accessed Jan. 13, 2011.

Page 79   "An organization that aims": *Obshchestvennaya zhizn'*, p. 119.

Page 80   "They would gather": Andrei Boltyansky, interview, 2008, ibid., p. 434.

Page 81   "With a cigarette dangling from her lips": Petr Shelish, interview, 2008, *Obshchestvennaya zhizn'*, p. 884 of the online version.

Page 81   conflict erupted between Azerbaijan and Armenia: Thomas de Waal, *Black Garden: Armenia and Azerbaijan Through Peace and War* (New York: New York University Press, 2004).

Page 82   solidarity with the Armenian people: *Obshchestvennaya zhizn'*, p. 115.

Page 82   Armenian children from Sumgait: Alexander Vinnikov, memoir, ibid., p. 450.

Page 82   Karabakh Committee: *Obshchestvennaya zhizn'*, p. 126.

Page 82   Article 70: Article 70, Penal Code of the RSFSR. http://www.memo.ru/history/diss/links/st70.htm. Accessed Jan. 17, 2011.

Page 82   the last Article 70 case: *Obshchestvennaya zhizn'*, p. 127.

Page 83   What the censors did not realize: Natalya Serova, interview, ibid., p. 621.

Page 83   a new election law: http://pravo.levonevsky.org/baza/soviet/sssr1440.htm. Accessed Jan. 17, 2011.

Page 83   A committee called Election-89: A flyer put out by the committee Election-89; reproduced in *Obshchestvennaya zhizn'*, pp. 139–40.

Page 84   "I have a dream": Anatoly Sobchak, *Zhila-Byla Kommunisticheskaya partiya*, pp. 45–48, cited in *Obshchestvennaya zhizn'*, p. 623.

Page 85   "Get that away from me": Yury Afanasiev, interviewed by Yevgeni Kiselev on Echo Moskvy, 2008. http://www.echo.msk.ru/programs/all/548798-echo/. Accessed Jan. 18, 2011.

Page 86   Tens, possibly hundreds, of thousands: Alexander Nikishin, "Pokhorony akademika A. D. Sakharova," *Znamya*, no. 5 (1990), pp. 178–88.

Page 86   Thousands of people fell into formation: "A. D. Sakharov," *Voskreseniye*, vol. 33, no. 65. http://piter.anarhist.org/fevral12.htm. Accessed Jan. 18, 2011.

Page 87   his last time up on the podium: Alexander Vinnikov, memoir, *Obshchestvennaya zhizn'*, p. 453.

Page 87   "The following day": Marina Salye, interview, 2008, *Obshchestvennaya zhizn'*, pp. 615–16.

Page 88   she needed immunity from prosecution: Ibid.

Page 89   "That is not your seat": Igor Kucherenko, memoir, *Obshchestvennaya zhizn'*, p. 556.

Page 90   the first meeting of the first democratically elected: Alexander Vinnikov, memoir, *Obshchestvennaya zhizn'*, online version only, pp. 568–69.

Page 90   "It was fantastical": Viktor Voronkov, interview, 2008, *Obshchestvennaya zhizn'*, p. 463.

Page 90 **"an acute sense of democracy":** Nikolai Girenko, memoir, *Obshchestvennaya zhizn'*, p. 473.

Page 90 **"The Mariinsky took on the look":** Viktor Veniaminov, memoir, *Avtobiografiya Peterburgskogo gorsoveta*, p. 620, cited in *Obshchestvennaya zhizn'*, p. 449.

Page 90 **"People had so longed to be heard":** Bella Kurkova, memoir, in *Obshchestvennaya zhizn'*, p. 552.

Page 91 **"I wish someone":** Author interview with Marina Salye, March 14, 2010.

Page 91 **"could derail a working meeting":** Vladimir Gelman, interview, *Obshchestvennaya zhizn'*, p. 471.

Page 92 **he opposed changing the name:** Dmitry Gubin, "Interview predsedatelya Lenosveta A. A. Sobchaka," *Ogonyok*, no. 28 (1990), cited in *Obshchestvennaya zhizn'*, p. 269.

Page 92 **honored their agreement:** Alexander Vinnikov, memoir, *Obshchestvennaya zhizn'*, pp. 453–54.

Page 92 **"We realized our mistake":** Author interview with Marina Salye, March 14, 2010; Vinnikov, memoir, *Obshchestvennaya zhizn'*, pp. 453–54.

Page 93 **"There were officers":** Bakatin, p. 138.

Page 94 **"The KGB, as it existed":** Ibid., pp. 36–37.

Page 95 **he planned to start writing a dissertation:** Gevorkyan et al.

Page 95 **"I remember the scene well":** Ibid.

Page 96 **"Putin was most certainly":** Anatoly Sobchak, interview, *Literaturnaya Gazeta*, February 2000, pp. 23–29, cited in *Anatoly Sobchak: Kakim on byl* (Moscow: Gamma-Press, 2007), p. 20.

Page 97 **A former colleague:** Author interview with Sergei Bezrukov, Düsseldorf, August 17, 2011.

Page 98 **"I told them, 'I have received'":** Gevorkyan et al.

Page 98 **the Committee for Constitutional Oversight:** Komitet Konstitutsionnogo Nadzora SSSR, 1989–91. http://www.panorama.ru/ks/iz8991.shtml. Accessed March 8, 2011.

Page 98 **the KGB ignored it:** Bakatin, 135.

Page 98 **conducted round-the-clock surveillance:** Ibid.

Page 98 **he claimed not to report to the KGB:** Gevorkyan et al.

Page 99 **"It was a very difficult decision":** Ibid.

FIVE. A COUP AND A CRUSADE

Page 102 **pogroms broke out in the streets:** "Playing the Communal Card: Communal Violence and Human Rights," Human Rights Watch report. http://www.hrw.org/legacy/reports/1995/communal/. Accessed Jan. 26, 2011.

Page 102 **ration cards:** *Leningradskaya pravda*, Nov. 28, 1990, cited in *Obshchestvennaya zhizn'*, p. 299.

Page 103 **The city came perilously close:** Vladimir Monakhov, interview, *Obshchestvennaya zhizn'*, p. 574.

Page 103 **Former dissident and political prisoner Yuli Rybakov:** Yuli Rybakov, interview, *Obshchestvennaya zhizn'*, p. 610.

Page 104 **sugar disappeared:** Vladimir Belyakov, memoir, *Obshchestvennaya zhizn'*, pp. 425–26.

Page 105 **"And we get there":** Author interview with Marina Salye, March 14, 2010.

Page 106 **Some people even claimed to know the date:** Alexander Konanykhin. http://www.snob.ru/go-to-comment/305858. Accessed March 10, 2011.

Page 108 **promises to the people:** "Obrashcheniye k sovetskomu narodu," in Y. Kazarin and B. Yakovlev, *Smert' zagovora: Belaya kniga* (Moscow: Novosti, 1992), pp. 12–16.

Page 108 **"taking into account the needs":** Kazarin and Yakovlev, *Smert' zagovora*, p. 7.

Page 109 **Igor Artemyev:** Igor Artemyev, memoir, *Obshchestvennaya zhizn'*, pp. 407–8.

Page 109   **no state of emergency:** Alexander Vinnikov, memoir, *Obshchestvennaya zhizn'*, pp. 454–55.

Page 109   **a "military coup":** Igor Artemyev, memoir, *Obshchestvennaya zhizn'*, p. 408.

Page 110   **"We told him that we are planning to go":** Author interview with Marina Salye, March 14, 2010.

Page 110   **the arrest did not take place:** Bakatin, p. 21.

Page 110   **Sobchak called Leningrad:** A. Golovkin and A. Chernov, interview with Anatoly Sobchak, *Moskovskiye novosti*, Aug. 26, 1991, quoted in *Obshchestvennaya zhizn'*, p. 627.

Page 111   **"Why did I do so?"** Sobchak, memoir, *Obshchestvennaya zhizn'*, p. 627.

Page 111   **Moscow's city council:** Kazarin and Yakovlev, p. 131.

Page 111   **ordered city services:** G. Popov, "Zayavleniye mera goroda Moskvy," in Kazarin and Yakovlev, pp. 68–69.

Page 111   **Moscow's deputy mayor, Yuri Luzhkov:** Center Labyrinth, Luzhkov biography. http://www.anticompromat.org/luzhkov/luzhkbio.html. Accessed March 13, 2011.

Page 112   **the Mariinsky Palace:** Yuli Rybakov, interview, *Obshchestvennaya zhizn'*, p. 612.

Page 112   **"We call on the people of Russia":** B. Yeltsin, I. Silayev, and R. Khasbulatov, "K grazhdanam Rossii," in Kazarin and Yakovlev, p. 42.

Page 112   **He was terrified:** Vyacheslav Shcherbakov, interview, *Obshchestvennaya zhizn'*, p. 681.

Page 112   **"What the hell did he do?"** Ibid.; author interview with Marina Salye, March 14, 2010; text of decree as dictated by Rutskoy and as read by Sobchak, provided by Salye.

Page 114   **"the flag was on a corner":** Elena Zelinskaya, interview, *Obshchestvennaya zhizn'*, p. 505.

Page 115   **the coup was not what it had seemed:** Author interview with Marina Salye, March 14, 2010.

Page 116   **"I had pushed five chairs":** Shcherbakov, in *Obshchestvennaya zhizn'*, p. 683.

Page 117   **"But I was not a KGB officer":** Gevorkyan et al.

Page 117   **"Kryuchkov simply would not":** Author interview with Arseniy Roginsky, Moscow, June 20, 2008.

Page 118   **The meat was delivered:** Letter from Marina Salye to Chief Comptroller of the Russian Federation Yuri Boldyrev, dated March 25, 1992, unpublished.

Page 119   **Boldyrev had written a letter:** Letter from Yuri Boldyrev to Petr Aven, dated March 13, 1992, document #105-177/n.

Page 119   **a man with an empty office:** Author interview with Irene Commeaut, Paris, June 2010.

Page 119   **eager, curious, and intellectually engaged:** Ilya Kolmanovsky interview with Alexander Margolis, St. Petersburg, June 2008.

Page 119   **"The Putins had a dog":** Marina Yentaltseva, quoted in Gevorkyan et al.

Page 120   **"I believed at the time":** Gevorkyan et al.

Page 122   **a simple kickback scheme:** *Otchet rabochey deputatskoy gruppy Komiteta po mezhdunarodnym i vneshnim svyazyam, postoyannykh komissiy po prodovolstviyu, torgovle i sfere bytovykh uslug Sankt-Peterburgskogo gorodskogo Soveta narodnykh deputatov po voprosu kvotirovaniya i litsenzirovaniya eksporta i importa tovarov na territorii Sankt-Peterburga*, with a resolution of May 8, 1992, #88; Marina Salye, "Putin—prezident korrumpirovannoy oligarkhii!" obtained from the Glasnost Foundation in Moscow, March 18, 2000.

Page 122   **"I think the city":** Gevorkyan et al.

Page 122   **"The point of the whole operation":** Salye, "Putin—prezident."

Page 123   **a three-page letter:** "Analiz normativnykh dokumentov, izdavayemykh merom i vitse-merom S. Peterburga," dated Jan. 15, 1992, bears the notation: "Given to B. Yeltsin on 15 January 1992."

Page 124   **Sobchak was handing out apartments:** See, for example, "Rasporyazheniye mera

Sankt-Peterburga o predostavlenii zhiloy ploshchadi Kurkovoy B. A.," 08.12.1992,
#1107-R; and "Rasporyazheniye mera Sankt-Peterburga o predostavlenii zhiloy
ploshchadi Stepashinu S. V.," 16.12.1992, #1147-R.
Page 125 **"And here are the papers":** Author interview with Marina Salye, March 14, 2010.
Page 125 **"This was different":** Ibid.
Page 126 **the Supreme Soviet had a presidium:** http://1993.sovnarkom.ru/TEXT/
SPRAVCHN/VSOVET/vsovet1.htm. Accessed April 2, 2011.
Page 127 **a decree dissolving the St. Petersburg city council:** Besik Pipia, "Lensovetu
stuknulo 10 let," *Nezavisimaya gazeta,* April 5, 2000. http://www.ng.ru/politics
/2000-04-05/3_lensovet.html. Accessed April 2, 2011.
Page 127 **in favor of supporting Putin:** Author interview with Marina Salye, March
14, 2010.
Page 129 **"a bureaucratic police regime":** "Pokhmelkin, Yushenkov, Gologlev i Rybakov
vyshli iz SPS," unsigned news story, newsru.com. http://www.newsru.com/
russia/14jan2002/sps.html. Accessed May 8, 2011.
Page 129 **Yushenkov was shot:** "V Moskve ubit deputat Gosdumy Sergei Yushenkov,"
unsigned news story, newsru.com. http://www.newsru.com/russia/17apr
2003/killed.html. Accessed May 8, 2011.
Page 129 **"Sometimes, when we journalists":** Masha Gessen, "Pamyati Sergeya Yushenkova," polit.ru, April 18,2003. http://www.polit.ru//world/2003/04/18/
615774.html. Accessed May 8, 2011.

SIX. THE END OF A REFORMER
Page 132 **"could be removed by those very same":** Gevorkyan et al.
Page 133 **a European Union event in Hamburg:** Vladimir Churov, quoted ibid.
Page 134 **The city's economy was in shambles:** Anatoly Sobchak, *Dyuzhina nozhey v spinu*
(Moscow: Vagrius/Petro-News, 1999), p. 72.
Page 135 **relative levels of standard of living:** Original reporting for Masha Gessen,
"Printsip Pitera," *Itogi,* Sept. 5, 2000.
Page 135 **"There was a concert":** Alexander Bogdanov, interview, *Obshchestvennaya zhizn',*
pp. 431–32.
Page 136 **"Not once during this time":** Radio Liberty interview with Yuri Boldyrev, March
9, 2010. http://www.svobodanews.ru/articleprintview/1978453.html. Accessed
Dec. 1, 2011.
Page 137 **"There was a show":** Ilya Kolmanovsky interview with Anna Sharogradskaya,
June 1, 2008.
Page 138 **a brutal attempt on his life:** Sobchak, *Dyuzhina,* pp. 73–78.
Page 138 **giving out loans and grants:** Boris Vishnevsky, "Kto i zachem kanoniziruyet
Sobchaka?" Radio Svoboda, Feb. 25, 2010. http://www.svobodanews.ru/content/
article/1968322.html. Accessed Oct. 27, 2011.
Page 139 **Almost all the building's residents:** "Lyudi oni horoshiye, no kvartirny vopros ih
isportil . . ." *Na strazhe Rodiny,* August 14, 1996; Brian Whitmore, "Is a Probe of City
Graft a Tool of City Hall?" *St. Petersburg Times,* April 9, 1998.
Page 140 **arranged a good post for him:** Gevorkyan et al.
Page 141 **all but running to the plane:** Ibid.; Boris Vishnevsky, *K demokratii i obratno.*
http://www.yabloko.ru/Publ/Book/Freedom/freedom_054.html. Accessed April 10,
2011.
Page 141 **taken verbatim from an American textbook:** Julie Corwin, "Russia: U.S. Academics
Charge Putin with Plagiarizing Thesis," RFERL website, March 27, 2006. http://www
.rferl.org/content/article/1067113.html. Accessed April 10, 2011.
Page 142 **the former mayor was aiming:** Peter Reddaway, "Some Notes on the Possible
Murder of Sobchak, the Political Career and Persecution of Marina Sal'ye, and Some
Related Cases," unpublished paper.
Page 142 **"the new Stalin":** Reddaway.

Page 143 **The request was urgent:** Author interview with Natalia Rozhdestvenskaya, March 2000.

Page 144 **he advanced the theory:** Arkady Vaksberg, *Le Laboratoire des Poisons: De Lénine à Poutine* (Paris: Buchet Chastel, 2007).

Page 144 **Vaksberg's car was blown up:** Reddaway.

SEVEN. THE DAY THE MEDIA DIED

Page 150 **its voter rolls swelled:** OSCE Mission report on the March 26, 2000, election, Russian translation. http://hro-uz.narod.ru/vibori.html. Accessed May 17, 2011.

Page 151 **over 52 percent of the vote:** 2000 election statistics. http://www.electoral geography.com/ru/countries/r/russia/2000-president-elections-russia.html. Accessed March 17, 2011.

Page 151 **Kremlin's historic Great Palace:** Andrei Kolesnikov, *Ya Putina videl!* (Moscow: Eksmo, 2005), p. 13.

Page 151 **suffered a trauma at birth:** Movement specialist Brenda Connors quoted in Paul Starobin, "The Accidental Autocrat," *Atlantic*, March 2005. http://www.theatlantic .com/magazine/archive/2005/03/the-accidental-autocrat/3725/. Accessed May 9, 2011.

Page 151 **Watch for the Left-handed:** Shamil Idiatullin and Olga Tatarchenko, "Pora perevodit' chasy na pravuyu ruku," *Kommersant*, May 18, 2000. http://www.kommer sant.ru/Doc/148145. Accessed May 19, 2011.

Page 152 **white-gold Patek Philippe:** "Kakiye chasy nosyat prezidenty i oligarkhi," unsigned story on newsru.com, posted Feb. 17, 2005. http://www.newsru.com/ russia/17feb2005/watch.html. Accessed May 19, 2011.

Page 152 **"an old man of short stature":** Kolesnikov, p. 16.

Page 152 **"I would like to report":** Vitaly Yaroshevsky, "Operatsiya 'Vnedreniye'-zavershena," interview with Olga Kryshtanovskaya, *Novaya Gazeta*, Aug. 30, 2004. http://www.novayagazeta.ru/data/2004/63/43.html. Accessed May 19, 2011.

Page 153 **"He called me in":** Author interview with Mikhail Kasyanov, Moscow, May 18, 2011.

Page 154 **defense spending would be increased:** Masha Gessen, "Lockstep to Putin's New Military Order," *New York Times*, Feb. 29, 2000, p. 21.

Page 155 **claimed no knowledge:** Sergei Parkhomenko, "Besedy na yasnom glazu," *Itogi*, May 11, 2000. http://www.itogi.ru/archive/2000/20/111020.html. Accessed May 21, 2011.

Page 158 **One thing was clear:** Original reporting for Masha Gessen, "Leningradskoye delo," *Itogi*, July 18, 2000. http://www.itogi.ru/archive/2000/29/112897.html. Accessed May 23, 2011.

Page 159 **"There are no charges":** Author interview with Nina Lepchenko, July 3, 2000.

Pages 160 **stopped being a threat:** Masha Gessen, "Leningradskoye delo," *Itogi*, July 18, 2000.

Page 161 **release him pending trial:** "Glava 'Russkogo video' Dmitry Rozhdestvensky umer ot serdechnogo pristupa," unsigned news story on lenta.ru. http://lenta .ru/russia/2002/06/06/rusvideo/. Accessed May 23, 2011.

Page 163 **debts would be forgiven:** Mikhail Kasyanov, *Bez Putina* (Moscow: Novaya Gazeta, 2009), pp. 70–73.

Page 163 **but also by the press minister:** Dmitry Pinsker, "Ulika nomer 6," *Itogi*, Sept. 26, 2000. http://www.itogi.ru/archive/2000/39/114667.html. Accessed May 25, 2011.

Page 163 **Gusinsky said publicly:** "Gusinsky ne budet ispolnyat' soglasheniya s Gazpromom, potomu shto oni podpisany pod ugrozoy lisheniya svobody. Ugrozhal yemu lichno Lesin," unsigned news story on www.polit.ru. http://old.polit .ru/documents/320557.html. Accessed May 25, 2011.

Page 164 **Putin refused to interfere:** "Putin schitayet, shto konflikt mezhdu Gazpromom i Media-Mostom—spor khozyaystvuyushchikh subyektov, reshat, kotoryi dolzhen sud," unsigned news item on www.polit.ru.http://old.polit.ru/documents/329155 .html. Accessed May 25, 2011.

Page 164 **reprimanding his press minister:** "Kasyanov snova publichno otchital Lesina. Na tom delo i konchilos'," unsigned news item on www.polit.ru.http://old.polit.ru/ documents/334896.html. Accessed May 25, 2011.

Page 166 **"Death is on board with us":** Boris Kuznetsov, *"Ona utonula . . .": Pravda o "Kurske," kotoruyu skryl genprokuror Ustinov* (Moscow: De-Fakto, 2005).

Page 167 **confirm there were no survivors:** "Gibel atomnoy podvodnoy lodki 'Kursk.' Khronologiya," unsigned item on RIA Novosti. http://ria.ru/society/20050812/ 41140663.html. Accessed June 1, 2011.

Page 168 **"I was screaming":** Author interview with Marina Litvinovich, July 1, 2008.

Page 169 **"'Do you believe that the guys'":** Kolesnikov, p. 35.

Page 170 **"'Cancel the mourning immediately!'":** Ibid., pp. 38–39.

Page 171 **"You saw it on television?":** *Programma Sergeya Dorenko ob APL Kursk*, aired Sept. 2, 2000. http://sergeydorenko.spb.ru/news-1-24.htm. Accessed June 1, 2011.

Page 173 **"It sank":** *Larry King Live*, "Russian President Vladimir Putin Discusses Domestic and Foreign Affairs," aired Sept. 8, 2000. http://transcripts.cnn.com/TRAN SCRIPTS/0009/08/lkl.00.html. Accessed June 1, 2011.

Page 174 **Testifying in a London court:** Alexander Voloshin, London Commercial Court testimony, November 14, 2011.

Page 174 **"I wrote about an American journalist":** Author interview with Boris Berezovsky, June 2008.

Page 174 **"I've always told people":** Yelena Bonner, press conference, Moscow, Nov. 30, 2000.

Page 175 **"What a shitty time":** Yuri Samodurov, press conference, Moscow, Nov. 30, 2000.

EIGHT. THE DISMANTLING OF DEMOCRACY

Page 177 **"In December 2000, I went":** "A Year of Putin," a roundtable discussion held in Moscow, Dec. 26, 2000. The speakers were Leonid Ionin, dean of applied political science at the Higher School of Economics; Duma deputy Vyacheslav Igrunov; political adviser Simor Kordonsky; philosopher Alexander Tsipko; and Carnegie Center scholar Andrei Ryabov.

Page 180 **"I spent six years":** Yuli Rybakov, interviewed by Marina Koroleva on Echo Moskvy, Jan. 17, 2001. http://www.echo.msk.ru/programs/beseda/13380.phtml. Accessed June 7, 2011.

Page 181 **an undercover KGB agent:** Leonid Drachevsky worked in Soviet embassies in Spain and Poland.

Page 181 **KGB officers from Leningrad:** Viktor Cherkesov and Georgy Poltavchenko.

Page 181 **a police general:** Petr Latyshev.

Page 181 **army generals:** Viktor Kazantsev and Konstantin Pulikovsky.

Page 182 **"I assert that the most":** Boris Berezovsky, "Lichniye svobody—glavny zakon demokraticheskogo obchshestva. Otkrytoye pismo prezidentu Rossiyskoy federatsii Vladimiru Putinu," *Kommersant*, May 31, 2000. http://www.kommersant.ru/ doc/149293/print. Accessed May 1, 2011.

Page 182 **group voting became routine:** OSCE Election Observation Mission Report 2004. http://www.osce.org/odihr/elections/russia/33101. Accessed June 8, 2011.

Page 183 **Darya Oreshkina:** Full disclosure: A couple of years after defending her dissertation on the topic, Darya became my life partner.

Page 183 **more of their power to decide:** Darya Oreshkina, *Kartograficheskiy metod v issledovanii elektoral'nogo povedeniya naseleniya Rossiyskoy Federatsii*, Ph.D. dissertation defended at Moscow State University in 2006.

Page 184 **"a powerful inoculation":** Ilya Kolmanovsky interview with Alexander Margolis, St. Petersburg, June 2008.

Page 184 **depended on their vote:** Golos press conference, Moscow, March 14, 2004.

Page 188 **An exhaustive study conducted:** Soyuz Zhurnalistov Rossii, "Predvaritel'niy otchyot o monitoringe osveshcheniya s SMI vyborov Prezidenta Rossiyskoy Federatsii 14 marta 2004 g." http://www.ruj.ru/news_2004/news_040331_1.html. Accessed Dec. 3, 2011.

Page 190 **"One cannot but weep":** "Putin obyavil o perestroike gosudarstva posle tragedii v Beslane," unsigned news item on newsru.com, and the full text of Putin's speech, Sept. 13, 2004. http://www.newsru.com/russia/13sep2004/putin.html. Accessed June 9, 2011.

NINE. RULE OF TERROR

Page 199 **"Just three weeks ago he was":** "Terrible Effects of Poison on Russian Spy Shown in First Pictures," unsigned story, *Daily Mail*, Nov. 21, 2006. http://www.dailymail .co.uk/news/article-417248/Terrible-effects-poison-Russian-spy-shown-pictures .html. Accessed June 22, 2011.

Page 199 **A few hours later . . . he was dead:** Author interview with Marina Litvinenko, London, April 24, 2011.

Page 203 **found evidence:** Alexander Litvinenko and Yuri Felshtinsky, *FSB vzryvayet Rossiyu* (New York: Liberty Publishing, 2004).

Page 203 **other evidence began to emerge:** Alexander Goldfarb with Marina Litvinenko, *Sasha, Volodya, Boris . . .* 2nd ed. (New York and London: AGC/Grani, 2010), p. 236.

Page 205 **"They were very happy":** L. Burban et al., "Nord-Ost. Neokonchennoye rassledovaniye. Sobytiya, fakty, vyvody," Moscow, April 26, 2006, Appendix 6.5, "Opisaniye sobytiy poterpevshey Karpovoy T. I." http://www.pravdabeslana.ru/nordost/ pril6.htm. Accessed June 23, 2011.

Page 205 **"Esteemed President":** Burban et al., *Khronologiya terakta.* http://www .pravdabeslana.ru/nordost/1-2.htm. Accessed June 23, 2011.

Page 208 **"You are welcome and":** Elaine Sciolino, "Putin Unleashes His Fury Against Chechen Guerrillas," *New York Times,* Nov. 12, 2002. http://www.nytimes .com/2002/11/12/international/europe/12RUSS.html. Accessed June 23, 2011.

Page 208 **the video of him lashing out:** See, for example, http://www.youtube.com/ watch?v=m-6ejE1KG8A. Accessed June 23, 2011.

Page 209 **Khanpash Terkibaev:** Author interview with Ahmed Zakaev, London, June 6, 2011.

Page 209 **gave him all the information:** "Litvinenko: FSB ubila Yushenkova za pravdu o Nord-Oste," unsigned story on grani.ru, April 25, 2003. http://grani.ru/Events/ Terror/m.30436.html. Accessed June 24, 2011.

Page 210 **Moscow, he said:** Anna Politkovskaya, "Odin iz gruppy terroristov utselel. My yego nashli," *Novaya Gazeta,* April 28, 2003. http://politkovskaya.novaya gazeta.ru/pub/2003/2003-035.shtml. Accessed June 20, 2011.

Page 211 **caused by an unknown toxin:** "K zaklyuchehiyu kommissionnoy sudebnomeditsinskoy expertizy o pravilnosti lecheniya Shchekochikhina Yuriya Petrovicha, 1950 goda rozhdeniya," *Novaya Gazeta,* July 1, 2004. http://2004.novayagazeta.ru/ nomer/2004/46n/n46n-s05.shtml. Accessed June 20, 2011.

Page 211 **possible secret-police involvement:** Author interview with Ahmed Zakaev, London, June 6, 2011.

Page 212 **Her plan was to act:** Sergei Sokolov and Dmitry Muratov, "Anna Politkovskaya otravlena FSB," *Novaya Gazeta,* Sept. 4, 2004. http://tapirr.narod.ru/politkov skaya2005.html#отравелена. Accessed June 20, 2011.

Page 216 **312 people died:** "Pravda Beslana." http://www.pravdabeslana.ru/pravda_ beslana.pdf. Accessed June 26, 2011.

Page 216 **not even heightened security:** Anna Politkovskaya, "Shto delalo MVD do

Beslana, vo vremya i posle," *Novaya Gazeta*, Aug. 28 2006. http://politkovskaya
.novayagazeta.ru/pub/2006/2006-77.shtml. Accessed June 26, 2011.

Page 219 **"Women should not be":** Alexei Chadayev's blog, March 21, 2006. http://
kerogazz-batyr.livejournal.com/365459.html?thread=4023699#t4023699. Accessed
Dec. 3, 2011.

Page 220 **"We disagreed occasionally":** Alexander Litvinenko, "Annu Politkovskuyu ubil
Putin," *Chechenpress*, Oct. 8, 2006. http://alexanderlitvinenko.narod.ru/myweb2/
article3.html. Accessed June 27, 2011.

Page 220 **he encountered a picket line:** "V Dresdene Putina nazvali ubiytsey," unsigned,
grani.ru, Oct. 10, 2006. http://grani.ru/Society/Media/m.112666.html. Accessed
June 27, 2011.

Page 220 **"That journalist was indeed":** Putin speaking at a press conference in Dresden,
Oct. 10, 2006. http://www.newstube.ru/Media.aspx?mediaid=511BE4A2
-5153-4F4E-BEA2-3086663E96D4. Accessed June 27, 2011.

Page 223 **"As I lie here":** Goldfarb and Litvinenko, p. 335.

Page 225 **Putin had him killed:** Author interview with Alexander Goldfarb, London, June
6, 2011; *Sasha, Volodya, Boris . . .*

TEN. INSATIABLE GREED

Page 227 **"The . . . elections . . . failed":** OSCE PA International Election Observation
Mission Statement of Preliminary Findings and Conclusions. http://www.osce.org/
odihr/elections/russia/18284. Accessed June 14, 2011.

Page 228 **condescending but approving editorial:** "Russians Inch Toward Democracy,"
unsigned editorial, *New York Times*, Dec. 8, 2003. http://www.nytimes.com/
2003/12/08/opinion/russians-inch-toward-democracy.html. Accessed June 14, 2011.

Page 228 **mammoth news story:** David Holley and Kim Murphy, "Election Bolsters Putin's
Control," *Los Angeles Times*, Dec. 8, 2003. http://articles.latimes.com/2003/dec/08/
world/fg-russelect8. Accessed June 14, 2011.

Page 228 **whole story right in the headline:** "Racists, Killers and Criminals Run for Duma,"
National Post, Dec. 6, 2003.

Page 228 **"a democrat's nightmare":** "Putin's Way," *Economist*, Dec. 11, 2003. http://www
.economist.com/node/2282403. Accessed June 14, 2011.

Page 229 **considerably less enthusiastic:** "Bush and Putin: Best of Friends," *BBC News*,
June 16, 2001. http://news.bbc.co.uk/2/hi/1392791.stm. Accessed July 11, 2011.

Page 229 **abrogation of an agreement:** Robert O. Freeman, "Russia, Iran and the Nuclear
Question: The Putin Record," a publication of the Strategic Studies Institute. http://
www.strategicstudiesinstitute.army.mil/pdffiles/pub737.pdf. Accessed July 11, 2011.

Page 229 **several billion dollars a year:** See, for example, "Russia Signs Arms Deals with
Arab States Totaling $12 Billion," unsigned news story on pravda.ru. http://english
.pravda.ru/russia/economics/22-02-2011/116979-russia_arms_deals-0/. Accessed
July 11, 2011.

Page 230 **appointed a liberal economist:** The economist was German Gref, and the think
tank was Tsentr strategicheskih razrabotok (Center for Strategic Initiatives).

Page 232 **something remarkable happened:** Author interview with Andrei Illarionov,
Moscow, June 2011; Andrei Illarionov, "Slovo i delo," *Kontinent*, no. 134 (2007),
pp. 83–147.

Page 234 **"The esprit de corps was like":** Author interview with William Browder, London,
May 13, 2011.

Page 235 **devising ways to squeeze cash:** Hoffman, *The Oligarchs.*

Page 236 **"Those who wanted to make":** Mikhail Khodorkovsky and Leonid Nevzlin,
Chelovek s rublem. http://lit.lib.ru/n/newzlin_l_b/text_0010.shtml. Accessed July
16, 2011.

Page 236 **"I would go to our oil rigs"**: Ludmila Ulitskaya and Mikhail Khodorkovsky, "Dialogi," *Znamya*, no. 10 (2009). http://magazines.russ.ru/znamia/2009/10/ul12.html. Accessed July 16, 2011.

Page 237 **"Until that point . . . I saw"**: Ibid.

Page 238 **"Before Pricewaterhouse came along"**: Author interview with Pavel Ivlev, New York City, July 2, 2011.

Page 238 **"We would set up"**: Author interview with Charles Krause, New York City, June 30, 2011.

Page 239 **I had heard it once**: This talk was given in Zvenigorod on Oct. 27, 2002.

Page 240 **Khodorkovsky told Litvinovich to return to Moscow**: Author interview with Marina Litvinovich, December 2009.

Page 241 **two to three times those in the government sector**: "Korruptsiya v Rossii—tormoz ekonomicheskogo rosta," a slide presentation acquired from the Khodorkovsky Press Center in Moscow, June 2011.

Page 241 **"Everyone thinks"**: Kolesnikov, *Ya Putina videl!*, p. 284.

Page 242 **He got the same smirk on his face**: Video footage of the meeting: http://www.youtube.com/watch?v=3KLzF3_-ShU&NR=1. Accessed July 17, 2011.

Page 242 **"It took three or four attempts"**: Author interview with Mikhail Kasyanov, Moscow, May 2011.

Page 242 **had "of course" been cleared by the Kremlin**: Author interview with Leonid Nevzlin, Greenwich, Conn., July 1, 2011.

Page 243 **"He did not go"**: Author interview with Andrei Illarionov, Moscow, June 2011.

Page 243 **"We should . . . fully support [Putin]"**: *Moscow Times*, Jan. 21, 2004. Full text: http://hermitagefund.com/newsandmedia/index.php?ELEMENT_ID=312. Accessed July 17, 2011.

Page 247 **he argued he should be released**: Sergei Magnitsky court testimony, unpublished document.

Page 248 **more corrupt than 86 percent of the world**: Transparency International, Global Corruption Reports 2003 and 2010. http://www.transparency.org/publications/gcr. Accessed July 17, 2011. The actual rankings are 86 for 2003 and 154 for 2010, but because of the changing total number of countries in the reports (133 in 2003 and 178 in 2010), I give the figures here as percentages.

Page 248 **"Everyone had their own turning point"**: Author interview with Andrei Illarionov, Moscow, June 2011. Illarionov's subsequent comments are from the same interview.

Page 249 **"different set of rails"**: Andrei Illarionov, "Drugaya Strana," originally published in *Kommersant*, Jan. 27, 2006. http://www.liberal.ru/anons/312. Accessed July 17, 2011.

Page 250 **he fired his cabinet**: "Kasyanov, Mikhail," unsigned Lentapedia dossier. http://lenta.ru/lib/14159606/full.htm. Accessed July 17, 2011.

Page 252 **To visit their client**: Author interview with Karina Moskalenko, Strasbourg, July 5, 2011.

Page 253 **now run by Putin's former deputy**: "Miller, Alexei," an unsigned Lentapedia dossier. http://lenta.ru/lib/14160384/. Accessed July 18, 2011.

Page 253 **lasted all of two minutes**: Yelena Lubarskaya, "'Yuganskneftegaz'utopili v 'Baikale,'" lenta.ru, Dec. 20, 2004. http://lenta.ru/articles/2004/12/20/ugansk/. Accessed July 18, 2011. Denis Skorobogat'ko, Dmitry Butrin, and Nikolai Kovalev, "'Yugansk' kupili ludi iz 'Londona,'" *Kommersant*, Dec. 12, 2004. http://www.kommersant.ru/doc/534631?isSearch=True. Accessed July 18, 2011. "Russia to Hold Yukos Auction Despite US Ruling," unsigned news story on MSNBC. http://www.msnbc.msn.com/id/6726341/. Accessed July 18, 2011.

Page 254 **in the course of a rigged auction**: "'Rosneft' kupila 'Baikalfinansgrup,' poluchiv control nad 'Yuganskneftegazom,'" unsigned news story, newsru.com. http://www.newsru.com/finance/23dec2004/rosneft.html. Accessed July 18, 2011.

Page 254   **net worth at $40 billion:** Luke Harding, "Putin, the Kremlin Power Struggle, and the $40bn Fortune," *Guardian*, Dec. 21, 2007. http://www.guardian.co.uk/world/2007/dec/21/russia.topstories3. Accessed July 18, 2011.

Page 255   **"we knew this was not money":** Author interview with Sergei Kolesnikov, Helsinki, June 2011.

Page 257   **the Black Sea project existed:** Roman Anin, "Dvortsovaya ploshad 740 tysyach kvadratnykh metrov," *Novaya Gazeta*, Feb. 14, 2011. http://www.novayagazeta.ru/data/2011/016/00.html#sup. Accessed July 19, 2011. Pavel Korobov and Oleg Kashin, "Vot chego-chego, a kontrollerov u nas khvatayet," *Kommersant*, April 20, 2011. http://www.kommersant.ru/Doc/1625310. Accessed July 19, 2011.

Page 257   **"Either you have me help you":** Author interview with Yuli Dubov, London, June 6, 2011.

Page 258   **Putin pocketed the 124-diamond Super Bowl ring:** Jacob Gershman, "Putin Pockets Patriots Ring," New York *Sun*, June 28, 2005. http://www.nysun.com/foreign/putin-pockets-patriots-ring/16172/. Accessed July 19, 2011. Donovan Slack, "For Putin, It's a Gem of a Cultural Exchange," *Boston Globe*, June 29, 2005. http://www.boston.com/sports/football/patriots/articles/2005/06/29/for_putin_its_a_gem_of_a_cultural_exchange/. Accessed July 19, 2011; "Vladimir Putin poluchil persten s 124 brilliantami," unsigned news item, *Kommersant*, June 30, 2005. http://www.kommersant.ru/news/984560. Accessed July 19, 2011. Putin's comment that he "could kill someone with this" was recounted by Robert Kraft's wife, Myra; see "Myra Kraft: Putin Stole Robert's Ring," *Jewish Russian Telegraph*, March 18, 2007. http://www.jrtelegraph.com/2007/03/myra_kraft_puti.html. Accessed Oct. 31, 2011.

Page 258   **New York's Solomon R. Guggenheim Museum:** Art consultant Nic Iljine recounts the incident in his essay "Guggenheim 24/7," in Laura K. Jones, ed., *A Hedonist's Guide to Art* (London: Filmer, 2010); see, for instance: http://www.theaustralian.com.au/news/world/book-details-strongman-vladimir-putins-artful-ways/story-e6frg6so-1225978192724.

Page 258   **costs about $300 in Moscow:** Here, for example, it is listed for 8,200 rubles: http://www.alcoport.ru/katalog/products/vodka/vodka-kalashnikov/vodka-kalashnikov-1l. Accessed July 19, 2011.

Page 259   **Andrei Illarionov discovered:** Author interview with Andrei Illarionov, Moscow, June 2011.

ELEVEN. BACK TO THE USSR

Page 262   **the Russian blogosphere consisted:** Interview with Bruce Eitling and John Kelly, Cambridge, Massachusetts, Nov. 7, 2008.

Page 264   **editors pulled their stories:** In March 2011, Dozhd, an Internet TV channel, canceled the program *Grazhdanin Poet* over a sketch skewering Medvedev. General Director Natalya Sindeeva explained in a statement that she did not want to insult Medvedev personally. http://tvrain.ru/teleshow/poet_and_citizen/. Accessed Nov. 10, 2011. I had several similar experiences as editor of www.snob.ru, where the publisher, for example, made me remove a reference to a British newspaper article in which Medvedev was called "Putin's assistant."

Page 264   **"We know they are now lying low":** "Putin poruchil spetssluzhbam 'vykovyryat' terroristov so dna kanalizatsii," unsigned news item on www.lenta.ru, March 30, 2010. http://lenta.ru/news/2010/03/30/drainpipe/. Accessed Nov. 10, 2011.

Page 265   **"We don't spread our legs":** "Putin obidelsya na sravneniye Obamy: My ne umeyem stoyat' 'vraskoryachku,'" unsigned news item on www.newsru.com, July 3, 2009. http://www.newsru.com/russia/03jul2009/raskoryachka.html. Accessed Nov. 10, 2011.

Page 265   **"I understand that an illness":** Petr Mironenko, Dmitry Butrin, and Yelena Kiselyova, "Rvyot i Mechel," *Kommersant*, July 25, 2008. http://www.kommersant.ru/Doc/915811. Accessed Nov. 10, 2011.

Page 265 "to be hit over the head with a stick": "Putin predrek oppozitsioneram 'oto-varivaniye dubinkoy,'" unsigned news item on www.lenta.ru, Aug. 30, 2010. http://lenta.ru/news/2010/08/30/explain/. Accessed Nov. 10, 2011.

Page 265 topless photographs of him vacationing: "Vladimir Putin Goes Fishing," photo gallery, *Guardian*, Aug. 14, 2007. http://www.guardian.co.uk/news/gallery/2007/aug/14/russia.internationalnews. Accessed Nov. 10, 2011.

Page 265 coverage of his diving: "Vladimir Putin, nashedshiy amfory VI veka, stal obyektom dlya nasmeshek rossiyskikh bloggerov I zarubezhnykh SMI," unsigned item on www.newsru.com, Aug. 11, 2011. http://www.newsru.com/russia/11aug2011/putin_amf.html. Accessed Nov. 10, 2011.

Page 265 planted there in advance by archaeologists: Putin's press secretary, Dmitry Peskov, later admitted that the vases had been planted. See Stepan Opalev, "Peskov pro Putina: Amfory nashel ne sam," www.slon.ru, October 5, 2011. http://slon.ru/russia/peskov_pro_putina_amfory_nashel_ne_sam-684066.xhtml. Accessed Nov. 10, 2011.

Page 265 increase the presidential term to six years: "Medvedev vnyos v Gosdumu zakonoproekt o prodlenii prezidentskikh polnomochiy," unsigned news item on www.lenta.ru, Nov. 11, 2008. http://lenta.ru/news/2008/11/11/medvedev/. Accessed Nov. 11, 2011.

Page 266 Every year, Russia slid lower: Transparency International, Corruption Perceptions Index. http://www.transparency.org/policy_research/surveys_indices/cpi/2010/results. Accessed Nov. 15, 2011.

Page 266 15 percent of the Russian prison population: Ludmila Alekseeva speaking at the Yegor Gaidar Prize ceremony, Moscow, Nov. 14, 2011.

Page 266 five gold wristwatches: "Zolotiye chasy dlya upravleniya delami Voronozhskoy oblasti. Prodolzheniye," *Rospil* blog, Oct. 6, 2011. http://rospil.info/news/p/983. Accessed Nov. 11, 2011.

Page 266 technical documentation on a planned railroad crossing: "Recheniye komissii FAS po zakazu s tsenoy kontrakta boleye chem 11.5 mlrd rubley," *Rospil* blog, Oct. 11, 2011. http://rospil.info/news/p/999. Accessed Nov. 11, 2011.

Page 266 two beds and two bedside tables: "MVD zaplatit 25 millionov rubley za otdelanniye zolotom krovati," unsigned news item on www.lenta.ru, Aug. 19, 2008. http://lenta.ru/news/2009/08/19/gold/. Accessed Nov. 11, 2011.

Page 266 "An actual politician": Anna Kachurovskaya, "Alexei Navalny: Tol'ko, pozhaluysta, ne nado govorit': 'Navalny sravnil sebya s Obamoy,'" *Snob*, Nov. 2010.

Page 266 a *New Yorker* profile: Julia Ioffe, "Net Impact: One Man's Cyber-Crusade Against Russian Corruption," *New Yorker*, April 4, 2011. http://www.newyorker.com/reporting/2011/04/04/110404fa_fact_ioffe. Accessed Nov. 11, 2011.

Page 267 an all-time speed record: "Proekt 'Rospil' sobral perviy million na 'Yandexden'gakh'," unsigned news item on www.lenta.ru, Feb. 3, 2011. http://lenta.ru/news/2011/02/03/million/. Accessed Nov. 11, 2011.

Page 270 Medvedev would be his prime minister: "Putin vydvigayetsya na prezidentskiye vybory 2012 goda," unsigned news item on www.gazeta.ru, Sept. 24, 2011. http://www.gazeta.ru/news/lastnews/2011/09/24/n_2022837.shtml. Accessed Nov. 12, 2011.

EPILOGUE. A WEEK IN DECEMBER

Page 274 just over 23 percent of the vote: Aleksei Zakharov, "Rezultaty vyborov na tekh uchastkakh, gde ne byli zafiksirovany narusheniya," www.slon.ru, Dec. 5, 2011. http://slon.ru/calendar/event/723777/. Accessed Dec. 11, 2011.

Page 275 "'Democracy is in action'": David Herszenhorn, Ellen Barry, "Majority for Putin's Party Narrows in Rebuke from Voters," *New York Times*, Dec. 4, 2011. http://www.nytimes.com/2011/12/05/world/europe/russians-vote-governing

-party-claims-early-victory.html?n=Top/News/World/Countries%20and%20 Territories/Russia?ref=russia. Accessed Dec. 11, 2011.

Page 280 **Mikhail Gorbachev has called for a revote:** "Mikhail Gorbachev—Novoy," *Novaya Gazeta*, Dec. 7, 2011. http://www.novayagazeta.ru/politics/49918.html. Accessed Dec. 12, 2011.

Page 280 **"The problem with the Soviet regime":** Masha Gessen, "When There's No Going Back," *International Herald Tribune*, Dec. 8, 2011. http://latitude.blogs.nytimes. com/2011/12/08/when-theres-no-going-back/?scp=2&sq=masha%20gessen&st=cse. Accessed Dec. 12, 2011.

Page 281 **"irritated urban communities":** Natalya Raybman, "Surkov: Nuzhno sozdat' partiyu dlya razdrazhennykh gorozhan," *Vedomosti*, Dec. 6, 2011. http://www .vedomosti.ru/politics/news/1444694/surkov_nuzhno_sozdat_partiyu_dlya_ razdrazhennyh_gorozhan. Accessed Dec. 12, 2011.

Page 283 **"inciting enmity against a specific social group":** Olga Korol', "Ex-press-sekretaryu prezidenta Tatarstana Murtazinu dali real'niy srok," *Komsomol'skaya Pravda*, Nov. 26, 2009. http://www.kp.ru/online/news//577494/. Accessed Dec. 12, 2011.

Page 285 **"Why does everything in this country":** Boris Akunin blog entry, "I Could Not Sit Still," Dec. 9, 2011. http://borisakunin.livejournal.com/45529.html. Accessed Dec. 12, 2011.

Page 289 **Protests were held today:** Konstantin Benyumov, "Vstavay, strana ogromnaya! Mitingi protesta 10 dekabrya proshli v 99 gorodakh Rossii," onair.ru. http://www .onair.ru/main/enews/view_msg/NMID_38499/. Accessed Dec. 13, 2011.

Page 289 **the government has no comment:** "Dmitry Peskov ne kommentiruyet miting na Bolotnoy ploshchadi," unsigned news item, www.gazeta.ru, Dec. 10, 2011. http:// www.gazeta.ru/news/lenta/2011/12/10/n_2130194.shtml. Accessed Dec. 12, 2011.

AFTERWORD

Page 297 **so that Putin could be photographed performing this feat:** http://bigcats-ru. livejournal.com/116816.html. Accessed October 14, 2012.

POSTSCRIPT

Page 308 **"It is not enough to ban propaganda of homosexuality!":** "Istorichesky Protsess," a Russia 1 talk show that aired on April 4, 2012, https://www.youtube.com/watch?v =oyvE16z6FrI, accessed April 25, 2014. This remark by Kiselev begins at the 1:15 mark.

Page 308 **he explained that gays and lesbians were the Antichrist:** Maxim Shevchenko, "Gei kak oruzhiye antikhrista," https://www.youtube.com/watch?v=mr8h0xod4hM; "Kto takiye gei," https://www.youtube.com/watch?v=2esxPq2qJG0, accessed April 25, 2014.

Page 309 **a sign of the coming apocalypse:** "Po mneniyu patriarkh Kirilla, priznaniye od-nopolykh brakov vedyot chelovechestvo k apokalipsisu," unsigned news item, NTV, July 21, 2013, http://www.ntv.ru/novosti/633297/, accessed April 25, 2014.

Page 309 **God's wrath against the sodomites:** "Spetsialniy korrespondent: Litsedei," Russia 1, aired November 12, 2013. https://www.youtube.com/watch?v=Jhzb5GIEvHo, accessed April 25, 2014.

Page 309 **Putin regime's antigay campaign was a distraction:** For example: Harvey Fier-stein, "Russia's Anti-Gay Crackdown," *New York Times*, July 21, 2013, http://www .nytimes.com/2013/07/22/opinion/russias-anti-gay-crackdown.html?_r=0, accessed April 25, 2014; Laura Smith-Spark, "Why Russia's Sochi Olympics Are Now a Bat-tleground for Gay Rights," CNN, August 10, 2103, http://www.cnn.com/2013/08/10/ world/europe/russia-gay-rights-controversy/, accessed April 25, 2014.

Page 311 **feeding them bogus statistics:** Max Seddon, J. Lester Feder, "Discredited U.S. Anti-Gay Activist Addresses Russian Parliamentarians over 'Family Values,'" *Buzzfeed*,

October 28, 2013, http://www.buzzfeed.com/maxseddon/discredited-us-anti-gay
-activist-addreses-russian-parliament, accessed April 25, 2014.

Page 311 **secured a plan to hold its annual conference in Moscow:** At the time of this
writing, the congress was planned for September 10–12, 2014. In a press release
announcing that the gathering will be held in Moscow, World Congress of Families
executive director Larry Jacobs said, "'We're convinced that Russia does and should
play a very significant role in defense of the family and moral values worldwide,
Russia has become a leader of promoting these values in the international arena."

Page 312 **a subtle veil over the statement's homophobia:** The Russian transcript of the
speech is here—http://kremlin.ru/news/19825—and the official English translation
here: http://eng.kremlin.ru/news/6402, accessed April 25, 2014.

Page 313 **mentioned me and my family by name:** In this interview to Russia's biggest
tabloid, a leader of the antigay campaign, St. Petersburg politician Vitaly Milonov,
says, "The State Department is very aroused over homosexual rights. They say you
are not supposed to pick on homosexuals, you are supposed to stroke their hair
instead and give them the right to get married and take children out of orphanages
so that these poor children can grow up in perverted families like Masha Gessen's."
Vladimir Vorsobin, "Vitaly Milonov: 'Priyatno, kogda rugayut ne za to, shto ty podo-
nok in negodyay, a za tsitirovaniye Biblii,'" *Komsomolskaya Pravda*, March 12, 2013,
http://www.kp.ru/daily/26043/2957813, accessed April 25, 2014.

Page 314 **"a broadening of the sphere of gay culture":** Olga Pavlikova, "Assotsiatsiya s YeS
oznachayet rasshireniye sfery gey-kultury," *Slon*, December 10, 2013, http://slon.ru/
russia/assotsiatsiya_s_es_oznachaet_rasshirenie_sfery_gey_kultury-1032020.xhtml,
accessed April 25, 2014.

Page 315 **The document, published in its entirety:** "Minkultury izlozhilo 'Osnovy gosudarstvennoy kulturnoy politiki,'" *Izvestia*, April 10, 2014, http://izvestia.ru/news/
569016, accessed April 25, 2014.

Page 315 **"This is not another Cold War":** "Full Transcript: President Obama Gives Speech
Addressing Europe, Russia, on March 26," *Washington Post*, March 26, 2014, http://
www.washingtonpost.com/world/transcript-president-obama-gives-speech
-addressing-europe-russia-on-march-26/2014/03/26/07ae80ae-b503-11e3-b899
-20667de76985_story.html, accessed April 25, 2014.

Index

Brilliant, brave, and eloquent, Masha Gessen writes books that crystallize—and transcend—our time

Masha Gessen is internationally renowned for her courageous, impeccably researched reporting, but her work pushes beyond the bounds of the subjects that capture her imagination—history, biography, science, current events. Her books become nonfiction classics, enduring accounts of lives, nations, and ideas in flux. A Russian immigrant with startling grace in her adopted language and uncanny fluency in her adopted culture, she gains access other journalists only dream of and is unparalleled in her ability to translate seemingly incomprehensible events and attitudes into human and recognizable terms. At the same time, she is uncompromising in her pursuit of sometimes shocking and discomfiting realities. Speaking truth to power, she illuminates our most necessary stories.